Contents

Introduction, The video signal, Video source synchronization, Video bandwidth requirements, Adding colour to the signal, Colour difference signals, Component analogue video systems, Magnetic recording, Magnetic replay, Implications for video recording, Use of frequency modulation for video recording, Use of helical scan to improve write/read speeds, Control track, Timebase correction, Dropout compensation.

Introduction, The denary (decimal) system, The binary system, Binary-coded decimal, 2's complement coding, The hexadecimal system, Bit rate requirements, Simple digital codes, Organization of digital data, Causes of errors in digital systems, Error detection.

The original quadruplex cue track, The development of a longitudinal timecode (LTC) word, The biphase mark code, User bits, The form of the LTC word, LTC byte arrangement, The detail of the 625/50 LTC, The detail of the 525/60 LTC, The requirement for vertical interval timecode (VITC), The form of the VITC word, The cyclic redundancy check bits, The detail of the 625/50 VITC, The detail of the 525/60 VITC, The time address and the associated colour TV signal, The 525/60 drop-frame code (M/NTSC), M/PAL drop-frame code, Digital VITC, Timecode and 1125/60 television systems, 24 frame film timecode.

The U-Matic format, The 1in C-format, Betacam, Beta SP and MII formats, D-1 component digital format, Audio sector timecode and equipment type information, D-2 composite digital format, D-3 composite digital format, D-5 digital format, Digital Betacam, The Hi-8 video format, Domestic and professional R-DAT, Timecode in the R-DAT system, DASH and Prodigi, ¼in centre-track analogue audio, Audio analogue multi-track, Recording levels.

Introduction, EBU/IRT and EBU/TDF timecodes, SMPTE film codes, DataKode®, Aaton and Arriflex timecode systems, Machine-readable film timecodes, Film transfer to PAL video, 3-line VITC, Film transfer via 3/2 pulldown, Control of 4:3 scanning for the presentation of wide-screen films.

Preface to the second edition

Since the first edition of *Timecode: A user's guide* was published, major developments in technology and data handling systems have had a major impact in timecode formats and applications. Digital VITC is now established, timecode can be placed in the audio sectors of digital VCR recordings, there is now a standard for the extended use of the timecode word's user bits, time data are frequently carried in the RS422 digital interface and there is now a standard for timecode in High Definition Television.

Within Europe, the EBU has published the uses to which some of its members have put the binary groups within the timecode word. Uses include the control of Telecine 'panscan' for the selection of which area of a wide-screen 16:9 aspect ratio picture will be transmitted in 4:3, and the inclusion of date information. Additionally, some broadcasters are using the AES/EBU digital interface to carry time-related data, and proposals have been made for the carrying of time-related data in a form not related to the digital sampling rate.

Perhaps the most significant development in time-and-control code has been concerned with its use in the field of video assisted film post-production. Timecode is now no longer the 'Cinderella' of post-production, confined to looking after the housekeeping while its older sisters, pictures and sound, enjoy all the glamour and adulation. Timecode has met her 'Prince Charming' in the form of KeyKode®, and the 'glass slipper' of recognition has been the powerful data logging and management systems such as Excalibur and Keylink, coupled with intuitive non-linear editing systems such as Avid, D/Vision and Lightworks. Timecode is now the 'business manager' to her older sisters, allowing them to be edited more flexibly and efficiently, and easing the production of film and video versions of programmes, commercials and feature films for worldwide distribution. As this edition is being written, 3-line VITC is being developed to enable non-linear editors to manage a variety of film, video and audio timecode databases more effectively.

This edition aims to explain and de-mystify these new forms of and uses for timecode, and I would like to thank all who so freely gave me both their knowledge and time in its preparation, especially David Bryant of Filmlab Systems, Tony Harcourt of Kodak Limited, Anita Sinclair and Mick Colthart of Lightworks Editing Systems Limited, Francis Rumsey of the University of Surrey, and Jon Hocking of Wren Communications.

Preface to the first edition

Probably every person involved in the making of television programmes will come across 'timecode' at some stage in the production process. It can be a powerful tool in post-production, yet is often poorly understood. As a result, it can cause embarrassing and expensive problems when it fails. Most timecode failure can be avoided if its characteristics, and those of the various recording machines that process it, are properly understood. On location it can make various production processes much easier and less time-consuming, yet few people are aware of its full potential.

Recording formats have evolved rapidly in recent years, with location professional R-DAT and digital VCRs already with us. Timecode implementation in digital recording formats can differ markedly from that in traditional analogue systems. MIDI control systems can now interface with timecode, and the IEC has rationalized the EBU and SMPTE videotape codes. There have been exciting developments in the application to film and timecode data can be carried within the data stream of the AES/EBU digital audio interface.

This book aims to explain timecode in all its manifestations. It is intended to be of use to the operator working in the field or edit suite, to the person involved with installation and maintenance of timecode equipment, and to anyone interested in the development of either software or hardware for handling the code. The potential of timecode as a tool for use at all stages is explained, and causes of timecode failure are discussed, together with possible solutions.

The opening chapters of the book explain the underlying theory, and appendices contain technical detail. These, together with a comprehensive bibliography, make this book of value both as a manual and as a work of reference. Mathematics is kept to a minimum, and any necessary theory is included and explained, making the book accessible to the widest range of possible users.

Timecode
A user's guide
Second edition

John Ratcliff

Focal Press
An imprint of Butterworth-Heinemann Ltd
Linacre House, Jordan Hill, Oxford OX2 8DP

A member of the Reed Elsevier plc group

OXFORD LONDON BOSTON
NEW DELHI SINGAPORE SYDNEY
TOKYO TORONTO WELLINGTON

First published 1993
Reprinted 1994
Second edition 1996

© Butterworth-Heinemann Ltd 1993, 1996

British Library Cataloguing in Publication Data
Ratcliff, John
    Timecode: A User's Guide – 2Rev.ed
    I. Title
    621.38833

ISBN 0 240 51404 1

Library of Congress Cataloguing in Publication Data
Ratcliff, J. D.
    Timecode: a user's guide/John Ratcliff.
    p. cm.
    Includes bibliographical references and index.
    1. Video tapes – Editing. 2. Time code (Audio-visual technology)
    I. Title.
    TR899.R38   95-30824
    778.59–dc20   CIP

Printed and bound in Great Britain by Clays, Bungay, Suffolk

Acknowledgements

I should like to express my thanks to the following individuals and companies for the help and information they have given me, and for supplying and giving permission to reproduce photographs: Pascale Geraci, Aaton des Autres; Chris Cadzow, Avitel Electronics Limited; Maybridge Electronics; Chris Thorpe Projects; Digital Audio Research; Hayden Laboratories Limited; John Lisney, Head of School of Television, Ravensbourne College of Design and Communication; Barrie White and Neil Papworth, freelance sound recordists; and Chris Harnett, MITV. My thanks go also to Andrew Wood, final year graphics student at Ravensbourne College, for providing many of the illustrations from my rough sketches, and to my Editor, Margaret Riley of Focal Press for her encouragement.

The words KODAK, KEYKODE, EASTMAN, ESTAR, DATAKODE and the KEYKODE device are trade marks of Eastman Kodak Company, which also owns the copyright in the diagrams printed in Figures 5.10 to 5.12. Both trade marks and diagrams are reproduced by permission and their use does not imply that this publication is endorsed by or connected with Eastman Kodak Company, or that Eastman Kodak agrees with its content.

CHAPTER 1

Basic video and magnetic theory

Introduction

Timecode was originally developed in order to clearly identify positional information on videotape in a manner similar to traditional motion-picture film. On film, this information is printed in human-readable form along the film edge, and the individual frames are clearly seen by inspecting the film. Videotape frames are recorded as magnetic imprints that cannot be seen by inspection, so when the timecode was introduced, it needed to contain details of the frames. The introduction of colour to the original monochrome signal increased the complexity of the video signal, so care had to be taken in joining non-contiguous sections during editing if disturbances in the picture were to be avoided. Developments in post-production meant that the sound could be dealt with separately, as long as a guide video was provided, together with timecode. There have recently been great strides forward in the marriage between film and videotape for the purposes of post-production. This chapter explains the video and magnetic theory relevant to the recording and replay of timecode on video- and audiotape in order that the timecode processes described later may be easily understood.

The video signal

A scene viewed by the television camera is converted into an electronic signal by scanning the image formed by the lens in a series of horizontal lines, much as one would read text in a book. These lines are grouped together in frames (pages in the book in our analogy). The rate at which individual pictures are reproduced has to be high enough to minimize flicker. The technology available when television was developed did not permit a frame rate sufficiently high to achieve this, so each frame was split into two fields, each field containing alternative lines (Figure 1.1).

Originally the frame rate was linked to the nominal frequency of the mains. This meant that in Europe a rate of 25 frames (50 fields) per second (fps) was chosen, and in the USA the rate was 30 frames (60 fields) per second. When colour was added to the original monochrome signal it was coded into a very stable high-frequency sine wave, the frequency of which had to be chosen very carefully to keep interference to a minimum for those people who still viewed in monochrome.

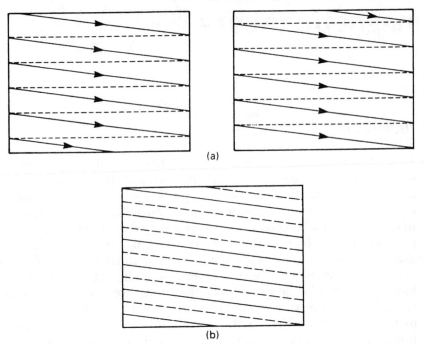

(a)

(b)

Figure 1.1 A television frame comprises two fields (a), which are interlaced (b) to produce a frame.

In the PAL system developed in the UK, each frame contains 625 lines of video information, divided into two fields of $312\frac{1}{2}$ lines. Each line of picture information contains a signal allowing the colour information to be decoded. In some countries on the European mainland the French SECAM system is used. This has the same frame rate and number of lines per frame as PAL, and a stable high-frequency sine wave is also used to carry the colour information, but the decoding information is placed in the start of each field. In the USA, Japan and a number of other Asian countries the NTSC system is employed. In this system the colour information is also coded into a high-frequency sine wave but in a simpler manner than either the PAL or SECAM systems. There are 525 lines to each frame, divided into two fields of $262\frac{1}{2}$ lines.

Video source synchronization

In all sequential scanning systems it is important that all items of equipment concerned with viewing or processing the scene maintain

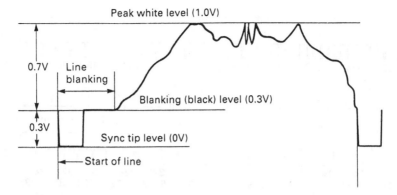

Figure 1.2 Video information extends from 0.3V to 1.0V. Sync information extends from 0.3V to 0V.

synchronization, so that each is dealing with the same frame, field and line of the scanned picture at the same instant as the other items of equipment. Each line starts with a clearly defined and identifiable pulse (the line synchronizing pulse), followed by a short interval before the picture information starts. The period of time containing both this pulse and the interval is called 'line blanking' (Figure 1.2).

Each field of information is preceded by a complex series of narrow and broad pulses which define both the start of the field and the particular field within a frame (Field 1 or Field 2). The start of the frame is indicated by the field having a half-line space between the narrow pulses and the first synchronizing pulse. A series of lines containing no video information follows this series of pulses. The period of time containing this series of pulses and the blank lines is called 'field blanking' (Figure 1.3). In the PAL system, picture black (blanking level) is represented by a signal level of 0.3 V, peak signal level (peak white) is 1.0 V, and the synchronizing pulses go below blanking level down to 0 V. In the NTSC system picture content from blanking level to peak white is represented by 100 IRE units, and sync pulses by 40 IRE units. The 1 V peak-to-peak value remains the same, but sync tip level is 0.29 V below blanking. The combination of synchronizing pulses and detail of the scene brightness is called the luminance signal.

Video bandwidth requirements

As Figure 1.4 illustrates, there is a clear relationship between frequency and the ability of a system to resolve fine detail. A detailed examination of the arguments that relate the frequency response of a system with resolution obtained is out of place here, but a television system needs to be capable of handling a frequency range (bandwidth) of 25 Hz to 5.5 MHz in PAL systems, 30 Hz to 4.5 MHz for NTSC.

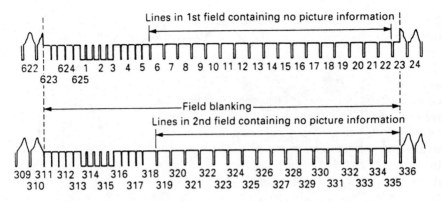

Figure 1.3 There are some 25 lines in each field clean of any picture information. 7 of these are used for field synchronization. This leaves 18 available for other purposes.

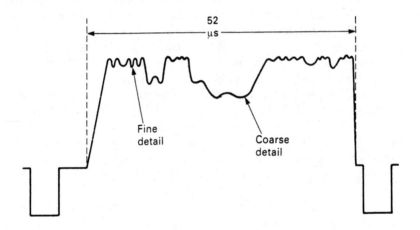

Figure 1.4 The ability of a video system to convey fine detail is dependent on its frequency response.

Adding colour to the signal

The perception of the human eye to colour information detail is much lower than to luminance because the eye contains fewer receptors for colour than for luminance. This is fortunate, as it permits colour information to be processed as a comparatively low-resolution signal. This 'chrominance' signal thus requires a narrower bandwidth than the luminance signal, typically about 1 MHz, and can be incorporated into an existing monochrome signal, as Figure 1.5 illustrates. Although the human eye is capable of identifying a large number of different colour shades (hues and saturations), it is possible to re-create most of them by combining just three colours (red, green and blue) in an additive mixing process, so that, for example, red and green combined in various proportions can produce an extensive range of oranges, yellows and browns. The colour information presented by the camera is mixed (matrixed) into two signals, called 'colour difference signals', which vary (modulate) the amplitude and phase of a high-frequency signal, called the colour sub-carrier, which is superimposed on the luminance signal. If this sub-carrier were to be an exact multiple of the line frequency, the patterning caused would be very obtrusive. To minimize this, the phase of the sub-carrier with respect to the start of each line is shifted by 90° on successive lines. In the NTSC and SECAM systems this phase shift results in a sequence that repeats every four fields. In the PAL system a further phase inversion on alternate lines reduces the effects of phase distortion in the transmission/reception process. This results in the phase relationship between the sub-carrier and the start of each field repeating only once in every eight fields (the eight-field sequence). These phase relationships have to be taken into account in the video post-production process if there is to be minimum disturbance to the colour (chroma) information during editing.

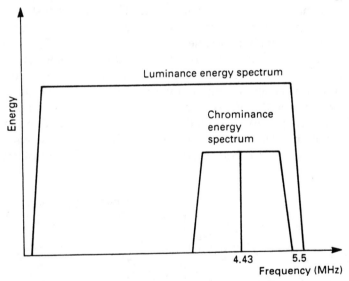

Figure 1.5 The chrominance information is contained within the luminance frequency bandwidth. Care has to be taken to minimize mutual interference.

With the need for an exact relationship between the colour sub-carrier phase, line and frame frequencies, television systems must run at very precise frequencies. In the PAL and SECAM systems this caused no particular problems; sync pulse generators were used that had highly stable internal clocks, instead of using the mains as a reference. However, engineers developing the NTSC system ran into problems with transmitting colour information at a precise 30 Hz frame rate, and had to reduce it to approximately 29.97 fps. When shooting or editing in NTSC, account has to be taken of this somewhat odd framing rate.

Colour difference signals

The red, green and blue colour components are not used in their raw form. Instead, the red (R) and blue (B) signals are each combined with the luminance signal by subtracting the luminance signal (Y) from the red and blue separately to give R–Y and B–Y. In this form they are known as 'colour difference signals'. It is these signals that modulate two separate feeds of colour sub-carrier. In the PAL and NTSC systems these two colour sub-carrier sine waves are identical in frequency, but are held 90° out of phase with each other. In the PAL system the phase swings on alternate lines between advance and retard (hence PAL or 'phase alternating line'). This reversal of phase on alternate lines was considered necessary in the development of the PAL system in order to minimize colour degradation should there be any decoder misalignment. The two modulated sub-carriers are added together to give a resultant sine wave whose amplitude and phase depends on the proportions of red and blue present in the original signal. It is this signal that is superimposed on the luminance signal as the chrominance signal. The SECAM system, on the other hand, employs sub-carriers of two different frequencies, carrying R and B information on alternate lines.

In all systems it is the amplitude of the modulated colour sub-carrier that represents the saturation of the colour. In PAL and NTSC systems the phase of the sub-carrier is compared with a reference signal (the 'colour burst') to determine the hue (Figure 1.6). The colour burst is inserted at the start of each picture information (active) line in the line blanking period, just after the line synchronizing pulse. In the SECAM system the decoding information is carried in several lines within the vertical interval.

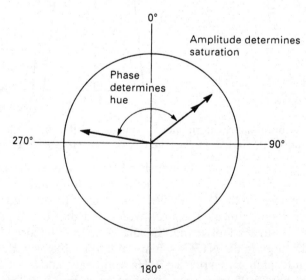

Figure 1.6 The instantaneous value (amplitude and relative phase) of the colour sub-carrier determines both intensity and hue of the chroma.

Any modulation process generates additional frequency bands ('sidebands') which extend both above and below the carrier frequency. In all systems these sidebands sit within the luminance bandwidth, making it impossible to remove the sub-carrier completely from the luminance signal.

Component analogue video systems

It is fair to say that if colour television were to be invented with the technology that exists today, a sub-carrier system would not be employed. Available technology has been exploited to develop colour television systems, known as component analogue systems, which avoid modulating the chrominance information onto the luminance signal. In the two component analogue VCR systems in use today, Betacam (and its development) Beta SP from the Sony Corporation, and MII, developed by National Panasonic, the colour difference signals are processed without the need for a colour sub-carrier. For distribution purposes, three signals have to be sent around a building instead of just one, but the additional complexity is more than compensated for by the improvement in picture quality and the reduction of signal degradation during post-production.

The two chrominance information signals are recorded onto tape in time-division multiplexed form, line by line. Both luminance and chrominance signals are recorded with timing signals, instead of the traditional synchronizing pulses, or colour burst, to allow a more favourable packing density on tape. The two chrominance signals, known as Pr and Pb, are recorded on a part of the tape completely separate from the luminance signal. They are time-expanded and demultiplexed on replay.

When a component VCR is recording signals decoded from a composite source, some form of sub-carrier phase identification is needed. This takes the form of a pulse placed in the chrominance channel and a line of sub-carrier ('vertical interval sub-carrier' or VISC) inserted into a line within the field blanking interval. The manner in which the chrominance is recorded, together with its limited bandwidth requirement, makes it possible to record two high-quality audio signals on frequency-modulated carriers along the chrominance tracks.

Magnetic recording

The basic principles of magnetic recording are reasonably well known; a plastic tape, coated with finely-divided magnetic powder, is passed at constant speed in intimate contact with a pair of magnetic poles called a 'recording head'. Currents flowing in the head coils cause corresponding variations in magnetic flux. The particles of magnetic powder are magnetized to varying degrees, depending on the strength of the current flowing in the recording head coils.

Magnetic replay

During replay the magnetized particles are caused to pass at constant speed in front of a similar head, where their external flux links with the head coil, generating a voltage. The strength of this voltage depends approximately on the rate of change of the magnetic flux rather than on its absolute level, so that the voltage that appears is the first derivative of the magnetic flux. This differentiation of the flux strength is modified by a number of factors, including the inductance and resistance of the head coil and the intimacy of contact between the tape and the face of the replay head (Figure 1.7). The consistency of the tape coating will also have an effect, variations in coating consistency resulting in corresponding variations in sensitivity. Should the particles of magnetic powder clump together, or be absent (perhaps as a result of poor adhesion), there will be a momentary loss of signal, or 'dropout'.

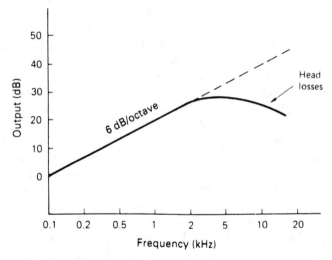

Figure 1.7 At high frequencies tape heads suffer from a variety of effects causing loss of available output voltage.

Implications for video recording

The variations in linear tape speed that are acceptable for audio signals are unacceptable for video processing where timing and synchronization are critical. For example, the accuracy of colour sub-carrier timing has to be within ±0.01 μs for video editing. In videotape recordings, variations in coating thickness and tape-to-head contact would cause unacceptable variations in brightness of the replayed picture. The video bandwidth extends over 18 octaves. Over this range, the differentiation effects described above would produce variations in replay output levels of over 108 dB. Differentiation also results in sine waves being effectively shifted

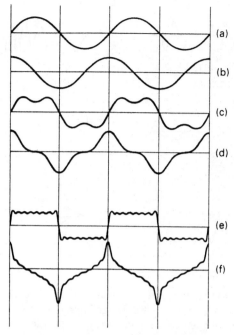

(a)

(b)

(c)

(d)

(e)

(f)

Figure 1.8 A sine wave (a) when differentiated becomes a cosine wave (b). A waveform comprising a sine wave and its 3rd harmonic (c) will produce the waveform (d) when differentiated. A square wave comprises a sine wave and an infinite number of odd harmonics; (e) comprises a fundamental sine wave and odd order harmonics up to the 15th. When differentiated the waveform (f) results.

in phase by 90°, and rectangular waves being reproduced as positive- and negative-going spikes (Figure 1.8). Obviously this is unacceptable, so some way has to be found of overcoming these problems.

Use of frequency modulation for video recording

The video signal is not recorded directly onto tape, but is used first to modulate the frequency of a constant-amplitude carrier. The resulting signal is recorded as a magnetic imprint on tape. In this way the effects that result from variations in replay levels that occur as a result of variations in tape/head contact and magnetic coating inconsistencies are reduced. Frequency modulation also allows the d.c. component of the video signal, representing brightness, to be recorded (Figure 1.9).

Although current magnetic tape and replay head technologies mean that wavelengths less than 1 μm can be recorded and replayed, there is still a requirement for tape-to-head speeds to be much higher than is realistically possible with longitudinal tracks traditionally used for analogue audio recordings. This is achieved by the use of helical scan techniques.

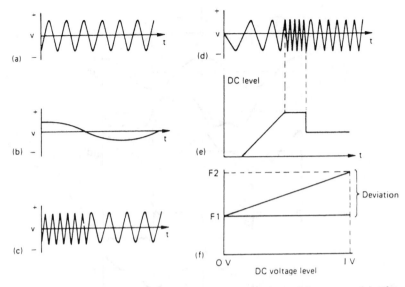

Figure 1.9 Unmodulated carrier has constant amplitude and frequency (a). This carrier is modified by a signal (b) to change its frequency but not its amplitude (c). Specific carrier frequencies (d) can represent specific voltage levels (e). Sync tip, blanking and peak white may thus be represented by an a.c. signal and so recorded onto tape. The difference in frequencies between sync tip and peak white is known as the deviation (f).

Use of helical scan to improve write/read speeds

The high tape-to-head speed required for video recording is obtained by having the heads mounted on a spinning drum, the complete assembly being called a 'scanner'. The tape is wrapped around the drum in an open spiral. This results in a series of recorded tracks being laid in shallow diagonal lines across the tape (Figure 1.10). In analogue video recording each of these tracks corresponds to an individual field of information. In digital video systems the information related to an individual field may be recorded over a number of tracks. In this manner, although the linear speed of the tape may be quite low, the writing speed will be very high. One typical system employs a linear (longitudinal) tape speed of 0.066 metres per second (m/s), but has a writing speed of 6.9 m/s, a writing-to-linear speed ratio of the order of 100:1.

Some video recording formats leave guard-bands between the recorded video tracks, others (notably component analogue and digital) may make use of azimuth recording techniques, where the write/read heads for luminance and chrominance tracks have azimuths offset in opposite directions. In azimuth recording, the heads are slightly wider than the recorded tracks, so will partially over-write (and over-read) adjacent tracks. The offset in the azimuth angles minimizes the resulting crosstalk

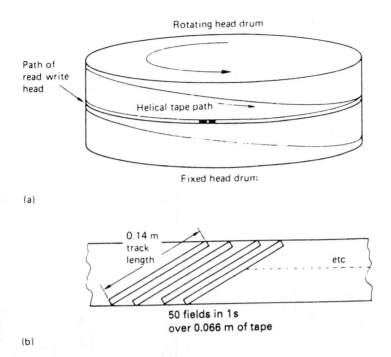

Rotating head drum

Path of
read write
head

Helical tape path

Fixed head drum

(a)

0.14 m
track
length

etc

50 fields in 1 s
over 0.066 m of tape

(b)

Figure 1.10 The videotape is wrapped as a part helix around a spinning drum
(a). Heads set in the drum write and read diagonal tracks on tape as it moves
relatively slowly through the transport system. Note in practice these diagonal
tracks are at a very shallow angle.

to acceptable levels. Some digital audio systems also employ helical
scanning techniques, both to minimize the linear tape speed (smaller
cassettes = longer recording times) and to accommodate the very high
rate of data that digital systems incur.

Control track

When material is recorded on tape as a series of stripes, some way has to
be found of ensuring that the scanning head (on both replay and over-
recording during editing) follows the originally-recorded tracks. If that
recorded material is video information, some way has to be found of
ensuring that the individually-recorded fields can be correctly identified,
particularly as regards the correct relationship of colour sub-carrier to
field. This relationship is still important even with a component analogue
recorder, as such a machine may well have to interface with equipment of
composite format during production, post-production and playout.

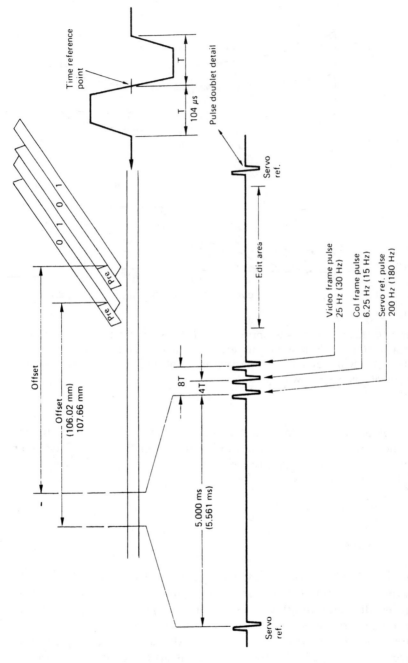

Figure 1.11 In the D-2 recording system the control track carries servo reference signals together with video and colour framing pulses. Figures given are for the PAL system, those for the NTSC system are in parentheses.

One way of achieving this is by recording, on a longitudinal track, a series of pulses which enables the scanning heads to follow the pre-recorded tracks correctly on replay. This track is called the 'control track'. It will often contain other pulses that identify the 8- or 4-field colour-framing sequence, and in digital video systems may carry information concerning the packaging, in segments, of the digital data on tape (Figure 1.11).

As the control track is frame-related, it can be used to control the editing process. However, it cannot be read while the tape is stationary or is moving at very slow speed (as when starting or stopping), because the replayed level is either non-existent or very low. A unique time identification for each frame, with this time related to the colour frame sequence in a known and unambiguous way, is the only satisfactory option.

Timebase correction

The timing accuracy necessary for the replay of video information is not possible using purely mechanical or electromechanical systems because of the inertia present with any mechanical device. The timing has to be corrected electronically. One method of doing this within a broadcast-quality system is to convert the off-tape demodulated signal into digital form. A digital signal can easily be stored until the correct time for transfer out of the machine, when it will be converted back into analogue form. This process is performed by a timebase corrector (TBC), a device which often incorporates a facility to adjust video and sync levels, and overall system timing and phase. Very often the vertical interval will be regenerated within the TBC, especially if it is external to the machine. Note that if the machine has to interface synchronously with the outside world, some form of external reference will be required by both the videotape machine and the TBC. The TBC may also be capable of outputting a correctly-timed video signal even while the machine is playing at non-standard speed, perhaps for special effects.

Dropout compensation

The high packing densities employed in video recorders, mean that momentary loss of output due to dropout is going to be much more noticeable than with audio. A dropout lasting just 1/15 000 s would result in the loss of a complete line of video. To minimize the effect, analogue video recorders employ devices called dropout compensators. Basically, these devices are short-term (1-line) stores constantly replenished by the FM video signal coming off tape. When a dropout occurs, signalled by a drop in the off-tape FM signal, the output to the demodulator is switched from the direct to the delayed signal in the store, and an uncorrupted line replaces the one with dropout.

CHAPTER 2

Digital processing

Introduction

Timecode is a digital signal. It carries information as a sequence of zeros (0s) and ones (1s), called 'digits'. These digits may represent quantities such as time or film footage, or they may carry 'command' and 'control' information. The assembly of these digits is called 'data'. Just as letters, numbers and characters have to be assembled into recognizable forms (languages) in order to be meaningful, so data must be arranged into recognizable forms in order to carry information. The arrangement of data is referred to as 'protocol'. Protocols define such matters as the number of digits used to form individual data words, the order in which data are presented within the words and the way in which the words are grouped together to carry information. There are a number of protocols used in the carrying of timecode data, depending on the application concerned. This need not be a problem because, as with languages, it is possible to translate from one protocol to another. This chapter will examine the various forms in which information may be carried within digital systems concerned with timecode, and starts by examining the nature of number systems.

The denary (decimal) system

All number systems use bases to permit a limited number of symbols to represent a large (in theory infinite) number of values. The number systems in use today use single symbols to represent quantities to a value one increment smaller than the base in use. These symbols are combined to represent higher quantities by the use of multipliers. At present most of the world communicates on a day-to-day basis using a base of 10, a number system called 'decimal' or (more accurately) 'denary'. The denary system numbers quantities from 0 to 9. So, for example, in base 10 the value 274 stands for

$(2 \text{xhundreds}) + (7 \text{xtens}) + (4 \text{xunits}) = (2 \text{x} 10^2) + (7 \text{x} 10^1) + (2 \text{x} 10^0)$

If a base of 5 were used 243 would stand for

$(2 \text{xtwenty-fives}) + (4 \text{xfives}) + (3 \text{xunits}) = (2 \text{x} 5^5) + (5 \text{x} 5^1) + (3 \text{x} 5^0)$, or 73 in base 10

Each multiplier is higher in value than the previous one by a factor determined by the base in use (ten in the case of denary). To prevent any ambiguity we should really include the base value as a suffix to the symbols used, so 274 should read 274_{10}. As denary systems are so ubiquitous such suffixes are invariably dispensed with. When dealing with other number systems prefixes or suffixes are, however, included to make the meaning clear.

The binary system

This system uses the number 2 as its base, and so its symbols range from 0 to 1. The multiplier values are units, twos, fours, eights etc, in the everyday (denary) counting system.

So the value 1101_2 represents (in denary terms):

$(1 \text{x} 8) + (1 \text{x} 4) + (0 \text{x} 2) + (1 \text{x} 1) = 8 + 4 + 0 + 1 = 13$

Since the binary number system uses only two symbols, it lends itself readily to processing by electrical, electronic and magnetic circuitry, as the symbols 0 and 1 can be represented by such methods as the opening/ closing of a switch, the polarity of a voltage, direction of current flow or the reversal of magnetic flux. Table 2.1 illustrates some possible coding methods. As we shall see, each of the methods illustrated presents a problem that might preclude its use in timecode but, nevertheless, noughts and ones lend themselves to simple processing. As timecode uses a form of binary code, it will be as well to examine it in more detail.

With any digital system the protocol determines the number of digits required to carry the information. For example, supposing we wish to

	0/1 indication	
Coding method	Logic 0	Logic 1
Voltage level	Zero voltage	Positive voltage
Voltage polarity	Negative (positive)	Positive (negative)
Frequency shift	f1	f2
Carrier phase	Advance	Retard
Carrier phase	Retard/advance	Advance/retard
Clocked	No clock edge	Clock edge
Clocked	Clock edges at bit edges	Clock edges at bit centres

Table 2.1 Various coding methods can be employed to store and transmit digital data.

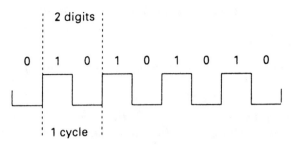

Figure 2.1 Two digits of binary information may require one complete cycle of signal.

quantify a range of weights – say a maximum of 15 g in minimum increments of 1 g – then four weighted binary digits will be required, with each digit representing a different weighted value, in this case 1 g, 2 g, 4g, 8 g. A table may then be constructed (Table 2.2) showing the arrangement of binary digits ('bits') to achieve the range of scaled weights.

Four things can be seen from Table 2.2. Firstly, each bit has a 'weighted' value which is determined by its position in the bit sequence. Secondly, the binary 'word' always contains the same number of bits, even if the leading bits are all set at zero. Thirdly, there is a maximum length to the word length, set at the design stage. Lastly, there is a minimum resolution (in this case 1 g) also set at the design stage. It is not the case, as with analogue systems, of how accurately the numbers can be read – they are present, or not present, unambiguously in the word. If higher resolution is required (or indeed if higher values than those obtainable with the set word length are required) then an extra bit will need to be added at one

	Weighted binary bit values			
Denary values	8	4	2	1
0	0	0	0	0
1	0	0	0	1
2	0	0	1	0
3	0	0	1	1
4	0	1	0	0
5	0	1	0	1
6	0	1	1	0
7	0	1	1	1
8	1	0	0	0
9	1	0	0	1
10	1	0	1	0
11	1	0	1	1
12	1	1	0	0
13	1	1	0	1
14	1	1	1	0
15	1	1	1	1

Table 2.2 Digits having weighted values can signal a range of discrete values.

or other end of the word, which will require a complete system redesign. In a binary system, a digital word n bits long can represent values in the range 0 to $2^n - 1$.

Commonly, microprocessors (found in edit controllers, timecode generators and timebase correctors) and digital communications systems deal in digital words eight bits long. Such groupings of eight bits are known as 'bytes'. The weighted values are as follows:

Weighted denary value	128	64	32	16	8	4	2	1
Bit value	1	1	1	1	1	1	1	1

If all the bits are set to 1 the equivalent denary value is:

$$128+ 64+ 32+ 16+ 8+ 4+ 2+ 1 = 255$$

Therefore, using a word 1 byte (8 bits) long enables all values between 0 and 255 to be identified. In this manner a range of alphanumeric and control codes can be incorporated within a single byte of digital bits.

To summarize: a word of digital bits can be used either to represent quantities (e.g. of time) by the use of weighted digits, or each combination of zeros and ones in the code can be used to represent an alphanumeric symbol or an instruction. In both cases the word length and range of values is set at the design stage.

Binary-coded decimal

Binary-coded decimal (BCD) codes are used to represent denary numbers in binary form. Table 2.2 showed that a 4-bit digital number could carry values from 0 to 15, so there is some redundancy if this were to represent a single denary number, as values 10 to 15 would not be required. A 4-bit digital word, especially one residing within an 8-bit byte, is sometimes referred to as a 'nibble'. To represent single denary numbers combining to give values from 10 to 99, two nibbles would be required: three nibbles would be required for values 100 to 999 etc. Thus the value 87_{10} would be represented by the bit sequence

10000111 (1000 & 0111)

Traditional (EBU/SMPTE or IEC) timecode uses a variation on BCD that accounts for the fact that not all binary words need to count to 9. The tens-of-seconds nibble needs to contain only the values 0 to 5. Where there are unused bits within each nibble, they are used to carry additional data.

Some other timecodes use longer word-lengths in order to obtain a greater range of values than permitted in ordinary BCD. For example, within the R-DAT format an 11-bit word is used to represent the number of audio samples per R-DAT frame; the EBU Radio Data System timecode uses 17 bits to represent values from 0 to 88 404 in order to store the date in Modified Julian Day form ($2^{17} = 131\ 072$).

2's complement coding

In situations where positive and negative value binary numbers are handled (audio signal processing and EBU panscan data in timecode are but two examples) it is convenient to convert the raw binary numbers into 2's complement form. In 2's complement the MS bit signs positive or negative values, and negative value numbers are converted into a form which permits the simple addition of positive and/or negative value numbers.

Positive numbers are given a leading zero. Negative numbers are given a leading zero, '0's and '1's are inverted and '1' is added, as the following example shows:

The value $+7_{10}$ converts to 0111_2
The value -4_{10} converts to 0100_2
0s and 1s are inverted to give 1011_2
A 1 is then added to give 1100_2 (1011 + 0001)
$7_{10} - 4_{10} = 3_{10}$
$0111_2 + 1100_2 = (1)0011_2 = 3_{10}$
The leading 1 falls out of the result.

The hexadecimal system

Reading long strings of 0s and 1s, though simple for computers, can be extremely tedious for humans. To make life simpler some digital signal processors interface with the human world by grouping digits together in blocks four bits long, and presenting the 16 possible values obtained in the form of a single symbol. This form of notation is called 'hexadecimal'. It uses the number 16 as a base, so the symbols range in value from zero to denary fifteen. Unfortunately, we do not have a purpose-built range of symbols for this system, so we use the symbols 0–9 from the denary system, and the symbols A, B, C, D, E, F to represent the denary values ten to fifteen. To reduce the possibility of confusion when dealing with hexadecimal symbols, a prefix is added to the number. This book will use the symbol '&'. The hexadecimal system of symbols with their denary equivalents is:

Hexadecimal:	&0	&1	&2	&3	&4	&5	&6	&7	&8	&9	&A	&B	&C	&D	&E	&F
Decimal:	0	1	2	3	4	5	6	7	8	9	10	11	12	13	14	15

In the hexadecimal system each multiplier is an order of sixteen greater than the preceding one, i.e. 'units', 'sixteens', 'two-hundred-and-fifty-sixes' etc. So the value &A3F represents (in denary terms):

$(10\times256) + (3\times16) + (15\times1) = 2560_{10} + 48_{10} + 15_{10} = 2623_{10}$

In the hexadecimal system ('hex' for short) just two symbols can be used to represent any of two hundred and fifty six different values (0–255 in denary). Computers and teletex make use of this property by using these symbol pairs as codes to represent numbers from 0 to 9, upper and lower case alphabetical symbols, punctuation marks, printer instructions (carriage return, back-space etc), and a whole range of control functions depending on the protocol. These codes can be incorporated into the timecode word.

Bit rate requirements

When we come to examine the rate at which bits need to be generated/ processed for timecode, or indeed if we wish to include data other than pure time information in the code, we need to determine what information timecode requires.

Firstly, timecode requires, at the very least, the ability to carry hours, minutes, seconds and frames data – though some systems carry time data specified in increments of 1/100 frame. Secondly, we need to consider whether a complete codework will be generated for every video or film frame, or whether the time data will be distributed over a series of frames. Thirdly, we need to consider whether the data should contain timecode information alone, or whether other information, such as control signals, should be included in the codeword.

We cannot simply generate one pulse or bit per frame (as a clock may generate one tick or swing of its pendulum per second) as timecode is used to carry information other than the passing of time on a regular basis. It may be used to identify various forms of time, for example 'time from start of tape', 'cumulative recorded material time' etc. There is the matter of reading simple pulses when a machine is starting from standstill. Control track code is a simple pulse identification system. When editing using control track pulses there is frequently some slippage in the edit point as machines run up to speed from standstill. Last there is the requirement to read the code at a variety of tape speeds so that it can be read during shuttle, slow motion or 'jog' operations, or even when the tape is stationary.

If a straightforward binary code were to be used to identify time, then up to 30 frames per second (fps) of information (for NTSC) would be required for every second of the day. This would require a 22-bit wordlength since there are 30 x 60 x 60 x 24 = 2 592 000 decimal number variations per day, represented by 1001111000110100000000 in binary. We could, of course, use a hexadecimal code, which would require only eight symbols (if we used one symbol for each of the elements tens-of-hours, units-of-hours, tens-of-minutes etc), but translated into a binary code at 4 bits per symbol this would require 32 bits per frame.

Binary coded decimal system requires 26 bits to identify each frame, as Table 2.3 shows. This is a rate of 650 bits per second (for PAL) or 780 bits per second (for NTSC). So where does this leave us regarding bandwidth requirements? If the coded bits were alternate 0s and 1s the resulting waveform might resemble a squarewave with a frequency of up to 390 Hz

(Figure 2.1) as each pair of alternate 0s and 1s represents one complete cycle. Control codes are carried by the timecode word, and there may also be other factors involved that determine the data rate. The timecode may, for instance, be mixed (multiplexed) with digital stereo sound as part of a digital interface, or be multiplexed with control codes for musical instruments. (Individual forms of timecode will be examined in detail in later chapters.) No matter what information is carried, if it is to be handled by a magnetic record/replay system or transmitted at varying bit rates, we are going to have a problem with long sequences of zeros or ones as this string represents d.c. as Figure 2.2 illustrates. As we saw in Chapter 1, magnetic replay systems will not be able to replay d.c. since this involves the differentiation of the waveform. If the data rate changes because of a machine speeding up or slowing down, it will not be possible to calculate the number of continuous ones (or zeros) that have passed. The raw data will have to be modified into a suitable form before it can be processed by a magnetic system. This modification is called 'channel coding'.

Hrs tens 0–2	Hrs units 0–9	Mins tens 0–5	Mins units 0–9	Secs tens 0–5	Secs units 0–9	Frames tens 0–2	Frames units 0–9
2 bits	4 bits	3 bits	4 bits	3 bits	4 bits	2 bits	4 bits

Table 2.3 Hours, minutes, seconds and frames data in BCD form can be stored in 26 bits.

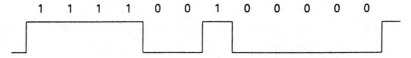

Figure 2.2 A string of consecutive 1s or 0s requires the ability to handle d.c.

Simple digital codes

A number of codes are available for the processing of digital data, each with its own characteristics. It may, as we have seen, be necessary to minimize d.c. content; there may be a requirement to read the code correctly when the connector has been wrongly wired causing the data to be inverted; the code may have to be self-clocking so that it can be correctly read over a wide range of replay speeds - there will certainly be a need for all the above in codes intended for LTC. Within many digital recorders there may be a requirement for a high packing density of the digital data.

    A number of digital codes are of interest where timecode is concerned, and these will now be examined.

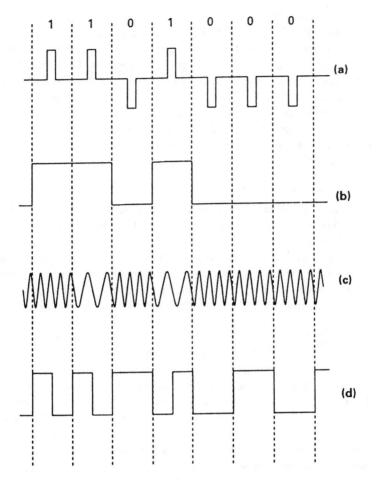

Figure 2.3 Return to zero codes (a) are self-clocking but require 3 identifiable levels. Non return to zero codes (b) are more robust but are not self-clocking. Frequency shift keying (c) requires a wide bandwidth. It is not polarity conscious, unlike RZ and NRZ codes. Biphase mark code (d) is self-clocking and not polarity conscious.

Return to zero (RZ) code

Illustrated in Figure 2.3a, this code uses three levels or states. These can be implemented in magnetic record/replay systems by using polarity reversal of recording current to identify 0s and 1s, with zero current representing absence of data. This code will be self-clocking, but it is not immune from phase reversal resulting from connector pins being reversed, since the positive and negative data pulses will be inverted. It has found a use in the EBU/IRT timecode for 16 mm magnetic stripe film.

Non return to zero code

This is illustrated in Figure 2.3b. This code has just two states. Polarity reversal indicates 0s or 1s. The code is not self-clocking since there is no way of distinguishing a run of 1s or 0s at other than a known speed. The code is subject to differentiation on replay. It is also polarity-conscious: if a connector is reverse-wired the ones and zeros will be inverted. These features make it unsuitable for direct recording of data on audiotape, but it is used for VITC, where the record/replay speed will be known (since the write/read speed of a helical scan video head is virtually independent of linear tape speed for a given format), where there is no possibility of polarity reversal, and where the recording system avoids signal differentiation on replay.

Frequency shift keying (FSK)

FSK code uses different frequencies to represent different logical values. For timecode with just two values (0 and 1), two frequencies will be required. Since specific frequencies represent specific logic levels, filters can be used to improve noise immunity, though this will prevent the recorded code being read at other than standard play speed. This code also has a poor packing density since several cycles will be required per logic digit for decoding. The code is illustrated in Figure 2.3c.

FM or bi-phase mark code

Originally known as Manchester-1 code, this is used for longitudinal timecode. It is, in effect, the limiting case of frequency-shift keying. It is d.c. free and self-clocking. There is always a transition on a clock edge, and an additional transition between edges to indicate logical 1. It is illustrated in Figure 2.3d. It can be read over a wide range of play speeds, hence its use for LTC, although its packing density and immunity from timing jitter are poor. The code is not polarity-conscious, as it is the presence or not of a transition that indicates 1 or 0.

Organization of digital data

One big advantage of processing information in digital form is that a series of 0s and 1s can be processed very easily, and at low cost, by electronic switches. Data can be handed on from one switch to the next very easily, and can be fed out from the system at a regular rate under the control of an electronic clock. Figure 2.4 illustrates the processes.

To facilitate the above processes it is convenient to organize the data stream into digital words or blocks, each of which has a known length and contains information identifying the start (or end) of the word. It might also be provided with some form of digital 'address' that will enable it to be placed correctly in the data stream in the event of the data words not being stored in order of time precedence. Figure 2.5 illustrates some common forms of data organization. The details of the LTC word will be covered in detail in Chapter 3.

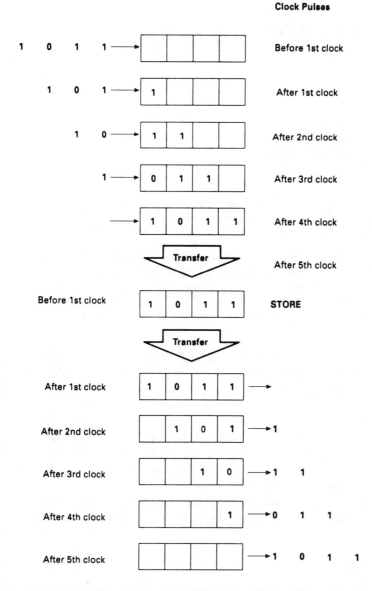

Figure 2.4 Digital data can be clocked into a shift register, then stored. They can later be clocked out. The clock rates need not be identical as long as strategies are employed to prevent the store from overflowing or emptying.

Causes of errors in digital systems

Errors can occur in digital processing systems for a variety of reasons. They result in data being misread, possibly with catastrophic results. Because of this, various techniques and working practices have been

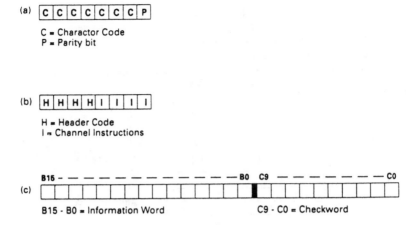

Figure 2.5 Common forms of data organization. ASCII codes carry alphanumeric and control characters in packets of 8 bits (a). 7 carry data, the 8th is parity. MIDI Header Codes comprise 1 byte divided into 2 nibbles (b). The Radio Data System packages data into blocks of 26 bits (c). 18 of these carry information, 10 perform identification and error checking.

evolved to reduce the incidence and effects of errors. For example, checking bits may be added to each data word. These provide at the least a simple warning that a single bit has been misread. At a more sophisticated level, they may take the form of a complex code added to each data word that will detect and correct many errors; the data word may be repeated a number of times within a video frame to minimize the effects of drop-out on tape; the data may be reprocessed every time they are copied to avoid the cumulative effects of noise and distortion that may eventually corrupt the data.

Causes of data corruption include phase distortion, timing errors, drops in signal level, electrical noise and spurious spikes added to the data.

Phase distortion

All reactive networks, whether capacitive or inductive, introduce phase shift. At low frequency this is usually unimportant. In video circuits phase shifts are always corrected for us, as if left uncorrected they would have a profound effect on the viewed picture. The magnetic replay process also causes phase shifts because it is one of differentiation. In all cases the result is to move the timing of pulse edges.

This problem of phase shift is not pronounced for longitudinal timecode at standard replay speeds, and tape machines specifically designed to handle timecode will usually have integral re-shaping or reprocessing circuitry so that a clean rectangular waveform is present at the timecode output of the machine. However, some machines are not designed for phase-corrected replay of timecode, and an operator may well be faced with timecode on an ordinary audio track (for example, with some industrial-grade formats). In these cases the timecode should be reprocessed externally, particularly if the code is to be copied across onto another machine. Reprocessing, also known as regenerating, completely cleans up a digital signal as long as the data have not been corrupted. Pulse edges are reshaped, noise and unwanted transitions (spikes) are removed, and timing errors minimized. Reprocessing should be thought of as a preventative measure rather than a cure, though as we shall see in a later chapter, reprocessing may be used to repair corrupted data. There is the possibility that noise reduction circuitry can cause unwanted phase shifts, so noise reduction should be switched off on any track being used for timecode.

Timing errors

Plainly, if a tape is to be replayed at other than standard speed (or at least within a few per cent of standard speed) the digital data are not going to be read at the correct rate. Most timecode readers will accept data over a wide range of spooling speeds, and feed it out at the standard rate after reprocessing. They may cause timecode numbers (addresses) to be repeated if the replay speed is slow, and can result in gaps in the addresses at high spooling speeds. Where timecode data are recorded on the helical tracks of videotape or R-DAT machines, the read head may scan more than one recorded track when playing at other than standard speed. In some formats it is possible for the timecode to be distributed among the programme data in such a way that it can be re-assembled (R-DAT is such a format); in others the replay head(s) can be dynamically repositioned to follow the recorded tracks.

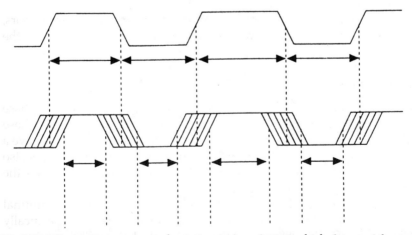

Figure 2.6 Timing jitter reduces the time window during which data may be read unambiguously.

One major cause of timing errors at standard speeds on helical scan machines is small variations in tape speed due to 'flutter'. Magnetic tape is slightly elastic; as it passes in front of tape heads and fixed guides, friction causes a stick-slip effect which superimposes small high-frequency variations on the standard speed, called 'jitter'. Figure 2.6 illustrates the effect on timecode pulse edges. The decision-making elements in a digital system have a certain latitude of replayed level beyond which the result is improbable. Timing jitter will reduce the window still further, as Figure 2.7a shows. The combination of timing jitter and partial dropout results in a trade-off between the two, known as the 'eye height' (Figure 2.7b). Any pulse transition falling outside this clear area of the 'eye' will result in possible misreading. If the misread bit was weighted to contain a significant proportion of the total value the result could be catastrophic.

All tape record/replay systems suffer from this problem, and, as we have seen in Chapter 1, video replay machines are equipped with timebase correctors to correct for this on their video output(s). Timing errors on videotape machines can be quite severe without the picture being affected because of the timebase corrector, but an audio machine slaved to unreprocessed longitudinal timecode coming directly off the video tape can hunt in speed as it attempts to follow the varying timecode rate. The solution to this problem is either to reprocess the off-VCR timecode, or to ensure that any synchronizer interface between video master and slave audio will smooth out these speed variations so that 'wow' is not noticeably present. This subject will be dealt with in detail in Chapter 9.

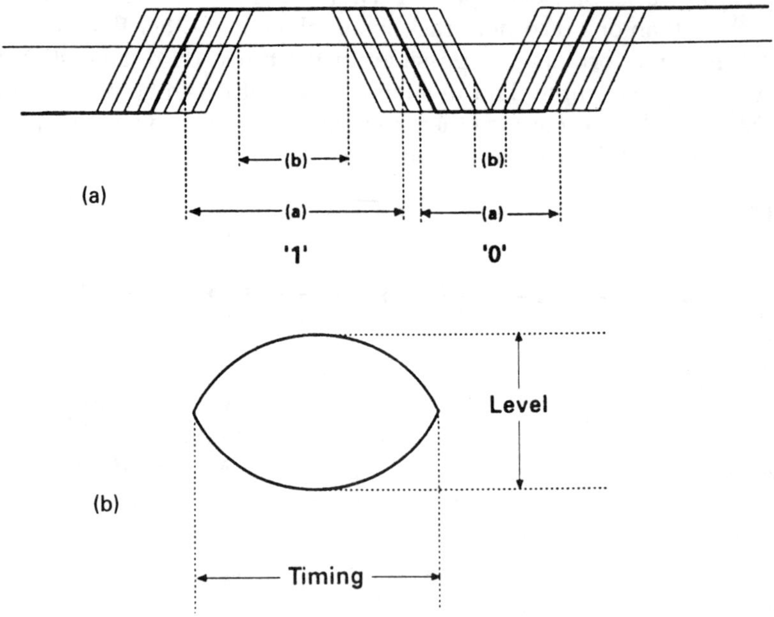

Figure 2.7 Timing jitter and amplitude variations combine to reduce the clear window (a), and can be traded off against each other (b) to give an 'eye height' diagram. This will specify system performance in terms of timing stability and amplitude variation.

Drop in replay level

Longitudinal timecode is often recorded at low levels of magnetic flux (compared with, say, peak level programme material) in order to minimize crosstalk. Variations in replayed level are therefore likely to cause problems. Dirty replay heads are a major cause of dropout. This is a particular problem with some video formats because of the low linear tape speeds. At the comparatively slow data rates employed by longitudinal timecode, dropout has to be quite severe before time data is lost, but if timecode is embedded either within the analogue video signal or within the bit stream of digital programme data, then even short-term dropout can cause severe loss of code. Analogue video recording systems, as we saw in Chapter 1, have their own specific ways of coping with this eventuality. Digital systems can handle loss of data in much more sophisticated ways as there is no need to handle the signal in real time. Compressors and limiters effectively reduce the dynamic range of any signal being recorded, as do automatic level controls. Because of this they should be bypassed on any track used to record longitudinal timecode.

Spikes appearing on the data

The usual cause of spikes appearing on a digital bit stream is poor installation. It may be that electrical machinery using the same mains supply is switching on and off, putting sudden spikes or noise signals onto the mains and these are finding their way onto the data-processing circuits. There is absolutely no excuse for digital systems crashing because of mains-borne interference. If the cost of a purpose-installed technical earth is prohibitive then interference suppressors should be fitted in the mains supplies. Chapter 7 deals with the matter.

Error detection

If all preventative measures fail and data become corrupted, then some form of warning (error detection) will enable strategies to be employed to prevent the errors causing problems.

The simplest form of error detection, as far as timecode is concerned, is to check the time data in the incoming word against the time data in the previous word. If the times are not contiguous then either the incoming word has been corrupted or there is a deliberate change in the time data. A corruption to the data is unlikely to last over more than a couple of frames so the incoming data can be examined for a few frames, while the regenerator generates a contiguous set of timecode words based on the last known (assumed) good word, Figure 2.8 illustrates this. Depending on the data arriving after the discontinuity, there will be a number of options open for action. These will be examined in Chapter 7.

It is possible to include a single bit of data within a digital word, usually (but not necessarily) at the end, whose value is chosen so that there is an even (or odd) number of 1s within the word, depending on the protocol. This additional bit is called a 'parity bit'. When the codeword arrives, the number of 1s can be checked to see whether there is an even (or odd) count. This process is known as 'parity checking'. A protocol requiring an even (odd) total of 1s in the word is called 'even (odd) parity'. Figure 2.9 illustrates the principle. A single parity check cannot guarantee to detect more than one single error per word, nor can it indicate which bit is in error. The longitudinal timecode word contains such a bit. It was not intended as a parity bit, it was intended to make the join between successive codewords smoother (see Chapter 3), but it is in effect a parity bit, and as such can be used for checking the validity of the word – though whether a single parity bit is of much use to an eighty-bit word is open to debate.

	Faulty Timecode Off tape	Regenerated Timecode	
	00:23:14:21	00:23:14:21	
	00:23:14:22	00:23:14:22	
	00:23:14:23	00:23:14:23	
	00:23:14:24	00:23:14:24	
	00:23:15:00	00:23:15:00	
	00:23:15:01	00:23:15:01	
	00:23:15:02	00:23:15:02	
	00:23:15:03	00:23:15:03	
Unreadable	*************	00:23:15:04	Re-generated
code off	*************	00:23:15:05	code fills in
tape	*************	00:23:15:06	missing addresses
	00:23:15:07	00:23:15:07	
	00:23:15:08	00:23:15:08	
	00:23:15:09	00:23:15:09	
	00:23:15:10	00:23:15:10	
	00:23:15:11	00:23:15:11	

Figure 2.8 A regenerator can continue generating a contiguous series of time addresses in the event of short-term loss of code. Long-term loss can be regenerated if all devices are connected to a common set of sync pulses.

More sophisticated forms of error detection are the Cyclic Redundancy Check Code (CRC or CRCC) and the Checksum, both of which are used with various forms of timecode. Both forms of error detection involve placing a codeword on the end of the data word before transmission or recording, and using it after reception or replay to check whether the time data have been corrupted. The value of the codeword is determined by the weighted values of the digits making up the time data. CRCs and checksums are extremely powerful tools for detecting errors. They both require additional bits to carry the checking data, which has implications for the data rate. The CRCC used in Vertical Interval Timecode can detect burst (i.e. consecutive bit) errors with a certainty of better than 99.5% (misdetection is less than 1/256 for a burst error of 10 consecutive bits or more).

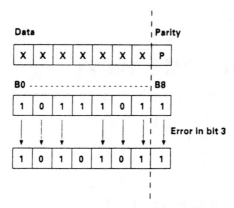

Figure 2.9 Even parity. If a single bit fails, an odd number of 1s results. This can be detected, but there is no indication of which bit has failed, nor will errors in an even number of bits be detected.

CHAPTER 3

The timecode word

The original quadruplex cue track

When practical videotape recorders were first being developed by the Ampex Corporation, a narrow-bandwidth, voice-quality audio track was incorporated onto the then current 2 inch VTRs in addition to the high-quality audio track. Although designed principally to record such material as talkback, the bandwidth of this longitudinal track allowed a 2400 baud (bits/second) digital signal to be recorded and replayed. At a video frame rate of 30 fps, this corresponds to a density of 80 bits per frame. The bit rate was limited by the need to read the signal while the tape was spooling.

The development of a longitudinal timecode (LTC) word

An 80-bit word will permit 2^{80} (equivalent to approximately 10^{24}) combinations of information to be incorporated in each frame. This is far in excess of that required to record hours, minutes, seconds and frames (approx 10^6 or 2^{20}). Longitudinal timecode requires 26 bits to record a frame-accurate time address, so additional data could be incorporated. This has been fortunate, as later developments have been able to use the spare capacity.

The biphase mark code

Although binary number systems lend themselves readily to processing by electronic circuitry, we saw in Chapter 1 that the output voltage of a magnetic record/replay device depends on the derivative (rate of change) of the recorded magnetic flux on replay rather than the absolute flux level, so runs of consecutive digits without any transitions in flux on replay cannot be decoded.

In Chapter 2 we saw that RZ, NRZ and FSK codes are all unsuitable for longitudinal timecode. To make the code self-clocking, while exploiting the full potential amplitude for code pulse transitions, and to make it immune from accidental polarity reversals, the clocking information is incorporated into the code itself, using the pulse edges rather than the instantaneous code polarity to carry the digital information.

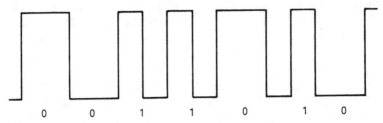

Figure 3.1 Biphase mark systems are independent of signal polarity, are self-clocking and d.c. free.

A digital zero is represented by the absence of any transition in the middle of the space between clock pulse edges, a digital one is represented by such a transition, positive- or negative-going as appropriate. The start of each bit space is marked by a transition, again positive- or negative-going as appropriate (Figure 3.1). Decoders in timecode readers enable the signal to be read over a wide range of replay speeds. The d.c. value of the code varies very little, simplifying the design of associated electronics. The ability to detect sharp pulse edges for timing accuracy will require a bandwidth capable of passing at least the 3rd harmonic of the fundamental frequencies.

User bits

The spare capacity permits timecode users to incorporate digital information of their own, grouped in the form of 4-bit words. These binary groups are commonly called 'user bits'. They can be used for a variety of purposes such as identifying take/shot numbers, calendar date, client code etc. The only limitation to their use is the ingenuity of the user. Several versions of the standard code have the option of putting a date into these groups, others incorporate alphanumeric character codes (ASCII code), and yet others can record details of a film shoot, such as scene, take and roll numbers.

There are eight of these groups per frame, so up to $8 \times 25 = 200$ 4-bit blocks of information can be sent per second in a 625/50 system. Eight bits (7 data, 1 parity) are required for each alphanumeric character, so four 8-bit characters can be sent per video frame.

The form of the LTC word

When applied to video- and audiotape recording, the code is continuous. Each codeword starts at the clock edge immediately before the first bit (bit 0). The bits are uniformly spaced, and there are eighty bits per frame. The resulting bit rate varies between 1920 bits/second (for 24 fps applications) and 2400 bits/second (for 30 fps). Used as a time and control code for television recorders, the previous EBU and SMPTE standards have been incorporated into the IEC standard 421:1986 (amended in 1990). Within the EBU this has been implemented as EBU standard N12: 1994. In the UK this has been implemented as BS 6865:1987 (amended 1993) and in the USA as SMPTE 12M:1994 (which also includes a specification for timecode for use with High Definition TV having 1125 lines/frame at 60 fps). This book will refer to the code as IEC timecode, and will highlight the difference in its implementation by the EBU and the SMPTE in terms of 625/50, 525/60 and 1125/60 versions of the code. The implementation of the SMPTE 24 fps code for film use will be dealt with at the end of this chapter, and again separately in Chapter 5.

Frames units 1st binary group	} Byte 1
Frames tens 2nd binary group	} Byte 2
Seconds units 3rd binary group	} Byte 3
Second tens 4th binary group	} Byte 4
Minutes units 5th binary group	} Byte 5
Minutes tens 6th binary group	} Byte 6
Hours units 7th binary group	} Byte 7
Hours tens 8th binary group	} Byte 8
Synchronization	Byte 9
Synchronization	Byte 10

Figure 3.2 The LTC word comprises 10 bytes. 8 of these carry time and control data, 2 carry synchronization and direction information.

LTC byte arrangement

In both versions of the code, the longitudinal timecode word can be thought of as comprising 8 bytes (64 bits) of data followed by 2 bytes (16 bits) of synchronizing information (Figure 3.2), making 80 bits in all, numbered 0–79. Twenty-six of the available bits are used to indicate the coded time down to the nearest frame. The time information is distributed throughout the length of the complete word.

Each data byte is divided into two 4-bit nibbles; 2, 3 or 4 bits of time data in the first nibble, and 4 bits of user data in the second. Bytes 2, 4, 6 and 8 contain additional information in the first nibble of each byte. This information differs slightly between the 625/50 and 525/60 versions of the code. The arrangement of the data in bytes, and the placing of the user information in the second nibble of each byte permits easy implementation of control data such as edit decision list information for an edit controller, shot listing on location, and the carrying of additional timecodes, enabling the video post-production of film. As the binary groups are arranged in groups of four bits, they can each be used to represent a hexadecimal number, or can be combined in pairs to carry 4 International Characters (ASCII, etc.) per timecode frame. In both the 625/ 50 and 525/60 versions of the code the time and user data occupy the same places within the complete word, as Figure 3.3 illustrates.

The assignment of the time bits can be summarized as follows:

Pictures	Units:	Bits 0–3:	arranged 1, 2, 4, 8:	count 0–9
	Tens:	Bits 8–9:	arranged 1, 2:	count 0–2
Seconds	Units:	Bits 16–19:	arranged 1, 2, 4, 8:	count 0–9
	Tens:	Bits 24–26:	arranged 1, 2, 4:	count 0–5
Minutes	Units:	Bits 32–35:	arranged 1, 2, 4, 8:	count 0–9
	Tens:	Bits 40–42:	arranged 1, 2, 4:	count 0–5
Hours	Units:	Bits 48–51:	arranged 1, 2, 4, 8:	count 0–9
	Tens:	Bits 56–57:	arranged 1, 2:	count 0–2

A twenty-four hour clock is used. The first frame of the day is reckoned as 00h 00m 00s 01f (00h 00m 00s 00f is reckoned as midnight at the end of the day – the count does not go up to 24h 00m 00s 00f).

Bits 64 to 79 make up that part of the overall timecode word called the 'synchronizing word'. This consists of a pair of 0s at its start, a 0 and 1 at its end, and a chain of 12 1s in between. The purpose of the synchronizing word is two-fold: it serves to indicate clearly the end of one word and the start of the next, since nowhere else in the word can twelve successive ones exist. It also indicates whether the tape is being played forwards or backwards since the pair of 0s will come first if the tape is being moved forwards, and a 1 followed by a 0 will indicate the tape being moved in reverse (Figure 3.4).

In both 625/50 and 525/60 versions of the code, bits 10, 11, 27, 43, 58 and 59 carry no time or user data. The implementation of these additional data bits varies between the two versions of the code, and will be dealt with separately.

The detail of the 625/50 LTC

The implementation of the additional data bits is as follows:

Bit 10
Unassigned. The use of this bit is reserved by the IEC. Until it is assigned it must be a permanent zero.

625/50 Systems	Bit no.	BCD wgt		525/60 Systems
	0	1		
	1	2	Frames	
	2	4	units	
	3	8		
	4			
	5		1st user	
	6		group	
	7			
	8	1	Frames	
	9	2	tens	
Unassigned	10			Drop frame flag
Colour frame flag	11			Colour frame flag
	12			
	13		2nd user	
	14		group	
	15			
	16	1		
	17	2	Seconds	
	18	4	units	
	19	8		
	20			
	21		3rd user	
	22		group	
	23			
	24	1	Seconds	
	25	2	tens	
	26	4		
Binary group flag 0 (BGF0)	27			Biphase mark correction
	28			
	29		4th user	
	30		group	
	31			
	32	1		
	33	2	Minutes	
	34	4	units	
	35	8		
	36			
	37		5th user	
	38		group	
	39			
	40	1	Minutes	
	41	2	tens	
	42	4		

Figure 3.3 The 625/50 and 525/60 LTC words compared.

Binary group flag 2 (BGF2)		43					Binary group flag 0 (BGF0)
		44					
		45		6th user			
		46		group			
		47					
		48	1				
		49	2	Hours			
		50	4	units			
		51	8				
		52					
		53		7th user			
		54		group			
		55					
		56	1	Hours			
		57	2	tens			
Binary group flag 1 (BGF1)		58					Binary group flag 1 (BGF1)
Biphase mark correction		59					Binary group flag 2 (BGF2)
		60					
		61		8th user			
		62		group			
		63					
	0	64		S			0
	0	65		Y			0
	1	66		N			1
	1	67		C			1
	1	68		H			1
	1	69		R			1
	1	70		O			1
	1	71		N			1
	1	72		I			1
	1	73		S			1
	1	74		I			1
	1	75		N			1
	1	76		G	W		1
	1	77			O		1
	1	78			R		0
	1	79			D		1

Figure 3.3 cont.

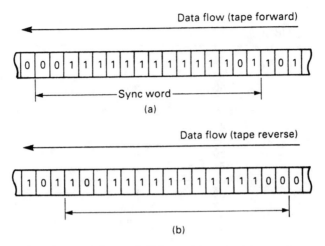

Data flow (tape forward)

| 0 | 0 | 0 | 1 | 1 | 1 | 1 | 1 | 1 | 1 | 1 | 1 | 1 | 1 | 1 | 1 | 0 | 1 | 1 | 0 | 1 |

Sync word

(a)

Data flow (tape reverse)

| 1 | 0 | 1 | 1 | 0 | 1 | 1 | 1 | 1 | 1 | 1 | 1 | 1 | 1 | 1 | 1 | 1 | 0 | 0 | 0 |

(b)

Figure 3.4 The 2 bits at either end of the synchronization word are not symmetrical. This enables the direction of tape motion to be determined.

Bit 11

This is the colour frame flag bit. Its purpose is to indicate whether or not the timecode has a specific relationship to the phase of the colour sub-carrier. As discussed in Chapter 1, the colour sub-carrier changes phase with respect to the line sync pulse every line in order to minimize patterning, and it takes eight fields, four complete frames in PAL systems, to return to its original phase at the beginning of the frame (the first of the broad pulses in the vertical interval in 625/50 systems). In the SECAM system the sequence is 2 frames (4 fields) long. In both these systems the colour sub-carrier, extrapolated back to the leading edge of the first line pulse of the first field of the day shall be crossing zero and going positive (Figure 3.5). The international standard is that the first frame of the day will be frame 1, fields 1 and 2. To achieve this relationship the timecode generator needs to be locked to the sync pulse generator generating the colour sub-carrier. When the relationship is correct, bit 11 in the timecode word is set to digital 1. The details are covered in Appendix 1.

Bits 27, 43 and 58

We have already seen that the binary groups can be set to carry additional information such as the eight-bit character set specified in ISO 646 and ISO 2022. Prior to 1993, bit 58 was unassigned, and bits 27 and 43 flagged the use of the binary groups to carry these characters. In 1993, however, the SMPTE proposed the use of bits 27, 43 and 58 to flag the extended use of the binary groups in a 'page-line index' through the use of time multiplexing the data over several timecode words. This extended use permits the carrying of an additional timecode, control codes, text and production information. A description of the page-line index is given in Appendix 5, the detail being given in SMPTE 262M. The following truth table applies to these bits in 625/25 systems:

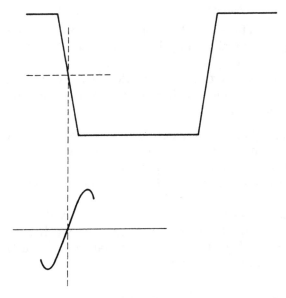

Figure 3.5 At the start of the 1st field of the day, the colour sub-carrier is crossing zero, going positive, at the same time as the leading edge of the 1st sync pulse is at half amplitude.

	Bit 27 BGF0	Bit 43 BGF2	Bit 58 BGF1
Character set unspecified	0	0	0
8-bit set to ISO 646 and ISO 2022	1	0	0
Page/line index	1	1	0

All other states are unassigned and should be set to zero as their use is reserved.

Figure 3.6 illustrates the arrangement of the binary groups for the ISO character sets. Groups 1/2, 3/4, 5/6, 7/8 each combine to define one ISO character.

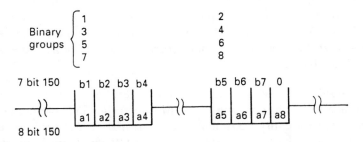

Figure 3.6 The eight 4-bit user groups may be combined to carry four alphanumeric characters to either ISO 646 or ISO 2022 standards.

The basic ISO 646 character set defines two 7-bit Latin code tables:

(a) Basic code table with all alphanumeric characters, punctuation marks, and control functions, together with ten free codes for national use and some limited graphics.
(b) International reference version (IRV), having the national characters filled, and a choice made where more than one graphic symbol is shown in the basic table.

The ISO 2022 gives code extension techniques by converting the code to 8-bit, based on the ISO 646 'Escape' command. This gives access to a library of centrally-registered characters such as ASCII and Teletext. The registration is done by the French National Standardization Office (AFNOR).

If bits 27 and 43 are set to 0 and 1 respectively, this indicates the use of the binary groups for carrying information when shooting with film. Although the SMPTE has an accepted standard, at the time of writing it has not been adopted in Europe.

Bit 59

This is the biphase mark correction bit. There are many occasions during post-production when non-contiguous sections of code (that is, code recorded as a continuous stripe, but where the time addresses do not increment up one at a time) may have to be joined together. This will happen when programme material comes from different parts of the master tape(s), or when Time of Day code has been recorded. When this occurs there is the possibility of losing the clock edge at the join, causing the timecode readers and synchronizers to miscount.

The following example explains the principle. Consider a 5-bit word containing 4 bits of data plus a spare bit. If we joined together two such words, the first containing 0101, with the spare bit set to 1, the second containing 0111, with the spare bit set to 1, the two words will join together in such a manner as to preserve the clock edges at the join (Figure 3.7a). However, should the first word contain an odd number of 0s, for example 1110, with the spare bit set to 1, then the clock edge will be lost at the join (Figure 3.7b).

The way round the problem is to ensure every word contains an even number of 0s (and hence an even number of 1s). Bit 59 is put in a state to make bits 0 to 79 of the timecode word contain an even number of 0s. At the time of writing the biphase mark correction bit is not a requirement for tape interchange.

Codeword timing

Synchronization of the codeword with the video signal is necessary if the codeword is to identify accurately an individual video frame. For the 625/50 version of the code, the start of the word (the half-amplitude point of the leading edge of bit 0) shall occur within the period of the field (broad) pulses at the start of the frame with which the codeword is associated (Figure 3.8).

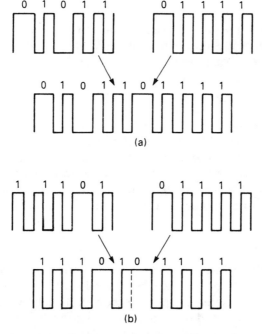

Figure 3.7 (a) A word ending with a positive-going transition will join the next word unambiguously. (b) If the word ends with a negative-going edge the transition will be lost.

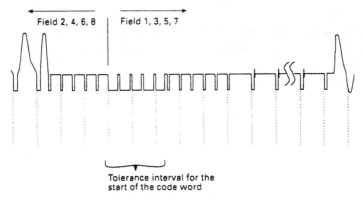

Figure 3.8 The LTC word must start within the first 2 lines of the frame in 625/50 systems.

The detail of the 525/60 LTC

Although the 525/60 code runs at 30 fps or so for video, the time data, synchronization and binary groups bits are arranged in exactly the same way as the 625/60 version. The remaining bits differ in their application.

Bit 10

This is the drop frame flag. It is used to indicate whether the frame rate is exactly 30 fps or if it is approximately 29.97 fps. It is set to '1' if a 29.97 (drop frame) rate is being used.

Bit 11

This is the colour frame flag bit. The NTSC system utilizes a 4-field colour sequence, the frames being labelled 'A' and 'B'. If an even timecode address identifies an 'A' frame, and an odd address a 'B' frame then this bit is set to '1'. Note that to maintain the sequence through an edit point, an even code address must be followed by an odd one. Drop frame working permits this because two consecutive frames are dropped at the start of each minute (except each tenth minute), and not one frame each 30 seconds.

Bit 27

This is the biphase mark correction bit. It performs exactly the same function as its counterpart in the 625/50 version of the code, so the detail will not be repeated here. One point worthy of note, however, is that the original version of this code did not provide this facility, so this bit was set to permanent zero. As a result some elderly NTSC editing systems cannot read timecode correctly with biphase mark correction in operation. Note that its position in the word differs from its 625/50 counterpart.

Bits 43 (BGF0), 58 (BGF1) and 59 (BGF2)

These are the binary group flags. They perform similar functions to their counterparts in the 625/50 version of the code, though their positions in the word differ from their 625/50 counterparts. There are SMPTE standards and recommendations for the use of the binary groups with film. These are covered in Chapter 5. These flags signal the various uses.

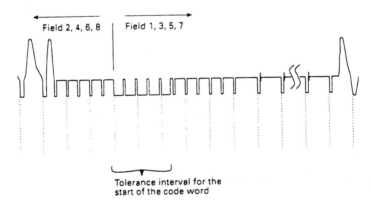

Figure 3.9 The LTC word must start within lines 6/7 of the frame in 525/60 systems.

Codeword timing

In the 525/60 version of the code, the start of the word (the half-amplitude point of the leading edge of bit zero) shall coincide with the start of line seven of the frame with which the codeword is associated, plus or minus one line (Figure 3.9). Note that the specification for the start of a field differs between 625/50 and 525/60 systems.

The requirement for vertical interval timecode (VITC)

Longitudinal timecode has several shortcomings when used to edit videotape. Chief among these are the impossibility of reading it when the tape is stationary, or when the tape is being jogged slowly to find an exact edit point. As a number of lines in the field interval are not used to carry pictures, it is possible to utilize some of them to carry timecode. Though some may carry chrominance information, test signals or teletext information, enough are available, with careful choice of line, to carry timecode during the editing stages of production. As the active line period is approximately 52 µs long in both 625/50 and 525/60 systems it is possible to incorporate a 90-bit code into one or more of these spare lines without exceeding the bandwidth limit (Figure 3.10).

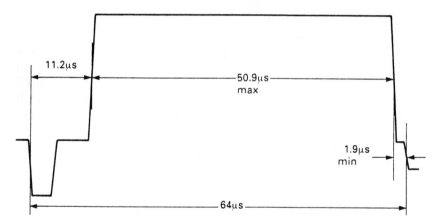

Figure 3.10 A 90-bit word may be incorporated within the active line period without exceeding the bandwidth limits.

The form of the VITC word

The VITC word is ninety bits long (bits 0–89). It takes the form of 8 bytes of time and user data, each byte (including the first) being preceded by a pair of synchronizing pulses. The eight data bytes are followed by 1 byte of cyclic redundancy check code (Figure 3.11). It is incorporated within the vertical interval in each field of the video signal, with a margin of a few lines before the active frame. There are differences in the lines specified as valid for the code between 625/50 and 525/60 versions, and these will be dealt with separately. It has traditionally been repeated twice within each field to guard against dropout. Since dropout may have a duration of more than one line, VITC is usually recorded on two non-adjacent lines with an intervening blank line between them. At the time of writing there is no agreed standard as to which lines VITC should occupy. Recent developments in timecode applications, and increasing pressure on the use of the vertical interval for additional signals, have led manufacturers to provide the options that include VITC on 1 line per field, and VITC repeated in a block over several consecutive lines. Since the code is incorporated within each field of the video frame, it is possible to include information within the codeword to identify the field.

Synchronization

Frames units
1st binary group   } Byte 1

Synchronization

Frames tens
2nd binary group   } Byte 2

Synchronization

Seconds units
3rd binary group   } Byte 3

Synchronization

Second tens
4th binary group   } Byte 4

Synchronization

Minutes units
5th binary group   } Byte 5

Synchronization

Minutes tens
6th binary group   } Byte 6

Synchronization

Hours units
7th binary group   } Byte 7

Synchronization

Hours tens
8th binary group   } Byte 8

Synchronization

Cyclic redundancy
check code

Figure 3.11 The VITC word comprises 8 data bytes containing time and control information, followed by a single byte for error detection. Each byte is preceded by two synchronizing bits.

The vertical interval version of timecode need not be self-clocking, since the reading speed of a videotape machine scanning head is virtually independent of tape speed within certain limits. The code is therefore not biphase, and a simple 'non return to zero' code is used. There is no synchronizing word because, being incorporated within a small part of a complete video field, the data are not presented as a continuous bit stream. As the video heads will always read the video tracks in the same direction, there is no need to indicate the direction in which the time address data are being presented.

A digital 1 is represented by a positive voltage substantially above blanking level (its actual level differs between the 625/50 and 525/60 versions). A digital 0 is repesented by a voltage at blanking level.

As the codeword occupies approximately 50 μs of the active video line, the data rate is 1.8 megabits/second. If the bits presented are a sequence of 1s and 0s, this rate of data represents a fundamental frequency of 0.9 MHz. To preserve the steep pulse edges required for timing accuracy, the third harmonic must be present. This implies a bandwidth requirement of at least 2.7 MHz. Not all industrial-grade (or domestic!) video recorders will support this.

In both 625/50 and 525/60 versions of the code, the time and user data occupy the same places within the complete word, as Figure 3.12 (pp. 44–45) illustrates, though the positions of the flag bits can vary, as with LTC.

The cyclic redundancy check bits

Parity checking is unsuitable for videotape applications because of the high risk of tape dropout. In place of the now unnecessary synchronizing word, the VITC word contains 8 bits of error protection in the form of a cyclic redundancy check word, bits 82–89. The generating polynomial is $G(x) = x^8 + 1$. There is no automatic error correction within the word but, as we see later, other techniques are employed to improve the immunity of the system to errors. As codeword is repeated several times per frame there is a high probability of the data being recovered without error.

The detail of the 625/50 VITC

Position within the field interval

In its 625/50 version, the VITC word is placed no earlier than line 6 (319), and no later than line 22 (335). However, there are constraints about which lines are most suitable, since the field interval is often used for processes other than field synchronization. In the SECAM system lines 7 to 15 (320 to 328) are occupied by field identification signals, so should be avoided. To avoid possible reading errors which may arise in the presence

625/50 Systems	Bit no.	BCD wgt		525/60 Systems
	0		Sync	
	1		bits	
	2	1		
	3	2	Frames	
	4	4	units	
	5	8		
	6			
	7		1st user	
	8		group	
	9			
	10		Sync	
	11		bits	
	12	1	Frames	
	13	2	tens	
Unassigned	14			Drop frame flag
Colour frame flag	15			Colour frame flag
	16			
	17		2nd user	
	18		group	
	19			
	20		Sync	
	21		bits	
	22	1		
	23	2	Seconds	
	24	4	units	
	25	8		
	26			
	27		3rd user	
	28		group	
	29			
	30		Sync	
	31		bits	
	32	1	Seconds	
	33	2	tens	
	34	4		
Binary group flag 0 (BGF0)	35			Field market bit
	36			
	37		4th user	
	38		group	
	39			
	40		Sync	
	41		bits	

Figure 3.12 The 625/50 and 525/60 VITC words compared.

	42	1		
	43	2	Minutes	
	44	4	units	
	45	8		
	46			
	47		5th user	
	48		group	
	49			
	50		Sync	
	51		bits	
	52	1	Minutes	
	53	2	tens	
	54	4		
Binary group flag 2 (BGF2)	55			Binary group flag 0 (BGF0)
	56			
	57		6th user	
	58		group	
	59			
	60		Sync	
	61		bits	
	62	1		
	63	2	Hours	
	64	4	units	
	65	8		
	66			
	67		7th user	
	68		group	
	69			
	70		Sync	
	71		bits	
	72	1	Hours	
	73	2	tens	
Binary group flag 1 (BGF1)	74			Binary group flag 1 (BGF1)
Field market bit	75			Binary group flag 2 (BGF2)
	76			
	77		8th user	
	78		group	
	79			
	80		Sync	
	81		bits	
	82			
	83			
	84			
Cyclic redundancy	85			Cyclic redundancy
check code	86			check code
	87			
	88			
	89			

Figure 3.12 cont.

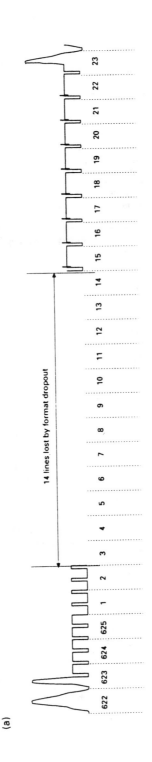

(a)

14 lines lost by format dropout

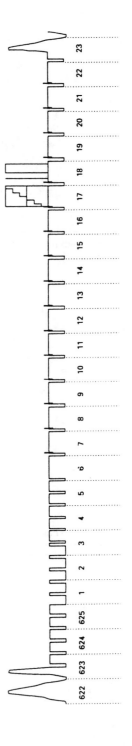

(b)

(c)

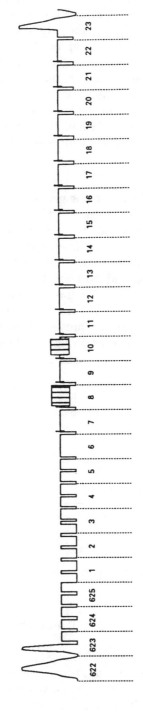

(d)

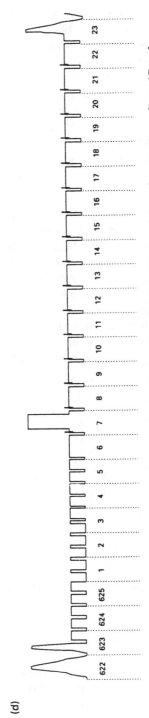

Figure 3.13 (a) In C-format VTRs, 14 lines are lost by format dropout. (b) Test signals may be present on lines 17 and 18. (c) VISC may be on lines 8 or 10 in component recorders. (d) Line 7 may contain the colour frame flag.

of skew, a margin should be allowed between the video head switching points and the recorded VITC word. For similar reasons an adequate margin should be used if dynamic tracking (DT or AST) heads are employed. Some lines may be used for other signals. C-format VTR machines suffer from format dropout (see Chapter 4), and 12 lines in the vertical interval will not be recorded unless the sync head option is employed. Component Analogue tape recorders put VISC on line 8 or 10 (321 or 323), and lines 17 and 18 may be used for engineering test signals. Figure 3.13 illustrates the possibilities and limitations. Common practice involves placing the VITC word on lines 19 and 21 in its 625/50 version, and most VITC generators and readers are factory-set at these lines.

Position within the line

The word occupies 49.655 μs (nominally), being generated at 115 x F_h ±2% bits/s, where F_h is the line repetition frequency. Hence the nominal bit rate is 1.796875 Mbits/s. This is a lower rate than previously specified but the previous bit rate does lie within the new tolerance. The word should start no earlier than 11.2 μs after the start of the line synchronizing pulse, and if the last bit is a '1' it should end no later than 1.9 μs before the leading edge of the synchronizing pulse for the next line. This gives a maximum duration of 50.9 μs available for the codeword. The pulses should be equally spaced. A logical '0' is represented by a level of 0–25 mV, and a logical '1' by a level of 500–600 mV. Figure 3.14 illustrates.

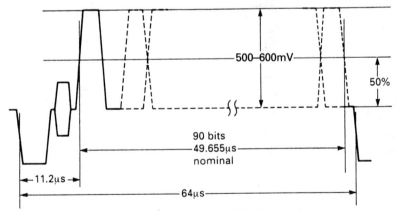

Figure 3.14 The position of the VITC word within the 625/50 line.

Bit assignment

Synchronizing bit pairs 0,1; 10,11; 20,21; 30,31; 40,41; 50,51; 60,61; 70,71; 80,81
Each of these pairs consists of a fixed '1' followed by a fixed '0'. Their distribution throughout the codeword is necessary because VTR machines suffer small timing errors (called 'velocity errors') along lines, which result in a degree of jitter. Although these errors are dealt with by

timebase correctors, the process can also replace the synchronizing pulses, colour bursts and the vertical interval, together with the timecode. If this is the case, it will be necessary to regenerate the code prior to timebase correction, while small timing errors still exist, re-inserting the code after timebase correction (Figure 3.15).

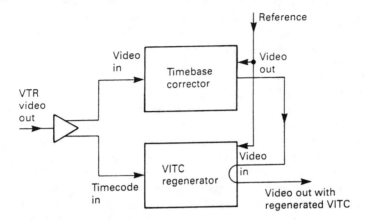

Figure 3.15 A timecode regenerator may be needed if the timebase corrector replaces the whole of the vertical interval.

Bit 14
This is unassigned. The IEC reserves its use. It should be fixed 0 until specified by the IEC.

Bit 15
This is the colour lock flag bit. It is set to logical '1' when the timecode is locked to its associated PAL colour signal in accordance with the 8-field sequence (4-field in SECAM), and the video signal has the preferred subcarrier-to-horizontal phase relationship. Its purpose has been covered in discussion of the 625/50 longitudinal code earlier in this chapter.

Bits 35, 55 and 75
These are the binary group flag bits. The detail has been covered in discussion of the 625/50 longitudinal code earlier in this chapter.

Bit 75
This is the field identification flag bit. VITC has no need of a biphase mark correction bit. The equivalent bit identifies the fields without reference to the field sync pulse sequence. It is set to logical '1' during fields 2, 4, 6 and 8, and to logical '0' during fields 1, 3, 5 and 7 in PAL (fields 2,4 and 1,3 for SECAM).

The detail of the 525/60 VITC

Position in the field

In 525/60 systems the VITC word is placed no earlier than line 10 (273) and no later than line 20 (283). To avoid decoding errors in the presence of skew, a margin should be allowed between the head switching points and the lines used for recording VITC. Some lines may be used for vertical interval test signals (VITS). The C-format VTR has 10 lines of format dropout in the NTSC system.

Position in the line

The word occupies 50.286 μs (nominally), being generated at 115 x F_h ±2% bits/s, where F_h is the line repetition frequency. Hence the nominal bit rate is 1.81125 Mbits/s. This is a higher rate than previously specified but the previous bit rate does lie within the new tolerance. The word should start no earlier than 10 μs after the start of the line synchronizing pulse, and if the last bit is a '1' it should end no later than 2 μs before the leading edge of the synchronizing pulse for the next line. This gives a maximum duration of 50.566 μs available for the codeword. The pulses should be equally spaced. A logical '0' is represented by a level of 0–10 IRE, and a logical '1' by a level of 70–90 IRE. Figure 3.16 illustrates.

Bit assignment

The sync pairs, time and user data bits, and the CRCC bits are identical to the 625/50 version of the code.

Bit 14
This is the drop frame flag (see p. 40).

Bit 15
This is the colour frame flag (see p. 40).

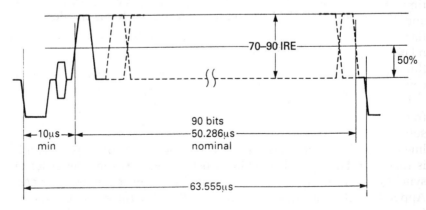

Figure 3.16 The position of the VITC word within the 525/60 line.

Bit 35
This is the field identifier flag bit. A logical '0' represents fields 1 and 3, in which the first pre-equalizing pulse follows the last line synchronizing pulse by one whole line. A logical '1' represents fields 2 and 4, in which the first pre-equalizing pulse follows the last synchronizing pulse by a half line.

Bits 55, 74 and 75
These are the binary group flag bits (see pp. 36–38).

Comparisons between LTC and VITC in both 625/50 and 525/60 versions

The bit contents of 625/50 LTC and VITC are compared in Figure 3.17 (pp. 52–53). The 525/60 LTC and VITC are compared in Figure 3.18 (pp. 54–55). The technical differences are covered in Appendix 2.

The time address and the associated colour TV signal

For purposes of electronic editing of composite television signals, the correct colour sub-carrier field sequence must be maintained across the edit point to avoid picture disturbance. The timebase corrector in a VTR or VCR system achieves this by shifting the start of the active line from the machine designated as 'slave' to bring the sub-carrier in phase with that on the recorder. This shift is a fraction of a sub-carrier cycle and is not noticeable when the cut or mix is between dissimilar pictures. However, cutting between identical pictures (perhaps for the purposes of shortening a sequence, or during an animation sequence) will result in this shift being noticeable.

These problems can be avoided by cutting on the correct frame to avoid the need for a shift in the picture. This can be determined by a timecode sync monitor (Figure 3.19) which displays the relationship on a picture monitor. The sub-carrier-to-sync relationship can be incorporated in the timecode by establishing a standard relationship between time-of-day and the 8- or 4-field sequence. If this relationship is correct, the colour lock flag is set to logical '1'. For this method to work, it is imperative that the relationship be determined at video and timecode generation, and carried through without ambiguity at all stages of production. This will be covered in detail in Chapter 9.

There are various ways by which timecode generators can identify frame 1 in the colour frame sequence. These include examination of the sub-carrier-to-sync relationship, by detecting a marker pulse inserted in line 7 of field 1, or from a flag generated by the SPG. The important point is that the timecode generator must have some form of colour-related synchronizing information if it is to generate colour-framed code. Appendix 1 examines the relationship between timecode and the colour frame sequence in detail.

VITC bit no.					LTC bit no.
0	1		Synchronizing bit		
1	0		Synchronizing bit		
2		1		1	0
3		2	Units of frames	2	1
4		4		4	2
5		8		8	3
6					4
7			1st user group		5
8					6
9					7
10	1		Synchronizing bit		
11	0		Synchronizing bit		
12		10	Tens of frames	10	8
13		20		20	9
14			Unassigned bit		10
15			Colour lock flag		11
16					12
17			2nd user group		13
18					14
19					15
20	1		Synchronizing bit		
21	0		Synchronizing bit		
22		1		1	16
23		2	Units of seconds	2	17
24		4		4	18
25		8		8	19
26					20
27			3rd user group		21
28					22
29					23
30	1		Synchronizing bit		
31	0		Synchronizing bit		
32		10		10	24
33		20	Tens of seconds	20	25
34		40		40	26
35			Binary group flag		27
36					28
37			4th user group		29
38					30
39					31
40	1		Synchronizing bit		
41	0		Synchronizing bit		

Figure 3.17 The 625/50 VITC and LTC words compared.

42	1		1	32
43	2	Units of minutes	2	33
44	4		4	34
45	8		8	35
46				36
47		5th user group		37
48				38
49				39
50	1	Synchronizing bit		
51	0	Synchronizing bit		
52	10		10	40
53	20	Tens of minutes	20	41
54	40		40	42
55		Binary group flag		43
56				44
57		6th binary group		45
58				46
59				47
60	1	Synchronizing bit		
61	0	Synchronizing bit		
62	1		1	48
63	2	Units of hours	2	49
64	4		4	50
65	8		8	51
66				52
67		7th binary group		53
68				54
69				55
70	1	Synchronizing bit		
71	0	Synchronizing bit		
72	10	Tens of hours	10	56
73	20		20	57
74		Binary group flag		58
75		Field marker bit/Phase correction bit		59
76				60
77		8th binary group		61
78				62
79				63
80	1	Synchronizing bit		
81	0	Synchronizing bit		
82				64
83				65
84	Cyclic			66
85	redundancy	Synchronizing		67
86	check	word		
87	code			.
88				.
89				79

Figure 3.17 cont.

VITC bit no.				LTC bit no.
0	1	Synchronizing bit		1
1	0	Synchronizing bit		0
2	1	Units of frames	1	0
3	2		2	1
4	4		4	2
5	8		8	3
6		1st user group		4
7				5
8				6
9				7
10	1	Synchronizing bit		
11	0	Synchronizing bit		
12	10	Tens of frames	10	8
13	20		20	9
14		Drop frame flag		10
15		Colour lock flag		11
16		2nd user group		12
17				13
18				14
19				15
20	1	Synchronizing bit		
21	0	Synchronizing bit		
22	1	Units of seconds	1	16
23	2		2	17
24	4		4	18
25	8		8	19
26		3rd user group		20
27				21
28				22
29				23
30	1	Synchronizing bit		
31	0	Synchronizing bit		
32	10	Tens of seconds	10	24
33	20		20	25
34	40		40	26
35		Field marker bit/Phase correction bit		27
36		4th user group		28
37				29
38				30
39				31
40	1	Synchronizing bit		
41	0	Synchronizing bit		
42	1	Units of minutes	1	32
43	2		2	33
44	4		4	34
45	8		8	35

46			5th user group		36
47					37
48					38
49					39
50	1		Synchronizing bit		
51	0		Synchronizing bit		
52		10	Tens of minutes	10	40
53		20		20	41
54		40		40	42
55			Binary group flag		43
56			6th binary group		44
57					45
58					46
59					47
60	1		Synchronizing bit		
61	0		Synchronizing bit		
62		1	Units of hours	1	48
63		2		2	49
64		4		4	50
65		8		8	51
66			7th binary group		52
67					53
68					54
69					55
70	1		Synchronizing bit		
71	0		Synchronizing bit		
72		10	Tens of hours	10	56
73		20		20	57
74			Binary group flag		58
75			Binary group flag		59
76			8th binary group		60
77					61
78					62
79					63
80	1		Synchronizing bit		
81	0		Synchronizing bit		
82					64
83					65
84		Cyclic			66
85		redundancy	Synchronizing		67
86		check	word		68
87		code			.
88					.
89					79

Figure 3.18 The 525/60 VITC and LTC words compared.

The 525/60 drop-frame code (M/NTSC)

Timecode locked to a 29.97 fps frame rate (as it must be for later post-production) will accumulate an error at 0.03 of a frame each second. Over a one-hour period the discrepancy between 'real-time' and 'colour-framed' time addresses will be 108 frames, i.e. 3.6 seconds, the timecode addresses falling behind in real time. To compensate for this, 108 frames have to be dropped every hour to allow the code to catch up with real time. Single frames cannot be dropped because of the need to maintain the 4-field colour frame sequence (colour frame A must be followed by colour frame B and vice versa), so a frame pair is dropped at the start of each minute, except minutes 0, 10, 20, 30, 40 and 50.

$(2 \times 60) - (2 \times 6) = 120 - 12 = 108$ frames

The frame count over, say, the end of the eighth minute in the hour will go:

01.08'59"28f
01.08'59"29f
01.09'00"02f
01.09'00"03f   etc,

whereas over the end of the ninth minute of the hour the count will go:

01.09'59"28f
01.09'59"29f
01.10'00"00f
01.10'00"01f   etc,

The dropping of these frames results in a discrepancy between real time and timecode addresses that varies by $\pm\,60\ \mu s$ over 10 minutes, illustrated in Figure 3.20. The discrepancy accumulates over a period of one minute when, as can be seen, the dropping of two frames slightly overcompensates. This overcompensation increases at the end of each succeeding minute until, at the ninth minute the time address is 60 μs in advance. This accumulated residual error is compensated for by not dropping the first two frames at the start of the 10th minute.

The above process does not exactly compensate for the discrepancies between real time and colour-frame time, because the NTSC frame rate is not exactly 29.97 Hz: it is 29.970 026 17 Hz. This difference results in a long-term residual discrepancy of 0.000 026 17 × 60 × 60 × 24 = 2.261 frames over a 24 hour period, equivalent to 86.4 μs. Good operational practice requires that the timecode generator be reset at regular intervals if long-term errors are not to accumulate. Commercial timecode generators are available which allow the 86 μs discrepancy to be corrected at a time when least disruption to programme making will occur. The correction is made daily, automatically, and at a time programmable by the user.

Figure 3.19 A timecode sync monitor display. Marker pulses on the right-hand edge indicate the field sequence. Markers on the bottom edge indicate S-C/H phase.

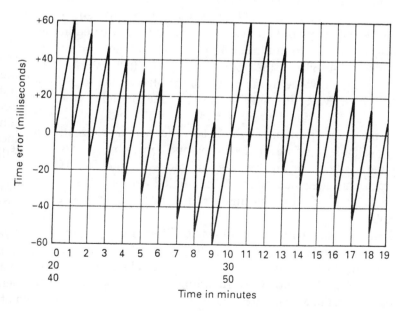

Figure 3.20 The short-term error in drop-frame code varies by ±60 μs over 10 minutes. It is corrected by not dropping a frame at the 10th minute.

M/PAL drop-frame code

The frame rate of system M is also approximately 29.97 fps. When this frame rate is combined with the PAL modulation system it is not possible to drop two frame sequences to resolve the colour frame error. Instead, the first four frames (1–4) are dropped from the count at the start of every 2nd minute (even minutes), except for minutes 0, 20 and 40. In this mode LTC bit 10 (bit 14 in the VITC equivalent) is set to '1'. The IEC refers to the drop-frame mode of M/NTSC and M/PAL as Mode 1. The non-drop-frame mode is referred to as Mode 0.

Digital VITC

D-VITC is an 8-bit digital representation of the analogue shape of the 90-bit VITC signal supported by analogue VCRs. It is recorded on lines 14 and 277 of the CCIR 601-2 component (4:2:2) digital video signal, with the option of additional insertion on lines 16 and 279. As it is recorded as a part of the data on the helical video tracks it can be read when the DVCR is either stationary or shuttling at too low a speed for LTC to be read.

CCIR 601-2 codes each video line with alternate data words of colour difference and luminance samples in the sequence C_b Y C_r Y C_b Y C_r Y etc, with a total of 1440 samples per line, clocked at 27 MHz, giving an active line duration of 53.333 μs (nominal). Each active line is preceded by a SAV (start of active line) code and terminated with an EAV (end of active line) code. D-VITC is placed on the luminance (it is not carried in the chrominance) lines prior to multiplexing with chrominance and has a nominal duration of 49.655 μs (625/50) or 50.286 μs (525/60). The luminance words range in value from 16_{10} (&10) for Black Level to 235_{10} (&EB) for Peak White. CCIR 601–2 specifies a 10 bit code for digital video (originally the digital video signal was specified to be 8 bit), and D-VITC is carried in the 8 most significant bits of the 10 bit code, with an alternative specification available to permit its recording and replay by older 8 bit systems. Consequently there are two sets of codes for the D-VITC data, a 3-character hexadecimal code for 10-bit digital video data and a 2-character hexadecimal code for 8-bit digital video data. Figure 3.21 illustrates the details.

There are slight timing relationship differences between 625/50 and 525/60 systems. Figure 3.22 illustrates these.

All unused luminance samples in the D-VITC line are set to &040 (10-bit) or &10 (8-bit). Corresponding lines in the chrominance data stream are set to &200 or &80 respectively.

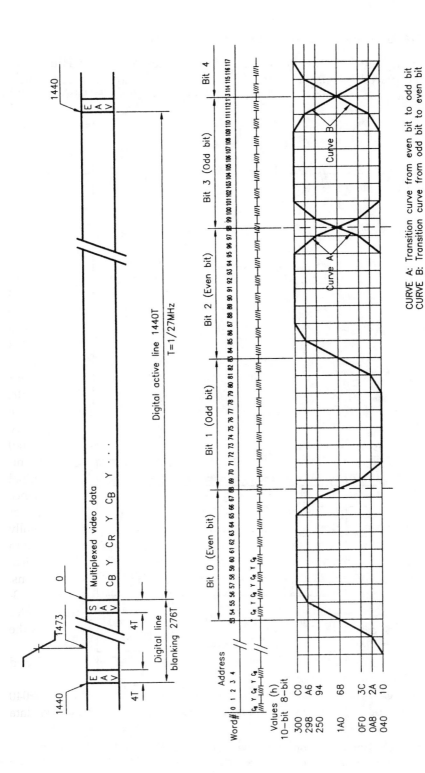

Figure 3.21 D-VITC waveform showing position in line, general form and both 10-bit and 8-bit hex values. Courtesy of *SMPTE Journal*.

Timecode and 1125/60 television systems

1125/60 high definition video has 1035 active lines, permitting a timecode to be placed in one or more of the 90 field blanking lines. The total duration for each line is 29.630 μs (60 fps) or 29.659 μs (59.94 fps), with

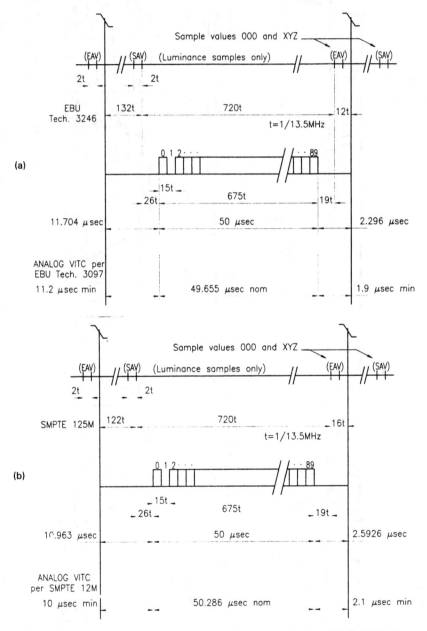

Figure 3.22 Timing relationships between analogue VITC and D-VITC (a) for 625/50 systems and (b) for 525/60 systems. Courtesy of *SMPTE Journal*.

active line times of 25.859 μs and 25.884 μs respectively (Figure 3.23). The synchronizing information is carried as a bi-directional pulse (Figure 3.24). Video information is carried by three parallel, time co-incident, signal paths which can be either RGB or luminance plus two colour difference ($E_{Y'}$, $E_{PB'}$, $E_{PR'}$). The system has an interlaced 2:1 format and an aspect ratio of 16:9. Both LTC and VITC are supported in this format, though there are significant differences from timecodes supported by 4:3 aspect ratio formats.

1125/60 LTC

This is carried as a continuous serial bit stream in 80-bit words, each word having a nominal duration of 33.33 μs (depending on the frame rate), at 1 word per frame. The start of the word (the first transition of bit 0) coincides with the start of Line 1 of each frame, ±1 line. The arrangement of time, binary group and synchronizing data are identical with 525/60

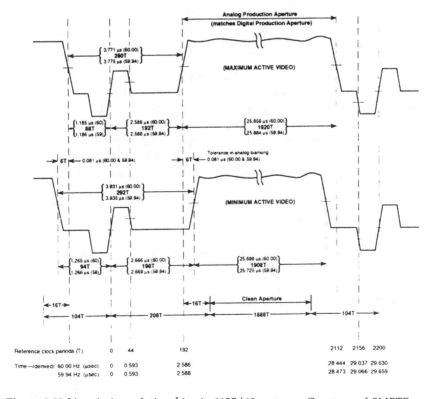

Figure 3.23 Line timing relationships in 1125/60 systems. Courtesy of *SMPTE Journal*.

LTC, but there are differences in the assignment of the other bits of the word:

Bits 10 and 11 are unassigned
Bit 27 remains the bi-phase mark correction bit
Bit 43 remains as the BGF0 flag bit
Bits 58 and 59 remain as BGF1 and BGF2 respectively.

1125/60 VITC

This is carried as a series of discrete 90-bit words, each word having a nominal duration of 23.18 μs, 1710 reference clock periods (depending on the frame rate). The start of the word is a minimum of 2.7 μs from the start of the line. It ends a minimum of 1.15 μs before the end of the line. The arrangement of time, binary group and synchronizing data are identical with 525/60 VITC, but there are differences in the assignment of the other bits of the word:

Bit 14 is the drop frame flag bit
Bit 15 is unassigned
Bit 35 remains the field marker bit ('0' representing colour fields 1, 3, 5 and 7; '1' representing colour fields, 2, 4, 6 and 8)
Bit 55 remains as the BGF0 flag bit
Bits 74 and 75 remain the BGF1 and BGF2 flag bit respectively.

1125/60 VITC can be placed on any line between 7 (569) and 40 (602) inclusive and can be inserted on multiple lines as long as time address, drop frame and colour frame data are identical. Rise and fall times of the pulse edges are 100 ns ± 25 ns. Logical '0' is represented by a voltage level of between 0–25 mV, logical '1' is represented by a voltage level of 500–600 mV. Amplitude distortions such as over/under shoot or droop must be limited to a maximum of 5% of the peak to peak amplitude of the signal.

24 frame film timecode

Time address, binary group and synchronizing bits are arranged in the same order as 525/60 LTC.

Bits 10 and 11 are unassigned
Bit 27 remains the Bi-phase mark correction bit
Bits 43, 58 and 59 remain BGF0, BGF1 and BGF2 flag bits respectively.

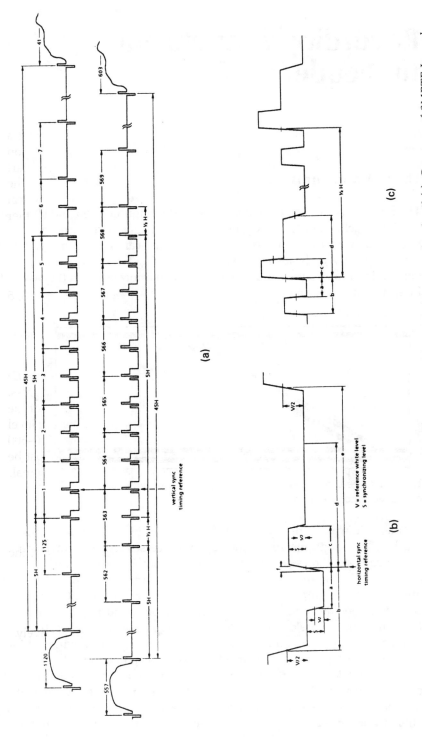

Figure 3.24 1125/60 Field blanking detail (a), Line blanking detail (b) and Field sync pulse detail (c). Courtesy of *SMPTE Journal*.

CHAPTER 4

Recording formats and timecode

The U-Matic format

The track layout of this format is illustrated in Figure 4.1 for the Hi-Band version. Each video track contains one field of video, recorded by a dedicated head (there are two heads on the scanning drum) and the switching between heads is accomplished during the broad pulses in the vertical interval. There is thus no loss of video information in the original inception of this format.

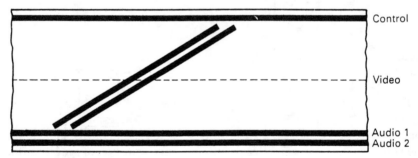

Figure 4.1 The U-Matic system did not originally provide for a dedicated timecode track.

Timecode was originally recorded on one of the audio tracks, usually Track 1. The sound recording and replay processes are performed by the same heads so there is no timing shift. However the raw timecode coming off tape had to be regenerated to correct the differentiation and timing jitter that occur on any magnetic analogue replay process. Operational considerations dictated that somewhere else be found for the timecode. Recordists in the field wished to record separate sounds on the two available tracks for later mixing, voice-over recording, or dubbing; editors also needed both audio tracks available for programme sound mixing. A dedicated track for longitudinal timecode was needed, but where could it be put? The answer lay in the property of different recorded wavelengths to penetrate to different depths from the surface of the magnetic medium. Short recorded wavelengths tend to lie close to the surface of the tape, whereas long wavelengths penetrate deeper. Figure 4.2 illustrates the point.

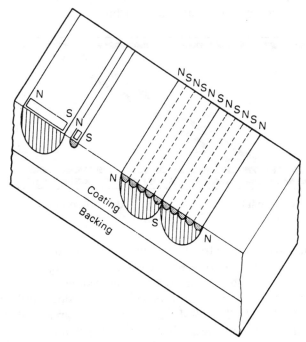

Figure 4.2 Short wavelengths are recorded near the surface of the tape, long wavelengths penetrate deeper. On replay they can be separated by filtering.

The video write speed of a Hi-Band U-Matic is 854 mm/s. The recorded wavelengths of the video are going to be a few micrometres long. The longitudinal speed of the tape is 95.3 mm/s. At 80 bits of LTC per frame, the shortest recorded wavelength will be in the order of 40 μm. With the video and timecode signals occupying such widely-spaced parts of the frequency spectrum, it is easy to ensure that mutual interference is filtered out. The timecode track is inside the two original audio tracks. The video tracks will overwrite the area occupied by this 'address track', as Figure 4.3 illustrates. The process of recording a magnetic imprint deep into the tape layer, for later overwriting on the surface is called 'burning in'; however, the term 'burning in' has come to mean the insertion, into the video waveform, of a signal that will allow the timecode to be displayed as human-readable characters, usually in a rectangular box towards the bottom of the screen. This facility can be of assistance in the off-line editing, or daily viewing process.

Depth recording of a timecode track will allow pre-striping of a tape with both code and control track for insert editing (see Chapter 9), but what of re-recording timecode after the video has been recorded? This is no problem as long as the replayed video is processed by a timebase corrector. The time address track will overwrite 11 lines of the recorded video waveform as Figure 4.4 illustrates. The last two active lines in each field, and the field synchronizing pulses of the succeeding field, will be overwritten. Longitudinal timecode on this version of the format is reprocessed by circuitry internal to the machine.

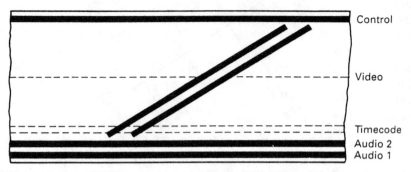

Figure 4.3 Longitudinal timecode can be 'burned in' underneath the video tracks on the U-Matic format.

VITC is not an option on this format because of the bandwidth requirement. Remember that to produce reasonable rectangular pulses of a particular frequency, the 3rd harmonic of that frequency must be present. 90 bits of information put into a 49.655 μs time slot would require a bandwidth of 2.7 MHz. The U-Matic format is not capable of this degree of video resolution unless regularly and carefully maintained.

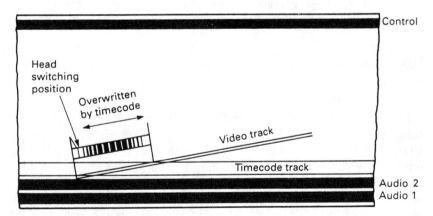

Figure 4.4 If timecode is re-written it will erase a portion of each video field. Since this contains only field sync information it can be reinserted by the timecase corrector.

The 1in C-format

A C-format VTR possesses a number of heads on the head drum to provide such operational facilities as confidence replay during record, video-only erase, variable-speed play and so on. The format has undergone a number of evolutions since its original introduction, and these will be outlined below. In every version the heads have to break contact with the tape once in each field, as Figure 4.5 illustrates. It can be seen that a head leaves the tape for 14° every revolution. This period is timed to begin in the early part of the field interval. Figure 4.6 illustrates the format dropout that results. The dropout starts after the 4th broad pulse in the vertical interval, and in the PAL implementation of the format has a duration of almost 12 lines. This means that in the PAL version lines 3–14 in fields 1, 3 etc, and lines 315 (in part), 316–326 entirely and line 327 (in part) in fields 2, 4 etc are lost (10 lines per field are lost in the NTSC version). These lines are replaced by the TBC, so VITC should not be placed in them.

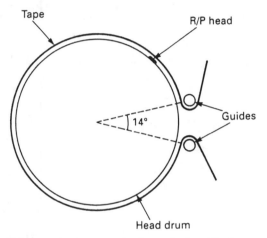

Figure 4.5 The C-format dropout results from the head losing contact with the tape for 14 degrees each revolution.

During variable-speed and stop-frame operation the number of lines subject to format dropout or prone to line time instability may increase, so VITC should not be put too close to this section. The reason for this is that when the tape is running at non-standard speed the effective tape-to-video-head velocity will change slightly so the format dropout duration will alter. When a helical-scan machine plays at a non-standard speed the effective diagonal angle between recorded tracks and the path followed by the video head will differ from that at standard playing speed. This will result in a 'noise bar' at some point in the viewed picture as the replay head crosses tracks. To avoid this, there is the option of providing a video head, known variously as an 'auto scan tracking' (AST) or 'dynamic tracking' (DT) head which will follow the recorded tracks over a wide range of playing speeds including 'stop'. The mounting for this head flexes in response to controlling signals and so is able to follow the slightly different track angle. On some machines the degree of flexibility

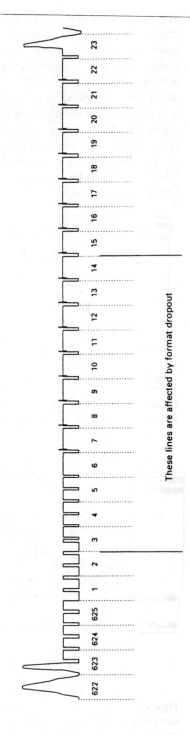

Figure 4.6 Format dropout affects the first lines in each field.

allows the head to track adjacent recorded field tracks, thus giving true frame information rather than a repeat field. This process results in the head requiring some settling time at the start of each track (Figure 4.7) and there may be some line instability at the start of each scanned section of the field. If VITC is present in this section it may be misread. If this occurs the DT or AST head should be switched off if possible. The alternative to losing part of the field interval to format dropout is to provide the information on separate tracks. The C-format originally specified three options for the tracks, which are illustrated in Figure 4.8.

Option 1

Two audio tracks at the top of the tape for programme sound.

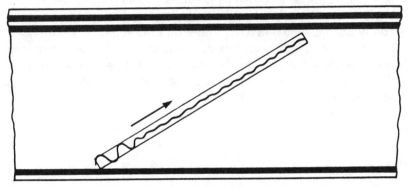

Figure 4.7 DT (AST) heads may require settling time at the start of each track. If this causes problems with VITC, switch the DT function off.

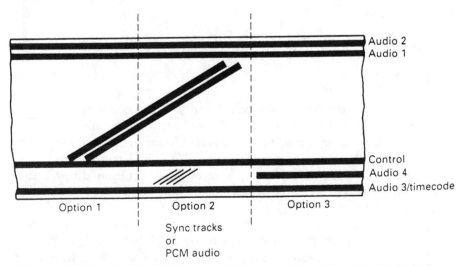

Figure 4.8 Option 1 of the C-format provides two audio tracks and a third which can carry either audio or timecode as specified. Option 2 can carry either the missing sync information or PCM digital audio as specified. Option 3 carries a fourth audio track.

One audio track at the bottom of the tape for either longitudinal timecode or cue audio.

Control track.

Option 2

Two audio tracks at the top of the tape for programme sound.

One audio track at the bottom of the tape for either longitudinal timecode or cue audio.

Diagonal sync tracks, recorded by a sync head mounted on the scanner, replace the information lost by format dropout and allow some overlap for stability during switching (18.75 lines on EBU versions, 15.75 lines in SMPTE). A recent variation on this option is to record time-compressed PCM sound in these tracks instead of syncs, in which case they will not be available for VITC. These tracks are recorded between audio track 3 and the control track.

Control track.

Option 3

Two audio tracks at the top of the tape for programme sound.

One audio track at the bottom of the tape for either longitudinal timecode or cue audio.

A fourth audio track, recorded between track 3 and the control track.

Control track.

On each of the options, audio track 3 can be combined with a suitable record/replay head and associated electronics to handle the wide bandwidth required to read timecode both at slow jog and high spooling speeds. The electronics associated with a dedicated timecode track will regenerate the code on replay. Code recorded on an unmodified audio track will not give the degree of flexibility required in the post-production environment.

In a PAL environment the longitudinal timecode is recorded at a peak-to-peak level of 185 nanowebers per metre (nWb/m) short-circuit flux. The SMPTE specify a recorded flux of at least 141 nWb/m. At the time of writing the SMPTE proposes that in the 525/60 environment VITC shall be recorded on lines 12 and 14 in C-format VTRs with sync head and lines 16 and 18 in C-format VTRs without a sync head.

Betacam, Beta SP and MII formats

In these systems the colour information is not modulated onto the luminance prior to recording. Instead, luminance and chrominance are handled separately, and recorded on different sections of the tape. The requirements for signal timing are as rigid as in a composite system, since luminance, chrominance and timing pulses all have to register for processing in vision mixers etc.

Within the recorder the luminance (Y) signal is recorded onto alternate tracks, one field per track. There is no need to record the vertical interval pulses as they will be replaced by the machine's internal TBC. The Pr and Pb signals are time-compressed on a line-by-line basis. Alternate lines of Pr and Pb are then recorded one after the other throughout the complete track, so that it consists of alternate Pr and Pb line samples multiplexed along its length. The chrominance tracks are alternated with the luminance tracks on tape.

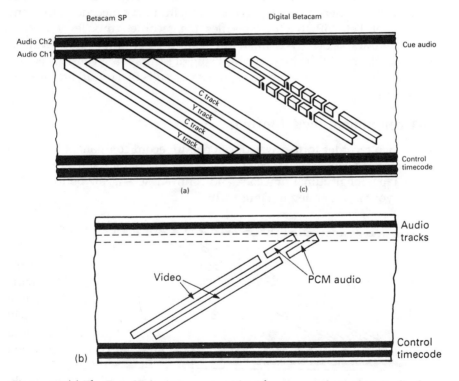

Figure 4.9 (a) The Beta SP format can provide either two analogue longitudinal audio tracks, or one audio analogue track with two digital audio channels. (b) The MII format provides the same options, although the footprint differs. Both provide for analogue FM audio to be frequency division multiplexed with the chrominance signal. (c) Digital Betacam provides four digital audio channels and a single linear analogue audio track. All three formats carry LTC.

These formats can carry information about the eight-field sequence. Although this is not required in a purely component environment, a recorder may be fed with a composite signal. When this occurs, a colour frame ID pulse is also recorded together with a line of colour framed sub-carrier information (vertical interval sub-carrier, or VISC). In the Beta SP format this signal is placed in line 8 (line 11 in NTSC) of the vertical interval to improve the accuracy of colour framing on replay. In the PAL system it runs at half the colour sub-carrier frequency; in the NTSC version it runs at sub-carrier frequency. The MII format also incorporates a VISC signal, but places it in line 10. In addition, the MII format indicates colour framing by use of variable-width control-track pulses. The original Betacam format had no provisions for handling VITC, though a modification is available to permit its use. If VITC has been recorded by a modified machine, or a Beta SP machine is loaded with oxide tape, there is the distinct possibility that an unmodified machine will not replay it. Hence the requirement for LTC. Beta SP does support VITC.

Figure 4.9 illustrates the track layouts of the Betacam, Beta SP & MII formats. All formats give a reprocessed longitudinal timecode output on replay. For Beta SP the IEC specifies the recorded flux level of the timecode track as 500 nWb/m short-circuit flux per unit of track width. The SMPTE specify the flux level as being at saturation level. This is the level at which a 1 dB increase in input level results in a 0.5 dB increase in output level.

D-1 component digital format

This video recorder format was developed to record component video in digital form. There is a reasonable quality cue audio track at the top edge of the tape; longitudinal timecode and control tracks at the bottom. The track layout is illustrated in Figure 4.10.

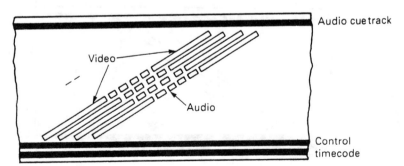

Figure 4.10 The D-1 format carries LTC but has no VITC facility. Digital audio is recorded in the centre of the tape.

The information in one video field is shuffled over several tracks to assist error protection. Because of this, it is inappropriate to rely on VITC alone, as no guarantee can be given that time data incorporated in the video waveform can be read at other than standard speed, which rather defeats the whole purpose of VITC. If digital audio is being fed to the machine via the AES/EBU interface (see Chapter 11), time data could be incorporated in the segmented audio tracks in the centre of the tape. The nature of audio requires a higher degree of error correction, and lower levels of concealment than are appropriate to video. The lower data rate requirements for audio mean that information can be duplicated on different sectors, and in different relative positions, as Figure 4.11 shows. As a result there is an extremely high expectation that audio data with embedded timecode data will be recovered unambiguously.

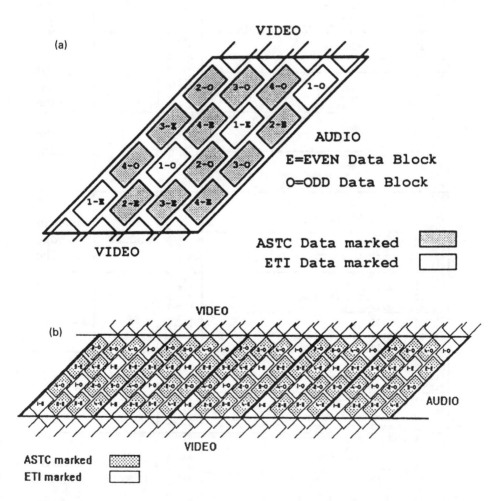

Figure 4.11 (a) Timecode and equipment type information are carried in the even and odd audio sectors respectively. (b) There are 6 audio sectors per video frame in 625/50 systems, and 5 audio sectors per frame in 525/60 systems.

Longitudinal Time Code Bit No.		Coding	ASTC Data	Audio Data Block USER No. EVEN	USER No. ODD
Bit 0	1		Bit 0		
Bit 1	2	Frame	Bit 1		
Bit 2	4	Units	Bit 2		
Bit 3	8		Bit 3		
Bit 8	10	Frame	Bit 4	USER0	USER1
Bit 9	20	tens	Bit 5		
Bit 10		Drop frame flag	Bit 6		
Bit 11		Color frame flag	Bit 7		
Bit 16	1		Bit 0		
Bit 17	2	Seconds	Bit 1		
Bit 18	4	Units	Bit 2		
Bit 19	8		Bit 3		
Bit 24	10		Bit 4	USER2	USER3
Bit 25	20	Seconds	Bit 5		
Bit 26	40	tens	Bit 6		
Bit 27		Biphase mark correction bit	Bit 7		
Bit 32	1		Bit 0		
Bit 33	2	Minutes	Bit 1		
Bit 34	4	Units	Bit 2		
Bit 35	8		Bit 3		
Bit 40	10		Bit 4	USER4	USER5
Bit 41	20	Minutes	Bit 5		
Bit 42	40	tens	Bit 6		
Bit 43		Binary group flag bit	Bit 7		
Bit 48	1		Bit 0		
Bit 49	2	Hours	Bit 1		
Bit 50	4	Units	Bit 2		
Bit 51	8		Bit 3		
Bit 56	10	Hours	Bit 4	USER6	USER7
Bit 57	20	tens	Bit 5		
Bit 58		Unassigned address bit	Bit 6		
Bit 59		Binary group flag bit	Bit 7		
Bit 4	Bit0		Bit 0		
Bit 5	Bit1	1st	Bit 1		
Bit 6	Bit2	Binary Group	Bit 2		
Bit 7	Bit3		Bit 3		
Bit 12	Bit0		Bit 4	USER8	USER9
Bit 13	Bit1	2nd	Bit 5		
Bit 14	Bit2	Binary Group	Bit 6		
Bit 15	Bit3		Bit 7		
Bit 20	Bit0		Bit 0		
Bit 21	Bit1	3d	Bit 1		
Bit 22	Bit2	Binary Group	Bit 2		
Bit 23	Bit3		Bit 3		
Bit 28	Bit0		Bit 4	USER10	USER11
Bit 29	Bit1	4th	Bit 5		
Bit 30	Bit2	Binary Group	Bit 6		
Bit 31	Bit3		Bit 7		
Bit 36	Bit0		Bit 0		
Bit 37	Bit1	5th	Bit 1		
Bit 38	Bit2	Binary Group	Bit 2		
Bit 39	Bit3		Bit 3		
Bit 44	Bit0		Bit 4	USER12	USER13
Bit 45	Bit1	6th	Bit 5		
Bit 46	Bit2	Binary Group	Bit 6		
Bit 47	Bit3		Bit 7		
Bit 52	Bit0		Bit 0		
Bit 53	Bit1	7th	Bit 1		
Bit 54	Bit2	Binary Group	Bit 2		
Bit 55	Bit3		Bit 3		
Bit 60	Bit0		Bit 4	USER14	USER15
Bit 61	Bit1	8th	Bit 5		
Bit 62	Bit2	Binary Group	Bit 6		
Bit 63	Bit3		Bit 7		

Fig 4.11 (c) The ASTC/ETI data structure. Courtesy of SMPTE *Journal*.

There is a longitudinal timecode track that can be read over a very wide range of speeds, using biphase mark code. Originally there was provision for two independent timecode words. It was thought useful to have two, so that one could carry the original time addresses from a source tape as a record of its history. However, dual timecode was not taken up and all current machines support standard format LTC. Peak flux level of the timecode track is identical with that specified for C-format.

Audio sector timecode and equipment type information

The D-1 format now supports audio sector timecode and equipment type information. These codes are internal to the VCR and are recorded in the user bit areas of the audio sectors of the helical tracks.

Audio sector timecode (ASTC) can be recorded and edited independently from the audio data by using advance preread heads and re-writing data lifted off in editing or re-recording. It is recorded in odd and even audio segments 2, 3 and 4 (Figure 4.11a), in the user bits. The ASTC word is 64 bits long (there is no provision for synchronizing word or cyclic redundancy check: the data will always be read in the same direction by the scanning head, and the code is repeated several times within each field). As each audio segment is recorded twice in each sector, the ASTC is also recorded twice per sector. There are 6 audio sectors per video frame in 625/50 systems, and 5 sectors per frame in 525/60 systems (Figure 4.11b).

Equipment type information (ETI) is derived from internal manufacturer's settings and is also recordable/editable independently of the audio data. It comprises pairs of data blocks of 8 bytes each, recorded alternately in the odd and even audio 1 segments (Figure 4.11a), in the user bits, giving 16 bytes of data which carry manufacturer identification, machine serial number, head drum (scanner) serial number and DVCR type. There are 4 undefined bytes (currently set at &00). The data in each of bytes 0–11 is coded up as ISO 646 (ASCII) alphanumeric characters as 2 hexadecimal (4 bit) words. Even ETI blocks carry user bytes 0, 2, 4, 6, 8, 10, 12 and 14. Odd data blocks carry user bytes 1, 3, 5, 7, 9, 11, 13 and 15. Figure 4.11c illustrates the ASTC/ETI structure.

D-2 composite digital format

The D-2 format was developed to provide, in digital form, the facilities expected of a C-format VTR. The track layout is illustrated in Figure 4.12. This format employs azimuth recording with no guardband between the helical tracks. The audio segments are located at either end of the video data tracks. The format incorporates a longitudinal timecode track. The channel code for LTC is standard biphase mark. It is recommended that LTC be recorded at a level of 250 nWb/m short-circuit flux.

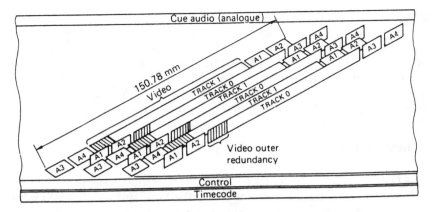

Figure 4.12 The D-2 format provides for timecode to be recorded on a longitudinal track. VITC is also supported.

Some D-2 models support a 'FORMAT' mode which enables an operator to pre-stripe a tape at three times normal speed, with control track and Timecode (generated internally). In the format mode the helical video and audio tracks are not laid down, which means that when editing a formatted tape all channels (video and audio) must be enabled. Formatting also requires the VCR to be fed a stable video feed, locked to reference video.

The format supports VITC, though not over the earlier lines of the range specified in the IEC 625/50 version, because the first few lines of each field are not recorded. This is to ensure that the first recorded segment of each field starts with the identical phase of colour sub-carrier. The details are shown in Figure 4.13. In 525/60 VCRs, VITC can be placed in any of the lines specified as they are always recorded, as Figure 4.14 illustrates. In common with all DVCRs, the audio channels accept the AES/EBU digital interface with its provisions for timecode.

D-3 composite digital format

Developed by National Panasonic, this format use 1/2in metal particles tape. The track layout is shown in Figure 4.15. As with D-2, 304 lines/field are recorded in the PAL version. This format provides a range of timecode facilities similar to those provided by D-2.

D-5 digital format

This format uses 1/2in metal particle tape. D-5 VCRs will record and play back CCIR 601 component digital video, but can be provided with the option of replaying D-3 digital composite recordings. The track layout is illustrated in Figure 4.15b. Longitudinal timecode is supported, as is the AES/EBU standard 2-channel interface.

Digital Betacam

Runs at a slightly slower longitudinal speed than Beta SP (96.7 mm/s as opposed to 118.6 mm/s) and has narrower tracks (20 μm as opposed to 86 μm for Y and 73 μm for Chroma). AES/EBU digital audio is supported, and carried in the audio sectors located in four segments in the centre of each helical track (Figure 4.9c). D-VITC can be supported as an option. LTC is carried on an outside track below the control track.

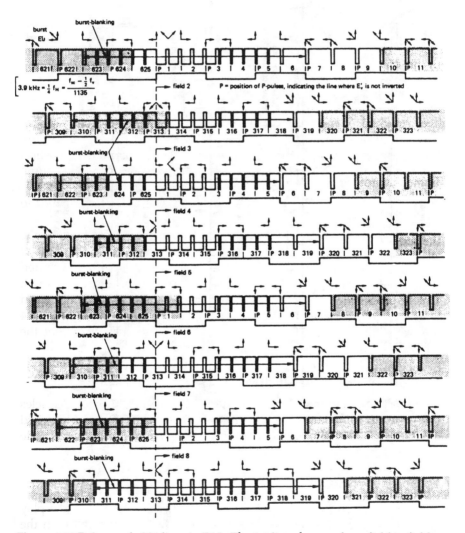

Figure 4.13 D-2 records 304 lines in PAL. The 1st line changes from field to field so that each field commences with the same line type. This aids colour processing in shuttle.

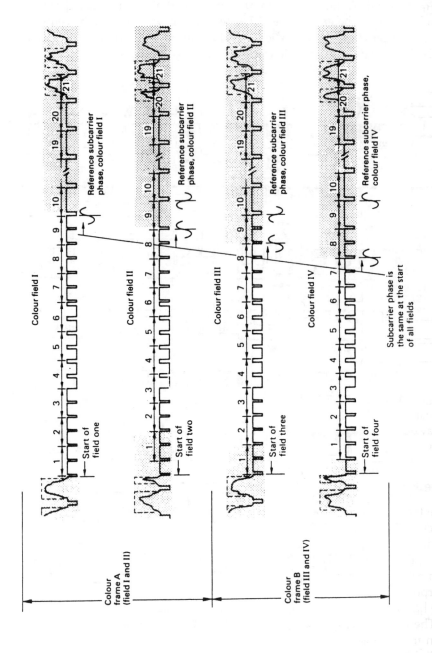

Figure 4.14 The recorded lines in the NTSC version vary from field to field. The first recorded line is chosen to ensure all fields start with the identical sub-carrier phase.

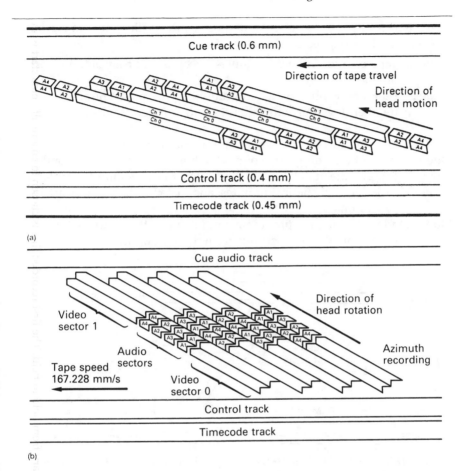

Figure 4.15 (a) The D-3 employs azimuth recording to lay down eight tracks of digital video as one field. (b) The D-5 also employs azimuth recording, this time to lay down CCIR 601 component video. Both formats support longitudinal timecode.

The Hi-8 video format

The track layout is illustrated in Figure 4.16. There are two longitudinal tracks. The track designated 'cue' is optional; the other carries analogue audio. The helical tracks carry video and FM audio. There is provision for an optional PCM audio sector within each of these tracks. There is no control track (though the cue track may in future be used for this purpose), its function being performed by a pilot signal recorded along the helical tracks. Each track carries one field of information.

There is provision within the PCM sector for six optional time information modes. The data are carried in four identification (ID) words. The individual modes are flagged by another 8-bit ID word, and a further ID word carries control information. These words are interleaved with the digital audio data. The assignment of these words is illustrated in Figure 4.17. The mode is flagged by the ID0 word:

Mode 1: Tape counter in hours, minutes, seconds and frames from start of tape.

Mode 2: Programme no. I, which indicates the programme number, take number, together with minutes and seconds from the start of each take.

Mode 3: Date in year, month, day of month and day of week.

Mode 4: Time of recording (time of day) in hours, minutes and seconds.

Mode 5: Programme no. II, which indicates the programme number together with hours, minutes and seconds from the start of programme.

Mode 6: Index, which is the programme number together with the time in hours, minutes and seconds from the start of the tape.

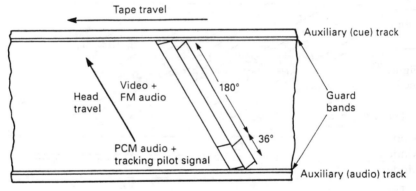

Figure 4.16 The footprint of the Hi-8 format has the option of PCM audio. Time data may be interleaved with audio data at the time of recording.

Domestic and professional R-DAT

This digital audio recording format was originally intended for domestic use. It achieves a recording time of two hours. Helical-scan azimuth recording is employed. There is no control track, its function being performed by automatic track-finding (ATF) sectors within the tracks. The track layout is shown in Figure 4.18. There are two optional longitudinal tracks provided, one at either edge of the tape. Timecode is recorded in the sub-data areas at either end of each audio data area. The normal tape speed is 8.15 mm/s, but different speeds are available, with three different basic sampling rates, 48 kHz (47.952 Hz for NTSC dropframe working), 44.1 kHz and 32 kHz. Domestic consumer versions of the format do not permit recording at the 44.1 kHz sampling rate. This is to deter direct digital copying of compact discs. There are two quantization standards. Table 4.1 illustrates the options available.

		Optional utility word	Control word
	ID0	ID1 ID2 ID3 ID4	ID5
Bit 7			1 = Dubbing protect
Bit 6	M O D	Time, date, programme no and index codes	B5,B6 1,0 Record start point 0,1 Record end point
Bit 5	E	(depending on mode)	1,1 Recording period 0,0 Ignore bits
Bit 4	C O		Channel 1 1 = audio 0 = other
Bit 3	D E		Channel 2 1 = audio 0 = other
Bit 2	W O R		B1,B2 0,0 Mono on both 0,1 Stereo 1,0 Bilingual
Bit 1	D		1,1 Other use
Bit 0			1 = Valid 0 = Bits 1 − 7 invalid

Figure 4.17 The time data in Hi-8 are recorded in optional utility words within the PCM audio segments.

The three 32 kHz modes are designated for the following applications:

Mode 1: Current broadcast and satellite television standards.
Mode 2: Extra long play (longitudinal tape speed is halved).
Mode 3: 4-channel recording.

The digital data are recorded in blocks of 288 bits. There are 196 blocks to one track. Each track contains 16 blocks of sub-code data in addition to audio (8 at each end of the track). The azimuth recording system employed results in the natural formation of track pairs (Figure 4.19). Each track pair is regarded as a frame, with audio data being conformed into frames for the purposes of editing. The duration of each frame is 30 ms (a frame rate of 33.3 fps).

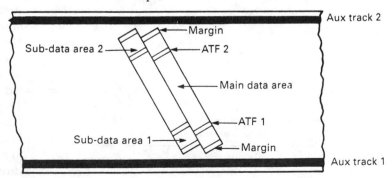

Figure 4.18 The R-DAT footprint places timecode within the subdata areas at the ends of each track.

| | Record/playback modes | | | | Prerecorded |
	Mandatory	Option 1	Option 2	Option 3	tape playback	
Number of channels	2	2	2	4	2	2
Sampling rate (kHz)	48	32	32	32	44.1	44.1
Quantization (bits)	16	16	12 non lin.	12 non lin.	16	16
Tape speed (mm/s)	8.15	8.15	4.075	8.15	8.15	12.225
Sub-code rate (kbit/s)	273.1	273.1	136.5	273.1	273.1	273.1
Playing time (13 μm tape)	120	120	240	120	120	80
Drum speed (rev/min)	2000	2000	1000	2000	2000	2000

Table 4.1 The R-DAT options compared. 48 kHz record/play and 44.1 kHz replay only are mandatory.

In its original domestic incarnation, the time data recorded in the subcode areas performed the functions of a sophisticated tape timer, providing three versions of tape time:

A – Time: Absolute time from the beginning of the tape
R – Time: Running time from the beginning of the recording
P – Time: Time from start of each programme item

Broadcasters were not slow to realize the value of the portable R-DAT machine. However, its usefulness as a post-production tool was limited by its inability to synchronize with other machines. As a result of pressure brought about by professional users, manufacturers and standards organizations acted to incorporate the IEC timecode into the format, together with video locking facilities, and to provide studio version machines with interface facilities that permitted communication with edit controllers and synchronizers.

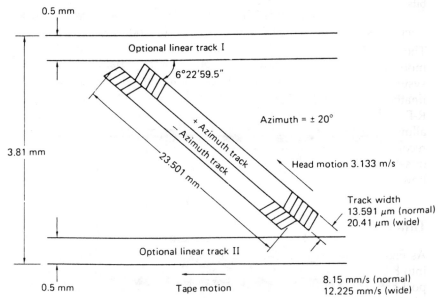

Figure 4.19 Azimuth recording employed in R-DAT results in the natural forming of 'track pairs'.

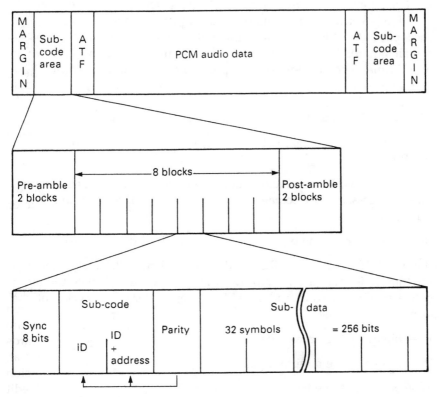

Figure 4.20 The sub-data areas carry 8 blocks of data. Each block contains 256 bits. These are grouped into 32 8-bit symbols.

The matter of incorporating IEC timecode into the format was not easy. The frame rate of R-DAT is not locked to an external clock in domestic models, and it differs from the frame rate of NTSC and PAL television systems and their non-composite derivatives (25 Hz and 29.97 Hz approximately). As a result traditional IEC cannot fit directly into one frame of R-DAT. To overcome this problem, incoming timecode is reprocessed to allow one 80-bit timecode word to be recorded per R-DAT frame. It is recorded in the sub-code areas, together with information regarding the offset between the two frame times. The following section will describe how this is done.

Timecode in the R-DAT system

As Figure 4.20 shows, each sub-code area of an R-DAT track is divided into 8 blocks, with an additional 2 blocks at each end forming pre- and post-ambles. Each block is divided into 36 byte-sized symbols. The first 4 of these symbols contain synchronizing and sub-data identification information, together with parity checking bits. The remaining 32 symbols are divided into 4 packs of 8 symbols, with each symbol containing 8 bits. There are thus 64 bits per pack, with the first four bits in each pack (the 'item area') defining its content. One of these packs contains the IEC time (but not user bit) information in a form known as 'pro-R time'. The make-up of each pro-R time pack, illustrated in Figure 4.21, is as follows:

PC-1 bits 4–7 define the pack as containing running time.

PC-1 bits 2 and 3 together with SPI-0 & SPI-1 define the contents as being pro-R time.

PC-2 bits F0 and F1 indicate the sampling frequency in use. This information is necessary to calculate the offset between timecode and RDAT frames.

Bits T0–T2 identify the type of timecode (25 frame, drop-frame etc).

Bits M0–M10 in the rest of PC-2 and all of PC-3 are collectively known as the 'timecode marker'. They provide information to calculate the offset between the timecode and R-DAT frames in terms of cycles of the sampling frequency.

PC-4 bits carry the hours data.

PC-5 bits carry the minutes data.

PC-6 bits carry the seconds data.

PC-7 bits carry the frames data.

PC-8 bits provide parity checks on the pack.

There are various methods of converting time data from IEC to R-DAT form. One of the simplest to implement is by means of a look-up table.

The timecode marker (TCM)

Because the frame rate of IEC timecode is slower than the frame rate of the R-DAT format, the time and R-DAT frames will cycle through, only occasionally coming into coincidence. If the R-DAT recorder is locked to the same source as the incoming timecode, the offset, though varying, will be predictable. If they are not locked together, or if one (or both) is giving an unstable output, then the offset will be unpredictable and will have to be calculated for each frame. Figure 4.22 illustrates. The nominal ratios between R-DAT frame rate and those of various other media are given in Table 4.2. Although this table shows simple ratios, it must be remembered that these will only be precise if the R-DAT machine and the video camera are locked to a common reference signal.

	B7	B6	B5	B4	B3	B2	B1	B0
PC1	0	Pack item 0	1	1	1	0	SPI0	SPI1
PC2	F1	F0	T2	T1	T0	(MSB)		
PC3	11 bit timecode marker							(LSB)
PC4	Hours (RH)							
PC5	Minutes (RM)							
PC6	Seconds (RS)							
PC7	Frames (RF)							
PC8	Pack parity							

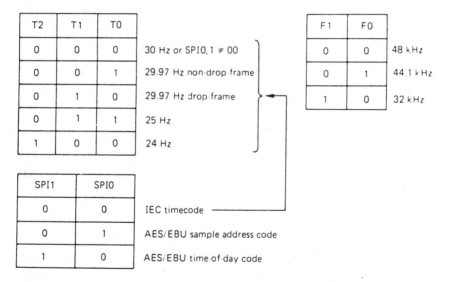

T2	T1	T0	
0	0	0	30 Hz or SPI0,1 ≠ 00
0	0	1	29.97 Hz non-drop frame
0	1	0	29.97 Hz drop frame
0	1	1	25 Hz
1	0	0	24 Hz

F1	F0	
0	0	48 kHz
0	1	44.1 kHz
1	0	32 kHz

SPI1	SPI0	
0	0	IEC timecode
0	1	AES/EBU sample address code
1	0	AES/EBU time-of-day code

Figure 4.21 The Pro-R time pack. It contains information about sampling frequency, frame rate and timecode type. Time and control data are carried in PC4–8. An 11-bit timecode marker carries the offset that results from the difference between R-DAT and video or AES/EBU frame rates.

To calculate the TCM, the IEC time address word is converted into its equivalent R-DAT time frame, perhaps by means of a look-up table. The difference in the start times of the IEC frame and its equivalent R-DAT frame obtained from this table provides an offset, 'or'. There will usually be a difference in time between the start of the R-DAT frame in the look-up

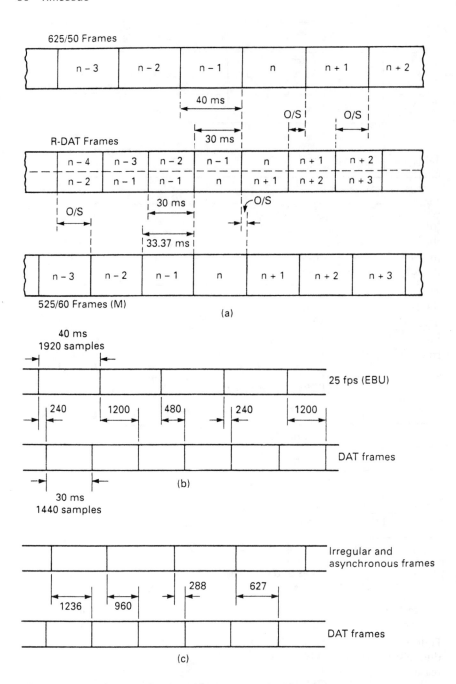

Figure 4.22 (a) In both 625/50 and 525/60 systems the timecode frame duration is longer than the R-DAT frame. (b) When the system is synchronous the time offset is predictable and can be calculated directly from the previous timecode market. (c) When the system has non-synchronous or unstable frame rates the offset cannot be predicted but must be individually calculated.

R-DAT frame rate is 33.33 Hz		
Time Code Type		Ratio Time Code : R-DAT
SMPTE	29.97 Hz	900:1001
	30 Hz	9:10
EBU	25 Hz	3:4
Film	24 Hz	18:25

Table 4.2 There are simple ratios between R-DAT, 525/60, 625/50 and SMTE film frame rates.

table and the actual R-DAT frame 'on'. The difference between the two (on—or) gives a time difference 't' between the reference DAT frame and the actual DAT frame. This time is divided by the periodic time of the master clock (its frequency will be that of the sampling frequency, hence the need to know it). The TCM is the number of clock count obtained. The TCM is converted into digital form and recorded as bits M0–M10 within the pack. Consequently the theoretical resolution of this system is sample accurate (cf LTC which can only be bit accurate – 1/80 LTC wordlength). Figure 4.23 illustrates the process for 625/50 code and a sampling frequency of 48 kHz.

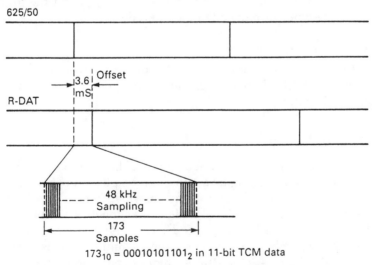

$173_{10} = 00010101101_2$ in 11-bit TCM data

Figure 4.23 The TCM carries, in digital form, the number of samples occurring during the offset between R-DAT frame and incoming timecode frame. For this reason the Pro-R pack must contain sampling rate information.

The timecode embedded within the AES/EBU digital interface signal may also be encoded within the time data pack. Bits SPI-0 and SPI-1 flag this condition. The AES/EBU code is placed in packs PC–4–PC–7, MSB in PC–4. PC–8 is for error detection. Figure 4.24 illustrates.

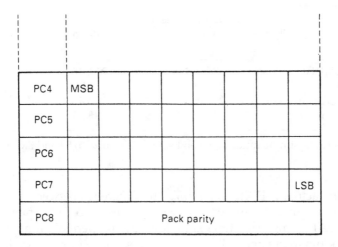

Figure 4.24 PC4–8 carry a 32-bit single code word when recording AES/EBU timecode (ProDIO code).

The user bits found within traditional timecode are incorporated in similar manner in a pack situated within a block of sub-data at the other end of the track pair.

Appendix 3 gives details of the R-DAT sub-codes and the formulae used to convert between the different timecodes.

R-DAT timecode in shuttle

Azimuth recording techniques, coupled with the relatively short recorded track lengths of R-DAT, make it possible to read pro-R time in shuttle, as Figure 4.25 illustrates.

DASH and Prodigi

Both these formats provide a number of digital linear multi-track options. DASH provides up to 24 digital audio channels plus 2 auxiliary analogue channels and timecode. A control track looks after tape speed stability. Prodigi provides up to 32 digital audio tracks together with two digital auxiliary audio channels and timecode. There is no control track as the clock signals are embedded within the digital audio channels in the form of sync words. Figure 4.26 illustrates a representative footprint of the two formats.

The Prodigi tape must be formatted prior to recording programme material unless all audio tracks are to be recorded simultaneously. This is because the error correction strategy employed calculates checkwords from data across all tracks. Formatting is done by putting the machine into record on all tracks with zero input on all channels. Formatting also provides an opportunity to record timecode.

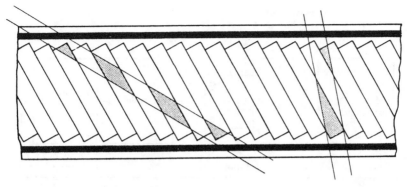

Figure 4.25 R-DAT permits replay of timecode in shuttle because an individual head will not replay track with the inappropriate azimuth, and because the individual data blocks are short and carry idents.

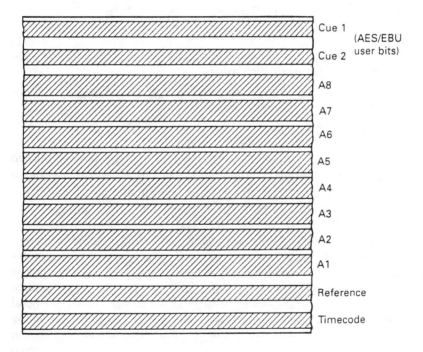

Figure 4.26 A typical DASH footprint.

The DASH format has separate digital audio and timecode/analogue headstacks. The Prodigi records all data, including timecode, on the same headstack, so an advance replay head is provided for 'punch-ins' (Figure 4.27 illustrates). Both formats support the AES/EBU digital audio interface.

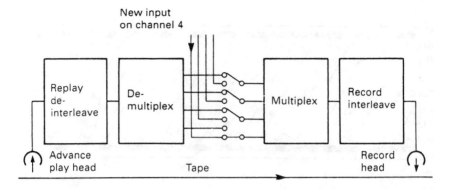

Figure 4.27 Prodigi provides an advance play head to permit de-multiplexing of words across the tracks for drop-ins, etc.

It is important, if the machines are to be used in audio/video post-production, that all recording (and formatting), as well as replay, are undertaken with the machine locked to reference syncs (not a synchronizer).

¹/₄in centre-track analogue audio

There are two track-width options for two-track analogue audiotape machines, NAB and CCIR. The NAB option has narrower track widths, with a wider guardband between them than with the CCIR standard, so can accommodate a longitudinal timecode track between them with minimal prospect of crosstalk. The LTC signal is recorded along a 0.38 mm wide track in the centre of a 2.0 mm wide band in the centre of the tape, as Figure 4.28 illustrates. The peak-to-peak level should be 6 ± 3 dB below peak-to-peak maximum audio level. Rise and fall times, and overshoot, are those specified in Appendix 2. The code should be recorded with a time constant of 0 Hz (i.e. no equalization), and without noise reduction, these requirements being intended to ensure that minimal phase distortion occurs. Crosstalk from timecode to audio should be better than 80 dB below maximum audio level. Crosstalk from audio to timecode between 40 Hz and 16 kHz should be better than 25 dB below timecode level. Input and output levels should be between 1 and 4 volts peak-to-peak. Input impedance should be greater than 5 kΩ; output impedance should be less than 40 Ω.

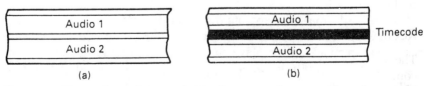

Figure 4.28 Timecode can be recorded in the centre of a two track analogue tape if sufficiently wide guard bands are provided to minimize crosstalk.

Although video machines record and replay audio off the same head (a condition necessary to maintain sync with the picture), audio machines are not so constrained, so can have separate head stacks optimized for their particular function. The manufacturer, therefore, has to consider how the timecode heads will be arranged. Will there be a common write/ read head, or will separate heads be provided? Will the timecode heads be incorporated into the audio headstacks or will they be placed upstream? However the manufacturer arranges things, the timecode address on tape must correspond to the audio material recorded physically alongside it. If the timecode heads are offset from the audio heads, the manufacturer will provide internal compensation for this offset, and may also provide a warning if this offset is in error.

Analogue audio machines lift the tape away from the heads during shuttle, and there are no control tracks to keep account of elapsed time. Instead, they have tachometer pulses, derived from transducers attached to a rotating idler. These pulses are arbitrary in their time spacing, being dependent on the effective diameter of the idler as well as the speed of the tape. They will give an indication of which direction the tape is moving. They may be presented to the outside world in a variety of forms including bi-directional pulses and frequency shift keying. It is important that any synchronizer can understand the particular form in which the tacho pulses will arrive, and the distance travelled (and hence time elapsed) by the tape. If this cannot be done then the audio machine will have to keep slowing down to examine the time addresses. This will make the location of sequences spaced apart on the tape exceedingly tedious. A number of synchronizers on the market will either learn the tacho pulse details automatically, or can be programmed to recognize specific machines by the installation of software.

Audio analogue multi-track

Timecode must be placed on the highest numbered track of a multi-track machine. Noise reduction should not be employed in order to minimize the possibility of phase distortion. The next highest track number should be left spare, and timecode should be recorded at –10 VU. These two precautions are intended to minimize crosstalk. It is important to ensure that timecode is replayed from the correct headstack. The arguments that apply to tachometer pulses on $1/4$in machines apply to 2in multi-track as well. Consideration should be given to incorporating dedicated electronics for the timecode track, to enable reading and reprocessing on replay.

Recording levels

The IEC now specifies the tracks and recording levels for time-and-control codes recorded in formats used with broadcast standard VCRs. These are summarized in Table 4.3, together with details of the relevant IEC publications and sections.

Format	IEC Publication and Section	Time-code track	Recording Level*	Notes
Transverse-track	347 [4] Section 4.5	Cue track	600–800 nWb/m p-p	1
Format B	602 [5], Amendment 1, Section 7.4.3	Audio track 3	720±70 nWb/m p-p	2
Format C	558 [6], Amendment 1, Section 8.5.3	Audio track 3	=> 186 nWb/m p-p	
Betacam SP	961 [7] Section 13	Dedicated time-code track	500 nWb/m rms	3
MII	1118 [8] Section 5.4	Dedicated time-code track	250±50 nWb/m p-p	
D1	1016 [9] Section 35	Dedicated time-code track	185±20 nWb/m rms	
D2	1709 [10] Section 9.5	Dedicated time-code track	500±20 nWb/m p-p	
D3	[11] Section 39	Dedicated time-code track	250±20 nWb/m p-p	
Analogue multi-track audio	94–6 [12]	Audio track having the highest number	Not standardized	4

Notes:
*Recording levels are expressed as the rms or peak-to-peak magnetic short-circuit flux level, per metre of record track width.
1. The transverse-track format is obsolete and is no longer recommended for programme exchanges.
2. A recording level of 720 nWb/m p-p corresponds to 254 nWb/m rms, for a sinusoidal signal.
3. The recording level shall be sufficient to ensure full saturation of the magnetic domains.
4. The audio track adjacent to the track carrying the time-code should preferably remain un-recorded. The recording level is chosen to give reliable time-code reading at speeds which are not close to zero, but should be low enough to avoid cross-talk into the audio tracks.

Table 4.2 IEC specifications for timecode tracks and levels.

CHAPTER 5

Timecode and film

Introduction

For many years, people working with film have employed a system of film footage numbering, commonly called 'key numbers'. These are printed along the edge of film stock at the time of manufacture as a latent image, becoming human-readable when the film is processed. The purpose of these numbers has been to facilitate the work of the negative cutter, once the film editor has done his or her work (Figure 5.1). In addition to the key number, a 'strip number', having a random relationship to the key number, has also been present to act as a check in the event of duplicated key numbers (always a possibility with a full-length feature film, where hundreds of thousands of feet of film may have been shot). The key number identifies the film type, the printer number (part of the quality control system), the perforation equipment and the footage count. As some scenes may be less than 1 ft long (especially in pop music videos) there may be no key number present in a particular shot. Recent developments in film production have resulted in the marriage of traditional film numbering systems with timecode. This chapter examines the coding systems available, together with the options expected to be developed in the near future.

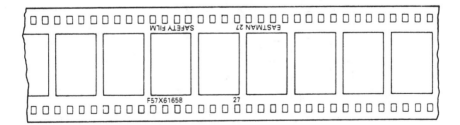

Figure 5.1 The original style key number

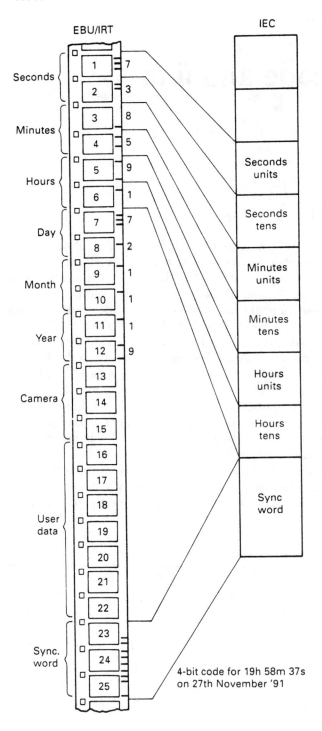

Figure 5.2 16 mm timecode recorded at the time of shooting within the camera as latent images along the opposite edge to the perforations.

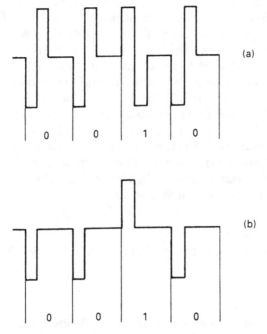

Figure 5.3 16 mm timecode recorded magnetically by either phase shift keying (a) or by a RZ code (b).

EBU/IRT and EBU/TDF timecodes

These codes were developed in the 1970s by the Institut für Rundfunktechnik in Munich, in collaboration with Télédiffusion de France. They both carry timecode information as defined in EBU document 3096, and provide time and date of shooting information together with the camera number. The code is recorded either optically or magnetically along the film edge of 16 mm film. Figure 5.2 illustrates the optical form of the code. Each codeword occupies 25 frames, and there are 4 bits of information per frame length, a data rate of 100 bits per second. The code is binary coded decimal. The optical form of the code is straightforward NRZ. The magnetic forms of the code differ slightly between the IRT and TDF versions, with IRT specifying pulse polarity (return to zero) to determine logical 1s and 0s, and the TDF version specifying phase shift keying. Figure 5.3 illustrates the differences. The code extends past midnight to 28 hours. This is to avoid the code resettling to 00.00.00.00 at midnight, which might cause problems in post-production.

SMPTE film codes

Timecodes for film are specified in SMPTE Recommended Practice RP 136-1990. There are two versions, B-format and C-format. The arrangement of time and data bits in both formats is that of the IEC 525/60 code covered in Chapter 3. There are differences in the synchronizing bits, as the two versions have different implementations. The C-format code is designed for application when the film is moving continuously both during filming and replaying. The codeword contains 80 bits, and should begin at a point adjacent to the centre of the frame bar (the frame line), though any point between the frame line and the centre line of the frame is acceptable (Figure 5.4). The bit allocation is identical to the 525/60 version of IEC longitudinal timecode. Arriflex have developed an in-camera recording system based on this format. The B-format code is recorded in blocks, each block being complete in itself. It is designed for use with equipment that has intermittent film motion, though it can also be played back in continuous mode. The format is illustrated in Figure 5.5. There are 112 bits to the complete word:

Bits 0–7 and 104–111
These are timing bits. They are alternate logical 1s and 0s. Bits 0–7 start 0,1; bits 104–112 start 1,0.

Bits 8–23 and 88–103
These are synchronizing words. They are identical, and have the same form as the LTC synchronizing word discussed in Chapter 3.

Bits 24–87 have the same allocations as bits 0–63 of the 525/60 version of IEC longitudinal timecode.

The gaps between the blocks are a minimum of 10% of the frame length (a frame length being the distance between two successive frame lines). To reduce the d.c. content of the code, the inter-block gaps should be filled

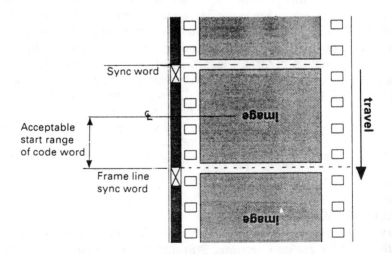

Figure 5.4 SMPTE C-format film timecode.

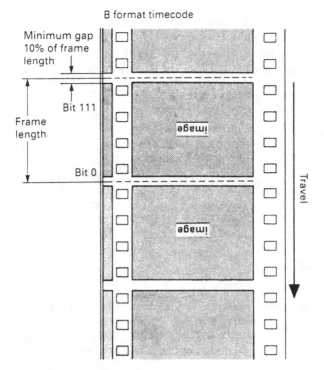

Figure 5.5 SMPTE B-format film timecode.

with alternate 0s and 1s. The lateral positioning of code on the film will depend on the particular format being used, and is laid down in various SMPTE Recommended Practices. The bit allocation between two formats is compared in Figure 5.6.

Both B- and C-format versions of the code employ biphase mark coding. They can each be recorded on film optically or magnetically. On final (release) prints, the timecode at the start of the picture is 01 h 00 m 00 s 00 f. All frames prior to the start of the picture are coded 01 h 00 m 00 s 00 f. On films with more than one reel the picture start is indicated by 01 h 00 m 00 s 00 f, with all preceding frames being similarly coded. Successive reels are numbered similarly, with the hour increasing by 1 for each successive reel.

Film binary groups data

At the time of writing the use of the binary groups is specified in SMPTE Recommended Practice 135-1990. This provides for information concerning the shoot to be placed in the user bits. The decision as to whether to provide/use this data is left to the discretion of the equipment manufacturer/user. The binary group flag bits indicate the use of the binary groups for carrying this data, which contains the date of the shoot together with camera, roll/tape, scene, take and production numbers, and details of the shot material (daylight/tungsten, day/night, sync/non-sync etc). Details of the code are given in Appendix 4. There is now an SMPTE standard 262m) for the 1.1 setting of the flag bits to indicate the use of the binary groups for additional data. Multiple timecodes, production data, titles, transmission and remote control data are all possibilities. Appendices 4 and 5 give an outline.

Type b code bits	Type C code bits	Detail
0 – 7		Alternating zeros and ones
8 – 23		Synchronizing word
8 – 9		Fixed Zeros
10 – 21		Fixed Ones
22		Fixed Zero
23		Fixed One
24 – 27	0 – 3	Units of frames
28 – 31	4 – 7	First binary group
32 – 33	8 – 9	Tens of frames
34	10	Drop frame flag
35	11	Colour frame flag
36 – 39	12 – 15	Second binary group
40 – 43	16 – 19	Units of seconds
44 – 47	20 – 23	Third binary group
48 – 50	24 – 26	Tens of seconds
51	27	Biphase mark correction bit
52 – 55	28 – 31	Fourth binary group
56 – 59	32 – 35	Units of minutes
60 – 63	36 – 39	Fifth binary group
64 – 66	40 – 42	Tens of minutes
67	43	Binary group flag bit
68 – 71	44 – 47	Sixth binary group
72 – 75	48 – 51	Units of hours
76 – 79	52 – 55	Seventh binary group
80 – 81	56 – 57	Tens of hours
82	58	Unassigned (zero till assigned)
83	59	Binary group flag bit
84 – 87	60 – 63	Eighth binary group
88 – 103	64 – 79	Synchronizing word
88 – 89	64 – 65	Fixed zeros
90 – 101	66 – 77	Fixed ones
102	78	Fixed zero
103	79	Fixed one
104 – 111		Alternating ones and zeroes

Figure 5.6 SMPTE code format bit allocations compared.

DataKode®

In the early 1980s, the Eastman Kodak Company developed a method of coating film stock with low-density gamma ferric oxide, approximately 0.005 mm thick. The film base was coated on the non-emulsion side. Time data could be recorded onto this coating magnetically, and later replayed either during film to videotape transfer or for viewing. Called DataKode®, this was not intended for release prints. The coating reduced the transmittance of the film stock slightly as additional dyes were required to keep the density neutral. This was of no consequence when shooting as the coating was on the film base; nor was it expected to cause any problems either to the printers or in the review rooms. However, as with all magnetic record/replay systems, contact between record/play head and magnetic surface is necessary to maintain consistent playback quality (freedom from dropout, resolution). The risk of scratches arising from this contact precluded the use of the picture area for this code, so although the coating covered the entire film surface only a narrow strip along the edge of the film stock could be utilized. There were further problems associated with the installation of record and confidence heads in camera instant-change magazines and the risk of mixing different types of film stock, so in the end the system was not adopted for 16 mm use.

Aaton and Arriflex timecode systems

Two companies, Aaton des Autres and the Arriflex Corporation, have developed in-camera timecode recording systems. Aaton have taken the route of encoding the time data in the form of matrices of 91 dots (13 columns of 7 lines) per frame, with specific sequences of timecoded frames alternating with additional information concerning the shoot. Their approach has been to develop a dedicated range of equipment to perform such tasks as setting the timecode and user bits, and creating databases for use in film/video transfer and subsequent post-production. The Arriflex approach has been to record time data in standard SMPTE RP136-1990 formats (both B- and C-formats are supported) though at the time of writing the SMPTE RP 135-1990 user bit options for the carrying of additional data are not implemented.

AatonCode

Of the 91 dots in the 7 x 13 matrix, 64 carry time and user bit information as standard SMPTE/EBU code; a further 27 bits carry control and synchronization information. The blocks are recorded two frames down from the gate, the offset being compensated for at the time of recording. The matrix is exposed onto film by a row of seven red LEDS. When code is running, these can be seen twinkling in the camera before the magazine is loaded, though this should not be taken as a confidence check as LEDs have been known to stick on or off. In the 35 mm film format these blocks are recorded on the outside of the sprocket holes on the opposite side of the film to KeyKode®. In the 16 mm film format the code is recorded between the sprocket holes, on the same side as KeyKode®, which is recorded outside the sprocket holes. With the Super-16 format the code is also recorded between the sprocket holes, and although there was some overlap between the AatonCode and KeyKode® (the human-readable characters within KeyKode® are larger than the machine-readable barcode), and also between AatonCode and traditional edge numbers, different emulsion dye colours are exposed so that each can be easily read.

The 64-bit 'core' of the Aaton code block is in accordance with SMPTE RP 135-1990, which means that the user bits can contain date, scene, take, roll, production and equipment identification codes. The 35 mm form of the code also incorporates a zero frame indicator.

In the 35 mm form of the code, human-readable data are contained in a sequence 'paged' over a number of frames, with each sequence containing one or two numbers or letters in the following sequence:

R	XX	XX	Roll number
TK	XX	XX	Take number
SC	XX	XX	Scene number
E	XX	XX	Camera number (may be designated CM)
P	XX	XX	Production number
YY	MM	DD	Date
HH	MM	SS	Time
s			Zero frame indicator

In the 16 mm form of the code 6 frames in 24 provide the following human-readable information:

Time	:HH	:MM	:SS	every second
Date	:YY	:MM	:DD	every three seconds
Equipment ID	:EQ	:XX	:XX	every three seconds
Production ID	:PR	:XX	:XX	every three seconds

Examples of the AatonCode are illustrated in Figure 5.7.

Arriflex Code

In the Arriflex Film Identification and Sync System (FIS), timecode is recorded as a series of stripes along the film, between the picture frames and the sprocket holes, on the same side as KeyKode®. Film exposure is from a single LED, either in the gate or within the magazine. If the LED is in the gate, and B-format code is being recorded, a microprocessor within the camera controls the generation of the codeword to compensate for the acceleration and deceleration of the film. If the LED is in the magazine, and C-format code is being recorded, the microprocessor calculates the loop size (from the ballistics of the film movement) and compensates accordingly. The camera timecode generator is momentarily jam-synched to an external source of code. The code source should not be removed after syncing, however, as the oscillator driving the transport and gate mechanisms requires a continuous feed of external timecode to maintain synchronization with the associated audio recorder. Confidence of

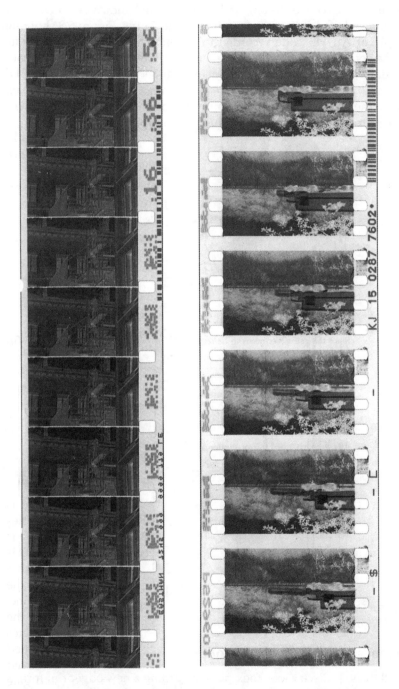

Figure 5.7 AatonCode recorded in-camera on the Super-16 format (a) and on 35 mm (b). There is no conflict with KeyKode®.

incoming code is achieved by either checking whether the LED is twinkling (if it can be seen) or by an external indicator LED. If the incoming code fails, the camera will revert to 24 fps. Figure 5.8 shows an example of ArriFIS code recorded on 35 mm film. During film/video transfer both SMPTE and KeyKode® are read and held on a microcomputer database, together with the videotape timecode. KeyKode® data can be put into the user bits of the videotape timecode. These data are later used by the controlling microcomputer to conform the EDL for the final cutting/process work. Figure 5.9 illustrates a typical arrangement.

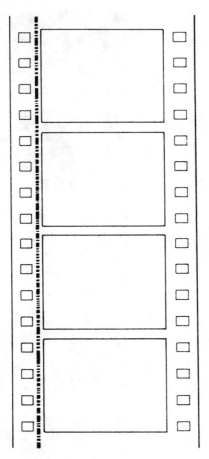

Figure 5.8 SMPTE code recorded in-camera by the ArriFIS system. There is no conflict with KeyKode®.

Machine-readable film timecodes

In 1988 the first discussions took place regarding a new edgeprint format, in 1990 the SMPTE proposed a standard for 'Manufacturer-printed latent image identification information' and in 1994 the standards were adopted as SMPTE 270 (for 65 mm film) and SMPTE 271 (for 16 mm film). This has

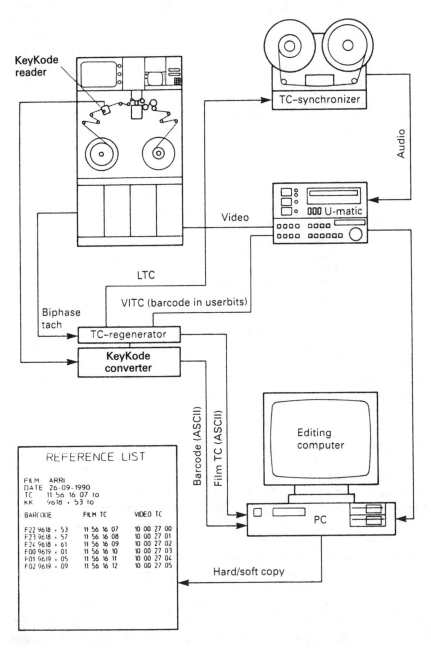

Figure 5.9 Film-to-video transfer involves KeyKode®, bi-phase (tacho) pulses and timecode. A small computer with a suitable database controls the process and logs the codes.

been implemented by film stock manufacturers, for example the Eastman Kodak Company with its KeyKode® number system. The code is put on the film stock during manufacture as a latent image, which becomes visible when the film is developed. The code is both human- and machine-readable. The machine-readable code is a barcode to USS128 standard. This particular barcode is specifically intended for use with reflective media. Two characters are embedded in one symbol. The code can identify the film manufacturer and the type of film stock, as well as time data. The manufacturer's identification codes are given in Table 5.1. The Film Type Identifier Codes are included at the manufacturer's discretion. The time data are embedded in a ten-digit number which indicates film footage and roll number. Figures 5.10–5.12 illustrate the 16, 35 and 65 mm forms of the code, as implemented by the Eastman Kodak Company.

Manufacturer	Code
Agfa-Gevaert N.V.	A
Eastman Kodak Company	K
Fuji Film Company	F
Other or non-designated	(nothing)

Table 5.1 KeyKode® manufacturers' codes.

Zero frame in the foot is the frame that is immediately above the zero frame mark. In the 35 mm format the code repeats every 64 perforations (every foot) with an identified mid-foot code 32 perforations after zero frame. In the 16 mm format the code increases by 1 every 20 perforations (6in). It is less wide than the 35 mm version in order to keep it out of the way of Aaton Time Code. The key number itself is numeric, and printed in both human-readable and barcode form. The key number is a 6-digit roll identification number and a 4-digit footage number. The barcode also contains the additional manufacturer and film type information mentioned earlier.

The barcode data consist of 16 digits, arranged into 8 characters: a 2-digit manufacturer's identification code, a 2-digit film type code, a 6-digit number (the 'prefix') to identify the roll, a 4-digit footage count, and a 2-digit offset (00 for the code at frame zero, 32 for the mid-foot code). The code is preceded by a start character. It is followed by checksum and stop characters. The checksum is the Modulo 103 sum of the start character and the weighted values of the 8 data characters.

Many manufacturers have developed equipment to both read the KeyKode® number system, and to convert it to IEC code (Figure 5.13). This facility permits the video off-line editing of film. The timecode can also be converted back to key number form again for the convenience of the negative cutter.

EASTMAN 16 mm KEYKODE™ Numbers

U S E R S ' G U I D E

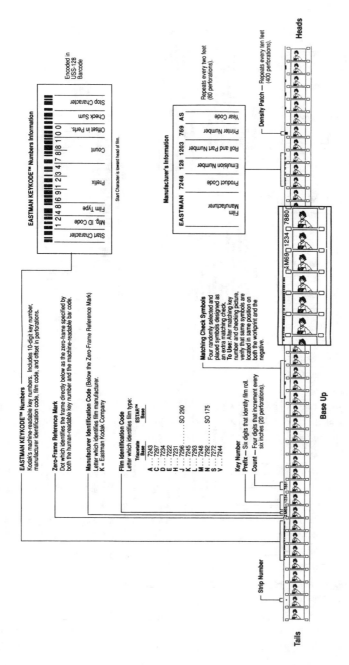

EASTMAN KEYKODE™ Numbers. Includes 10-digit key number, manufacturer identification code, film code, and offset in perforations.

Zero-Frame Reference Mark
Dot which identifies the frame directly below as the zero-frame specified by both the human-readable key number and the machine-readable bar code.

Manufacturer Identification Code (Below the Zero-Frame Reference Mark)
Letter which identifies film manufacturer.
K = Eastman Kodak Company

Film Identification Code
Letter which identifies film type:

	Triacetate Base	ESTAR™ Base
A	7243	
C	7297	
D	7234	
E	7222	
H	7231	
J	7296	SO 290
K	7245	
L	7293	
M	7248	
N	7292	SO 175
S	7272	
V	7244	

Key Number
Prefix — Six digits that identify film roll.
Count — Four digits that increment every six inches (20 perforations).

Matching Check Symbols
Four randomly selected and placed symbols designed as an extra matching check.
To Use: Alter matching key number and checking picture, verify that same symbols are located in same position on both the workprint and the negative.

EASTMAN KEYKODE™ Numbers Information

Start Character	Mfg. ID Code	Film Type	Prefix	Count	Offset in Perfs.	Check Sum	Stop Character

1 2 4 8 6 9 1 2 3 4 7 8 8 1 0 0

Encoded in USS-128 Barcode

Start Character is toward head of film.

Manufacturer's Information

Film Manufacturer	Product Code	Emulsion Number	Roll and Part Number	Printer Number	Year Code
EASTMAN	7248	128	1203	769	AS

Repeats every two feet (80 perforations).

Density Patch — Repeats every ten feet (400 perforations).

Heads

Base Up

Tails

Strip Number

Eastman Motion Picture Films © Eastman Kodak

Figure 5.10 The Eastman 16 mm Edgeprint Format with KeyKode®. Courtesy of Eastman Kodak Company. © Eastman Kodak Company, 1991.

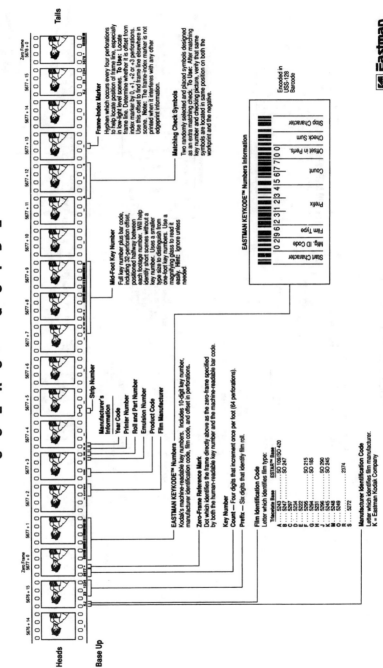

Figure 5.11 The Eastman 35 mm Edgeprint Format with KeyKode®. Courtesy of Eastman Kodak Company. © Eastman Kodak Company, 1991.

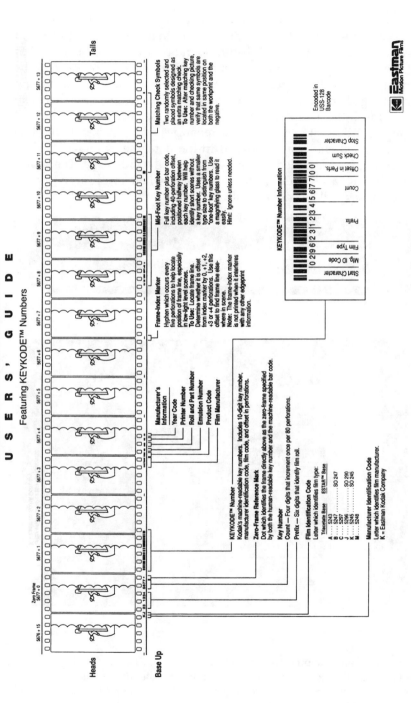

Figure 5.12 The Eastman 65 mm Edgeprint Format with KeyKode®. Courtesy of Eastman Kodak Company. © Eastman Kodak Company, 1991.

Film transfer to PAL video

Much film post-production is undertaken on videotape. This involves transfer of film to video at two separate points in the process: before video editing, and after video editing, before sound post-production. If the film and the accompanying audio are shot at 25 Hz frame rate there should be no problems with either pictures or sound transfer as long as everything is synced together. However, if the film has been shot at 24 Hz there can be problems. If the telecine/video transfer is done at 25 Hz, the film will be running 4.2% fast. The time discrepancies brought about this this change in speed shift can be logged in the database of the controlling microcomputer or recorded in the user bits on the videotape. The sound will be running fast however, and particularly where music is concerned the discrepancy will be very audible.

(a)

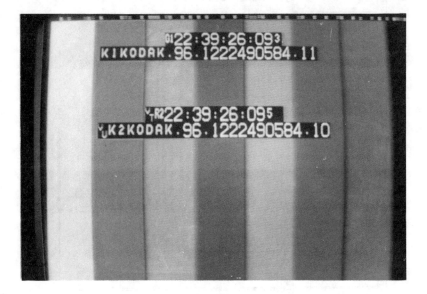

(b)

Figure 5.13 A timecode processor (a), which will display KeyKode®, TC generator path, TC signal type, and colour frame number (b), as well as performing a wide range of reprocessing and code translation functions. Courtesy Avitel Electronics Limited.

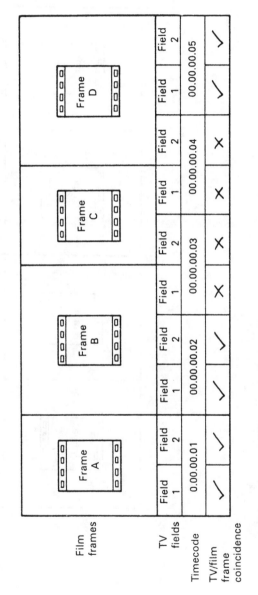

Film frames	Frame A		Frame B				Frame C		Frame D	
TV fields	Field 1	Field 2	Field 1	Field 2	Field 1	Field 2	Field 1	Field 2	Field 1	Field 2
Timecode	0.00.00.01		00.00.00.02		00.00.00.03		00.00.00.04		00.00.00.05	
TV/film frame coincidence	✓	✓	✓	✓	✗	✗	✗	✗	✓	✓

Figure 5.14 The relationship between 24 fps film and 30 fps video timecodes results in a 4 film frame/5 video frame sequence known as 3/2 pulldown. Frame A correlates exactly. Film frames B and D are recorded on 3 successive video fields. Film frame C is recorded on fields in different frames.

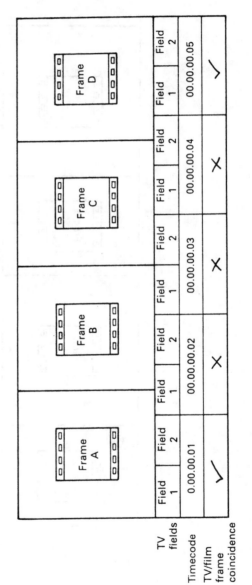

TV fields	Field 1	Field 2	Field 1	Field 2	Field 1	Field 2	Field 1	Field 2
	Frame A		Frame B		Frame C		Frame D	
Timecode	0.00.00.01		00.00.00.02	00.00.00.03	00.00.00.04		00.00.00.05	
TV/film frame coincidence	✓		✗	✗	✗		✓	

Figure 5.15 A linear 24/30 film/video transfer results in mixed film frame information on 3 out of 5 video frames.

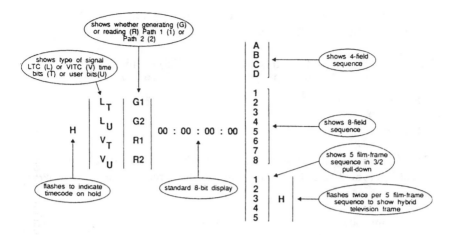

Figure 5.16 The film/video field/frame relationships that can be displayed on a picture monitor. Courtesy Avitel Electronics Limited.

A more elegant solution is to run the telecine at 24 Hz frame rate, locked to station syncs, and to make up the additional frames. Since telecine machines are working with optical images they can have RGB or component outputs, which means that sub-carrier phase is not a problem. An extra field can be added every twelve frames, the scans on the machine being modified accordingly, to maintain interlace. There will be short-term time discrepancies between timecode of film and real time, but these can be accommodated by a microcomputer and suitable database. The sound should either be transferred via a recorder locked to 25 Hz (the original tape running at 24 fps), or transferred to a machine (perhaps a digital sound station) which can run the sound at an equivalent 24 fps rate while being locked to 25 Hz.

Transfer of film to video intended for digitizing into a non-linear editing system can be much simpler, but will vary according to the non-linear system employed, and the capability of the telecine to run at 24 fps. In this respect, later versions of data management systems, such as Aaton's *Keylink* are able to convert 24 fps recorded code into a time-correct 25 fps 625/50 code. Chapter 10 discusses the options in detail.

3-line VITC

In 1994 Aaton and Evertz proposed a 3-line encoding format that can be generated during film-to-video transfer. The code is able to carry the in-camera code, audio recorder code, in-camera date, camera ident and Aaton Tags, all recorded at the time of shooting, as well as video tape code (of the recording VCR), video reel ident (of the recording VCR), 3/2 pull-down code (see next section) and KeyKode®, all recorded at film-to-video-transfer. The first VITC line carries traditional VITC CRCC, the other two lines each have their own unique CRCC to prevent confusion with traditional VITC information. Although the positioning of the 3-line VITC block is up to the user, the manufacturers recommend the following:

Block	625/50 lines	525/60 lines
1	19 – 20 – 21	18 – 19 – 20
2 (optional)	14 – 15 – 16	13 – 14 – 15
3 (White Flag) (optional)	12	12

The first line of a block is defined as that which lies closest to the vertical interval. The data are recorded in the three lines in the following manner:

	Time bits	User bits	CRCC
1st line	Videotape timecode	Aaton Tags or video reel ID	Normal
2nd line	Pulldown and Keykode®	KeyKode®	Inverted
3rd line	In-camera (production) or audio timecode	Audio user bits or in-camera date & ID	MS nibble inverted

The first line of the 3-line VITC is encoded with normal VITC CRCC so that it can be accessed by timecode readers installed in existing VCRs. The CRCC in the second line is inverted (i.e. '1's and '0's are inverted), and the third line has the bits in the most significant nibble of the CRCC inverted to prevent confusion from existing VITC readers. The White Flag line can be used to identify the first field of a video frame that results from a new image transfer.

The generators of the codes are manufactured as 1-U high 19in rack mounted units by a number of manufacturers, including manufacturers of non-linear editors, and may also contain or access data management systems (such as Aaton's Keylink or Avid's Phoenix). The ability to transfer *all* relevant time- and film-footage codes to videotape has profound implications not just for post-production, but also for the way a film is shot. These are discussed in Chapters 8 and 10. Appendix 8 carries the details of the bit arrangements within 3-line VITC.

Film transfer via 3/2 pulldown

Film shot at 24 fps cannot be run at 30 fps because of the large speed discrepancy between the two rates. To overcome this, and to permit easy comparison between film frame and corresponding video field, as identified by timecode, additional fields have to be inserted in a known sequence. This process, known as '3/2 pulldown', is illustrated in Figure 5.14. As can be seen, the sequence repeats every 4 film and 5 video (and timecode) frames, a ratio of 24:30. As the initial sequence starts with film from 00 and timecode from 00 it is possible to identify each point in the sequence from the timecode. If the video is running at 29.97 fps (as it will be with colour) then the telecine will need to run at 23.976 fps. The short-term time discrepancies can again be handled by a microcomputer.

It is possible to transfer film to video without 3/2 pulldown by using an optical multiplex system (linear transfer). In this case the film frames are mixed together in various proportions in each video field (Figure 5.15), with each film frame being transferred to an average of 1.25 video frames. This mix of frames is less than satisfactory. If 3/2 pulldown and linear transfer methods are compared we can see that with 3/2 pulldown three in five video frames (A, B and D) each contain information from one single film frame; with linear transfer only two video frames (A and D) in five each contain information from one single film frame. Equipment is available to display the correlation between film and video frames and fields and to display that correlation within the picture area, together with the timecode (Figure 5.16).

Control of 4:3 scanning for the presentation of wide-screen films

Within the EBU, although there is no restriction on the use of user bits by any individual organization for the exchange of recorded programmes, some broadcasters have devised some uses for them which the EBU has documented and distributed for the benefit of its members. One use, devised by the French broadcaster TDF, concerns the control of video scanning of wide-screen feature films for transmission in the standard 4:3 aspect ratio.

There are two ways in which wide-screen (16:9) format film can be transmitted; either it can be sent in 'letterbox' display, with black bars above and below the picture, or a panscan display can be presented, where a full-height section of the 16:9 film frame fills the screen, but parts of the sides are lost. The displayed section can be moved around to preserve as far as possible the artistic composition of the film frames.

If the film is transferred, in 16:9 format, to videotape before playout, codes can be placed in the user bits to select which area of the original picture will be transmitted. This is called 'Panscan'.

The user bits in the LTC carry the control data because:

1. LTC tracks are available on all current and proposed broadcast tape formats.
2. The data can be edited independently of picture and sound.

The data are sent twice, on separate frames, because:

1. LTC is not decoded until the end of the timecode word has been reached (at the end of the frame). This implies a delay in the picture while the scanning data are decoded.

2. Sending scanning data in advance permits applications that involve special effects stores, or which require panscan data in advance of the picture.

Panscan data is sent both during the picture to which it applies, and 15 frames ahead of that picture, so also carries information about the current frame (f) and the following frame ($f + 15$) to which it refers. The data are sent in binary groups 1–5. Groups 1 and 2 carry information for current frame (f), groups 3 and 4 carry information for frame ($f + 15$), group 5 carries aspect ratio data flags. Table 5.2a–b gives the details.

Bits	Information	Coding
0–3	Units of frames	IEC 461
4–7	Binary group 1	LSB of panscan data for picture N
8–11	Tens of frames, etc.	IEC 461
12–15	Binary group 2	MSB of panscan data for picture N
16–19	Units of seconds	IEC 461
20–23	Binary group 3	LSB of panscan data for picture $N+15$
24–27	Tens of seconds, etc.	IEC 461
28–31	Binary group 4	MSB of panscan data for picture $N+15$
32–35	Units of minutes	IEC 461
36–39	Binary group 5	Aspect ratio and panscan flag
40–43	Tens of minutes, etc.	IEC 461
44–47	Binary group 6	Reserved, set to zero
48–51	Units of hours	IEC 461
52–55	Binary group 7	Reserved, set to zero
56–59	Tens of hours, etc.	IEC 461
60–63	Binary group 8	Reserved, set to zero

Table 5.2a Allocation of panscan data in the timecode word.

Binary group 5	
Bit Information	Coding
D3 Unassigned	X
D2 Panscan flag	1: panscan data 0: no panscan data
D1 Image aspect ratio for picture $N+15$	1: aspect ratio of image $N+15$ is 16:9 0: aspect ratio of image $N+15$ is 4:3
D0 Image aspect ratio for current picture, N	1: aspect ratio of image N is 16:9 0: aspect ratio of image N is 4:3

Table 5.2b Aspect ratio stored in binary group 5.

Position	Shift Rec. 601 sample intervals	Code	MS nibble	LS nibble
Far left	−43	−43	D	5
Central	0	0	0	0
Far right	+44	+44	2	C

Table 5.3 Examples of panscan data stored as hexadecimal codes.

Data about frame	Binary group	
	MS nibble	LS nibble
N	2	1
N+15	4	3

Table 5.4 Allocation of panscan data in the binary groups.

Data are sent in eight-bit (byte) groups, by pairing binary groups. For each picture the data indicate the shift away from the centre of the picture in increments of ITU-R Rec. 601 colour-difference samples (approx. 148 ns) in 2's complement form (see Chapter 2). Accordingly, there are 43 increments left, one central position, and another 42 increments right, that define the shift in the scan. The value is coded as two hexadecimal numbers as Table 5.3 illustrates. In each binary group pair the LS nibble is carried in the lower number group, and the MS nibble in the higher number group as Table 5.4 illustrates.

CHAPTER 6

Timecode and MIDI

Introduction

MIDI (an acronym for Musical Instrument Digital Interface) is a digital control system developed to enable synthesizers, keyboards, sequencers, home computers, drum machines etc, to be interconnected via a standard interface. This standard specifies both the type of connector and data signal protocol and level. At its most basic level MIDI is a means of setting one instrument as slave to another. At its most sophisticated it can be used to create, store and replay complex musical compositions, and can be used to control ancillary equipment such as mixers and effects units. All communication in MIDI is carried in multi-byte serial 'messages'. The system is asynchronous, the data only being transmitted as required. Binary 0 is represented by a current flowing in the link, and binary 1 by no current flow. Each byte is preceded by a start bit and followed by an end bit. The data rate is 31.25 kBaud, ± 1%. This gives a duration of 320 μs for each 10-bit message. In the discussion that follows, the presence of these start and end bits will be assumed, and attention will be concentrated on the message bits. For most message types, the first byte of each message is a status byte, called the 'header', indicating the nature of the following data. As Figure 6.1 shows, these messages are of two broad types: channel and system.

Channel messages

Channel messages are intended for individual items of equipment, which are each identified by a number (the channel number) in the range 0–15. This number requires 4 bits (a nibble) of digital data. Each channel message consists of a header byte, followed by either one or two data bytes. The channel message header byte always commences with a logic 1, followed by a 3-digit message code, and a 4-digit channel number (Figure 6.2). Hence Channel Message Header 1 1 0 1 1 0 1 means:

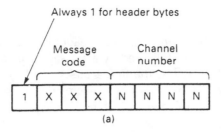

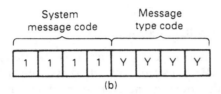

Figure 6.1 MIDI header bytes can identify (a) Channel Message Codes or (b) System Message Codes.

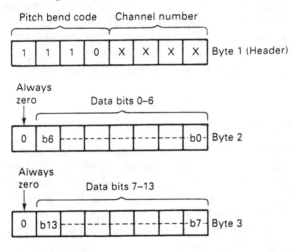

Figure 6.2 A Channel Message Code comprises a header byte followed by one or more message bytes.

1   Channel message
1 ⎫
0 ⎬ Overall key pressure
1 ⎭
1 ⎫
0 ⎪
0 ⎬ Channel 9
1 ⎭

System messages

As Figure 6.1 showed, the system message header byte always starts with a 4-bit system message code, followed by a message type code. Note that the system message header has the first 4 bits set to logic 1. The 4 least significant bits carry system messages. There are 16 messages (0–15) available, but not all are implemented. Of interest regarding timecode are:

1000 Clock signal
1010 Start
1011 Continue
1100 Stop
Code 0001 implements MIDI timecode, MTC.

The clock signal is used to keep, for example, sequencers accurately synchronized. The clock pulses are transmitted at a rate of 24 per crotchet (quarter note). They do not start and stop instruments, and they contain no time-specific information: they are the digital equivalent of a metronome. 'Start' messages will cause a sequencer to start its sequence from the beginning, regardless of where it stopped. The 'continue' message causes a sequencer to start up from where it left off, and the 'stop' message stops it. A device can be instructed to go to a position by means of a 'song position pointer', which is calculated by counting the semiquaver (sixteenth note) tempo intervals from the start of a particular sequence.

MIDI synchronizers

Synchronizers used with MIDI systems convert the clock signals into a form suitable for storage on magnetic tape or floppy disc, and reconvert back into MIDI form for replay. Simple synchronizers usually just record start, stop and clock signals. They do not generate time information as such, so there is no way of asking a machine to go to a particular time address, though the song position pointer can be used to point to a particular event, such as the start of a song.

More complex synchronizers will allow a degree of synchronization with IEC timecode pre-striped on tape, but they will only read timecode and locate it; they will not generate it. When the tape is replayed, timecode is converted to a MIDI message, usually by a microprocessor within the synchronizer – sometimes via a dedicated port rather than the MIDI interface which simplifies matters. The marriage of timecode with MIDI has been difficult because MIDI clocks and SPPs are tempo based, whereas timecode provides absolute time information. If the tempo of a piece of music is altered after being correlated with timecode, there is obviously going to be a discrepancy.

Some synchronizers *will* generate a timecode, but this is usually specific to the particular system, and although the manufacturer will probably provide 'backwards compatibility', there may well be difficulties in interfacing equipment from different manufacturers. Microcomputers equipped with suitable programs and databases are available to convert between timecode and MIDI clock, and to control peripheral devices such as synchronizers. It is now possible to accommodate changes in tempo by updating the database. Synchronizers are available to interface MIDI-controlled machines with traditional timecode-controlled ones. With the aid of the microcomputer, lists can be compiled to manage events and commands, and the data held in these lists fed to individual MIDI peripherals, to be acted on when the time arrives.

MIDI and IEC timecode

MIDI and IEC timecode frequently have to interface in post-production, not just for the marriage of music to pictures, but also for the generation of synthesized effects. To facilitate this, a system of accommodating real time within the MIDI message structure has evolved. It is called 'MIDI timecode' (MTC), and will be generated either by a synchronizer or by the systems-controlling sequencer. Operational aspects of MTC will be covered at the end of this chapter.

There are two forms of MTC messages, quarter-frame (IEC timecode frame) and full-frame. Each is identified by a header byte. The quarter-frame message is preceded by a System Common Header (&F1), the full frame message is preceded by a System Exclusive Header (&F0). Quarter-frame messages are sent regularly and carry real-time data. Full-frame messages also carry time data, but this is used to set up a device. A full-frame message may be used to send a machine to a particular location, or it may prepare a machine to act at a particular real-time point.

Quarter-frame messages

The time information in a quarter-frame message is held in a sequence of 8 data bytes, each preceded by a system header byte carrying the system common message code 11110001 (&F1). Four bytes of time data are carried per MIDI frame (hence the term 'quarter-frame'). The code carries time information compatible with that carried by IEC timecode. At 25 MIDI fps the quarter-frame MTC signal will give resolution down to 10 ms, but will take 80 ms to transmit, as the 8 bytes require 2 frames. This means that only one timecode word in two can be sent. In 24, 30 and 30 drop-frame formats MTC reads only even-numbered frames. In the 25- frame format MTC reads odd-numbered frames for one second and even- numbered frames the next.

The most significant nibble of each quarter-frame data byte has its MSB set to logic 0, the remaining three bits indicating which element of time is being updated. Figure 6.3a illustrates. The time units referred to in the most significant nibble are placed in the last 4 bits of the byte, with the LSB in bit 0 (the last bit). The nibbles are combined in pairs to form a data byte. The values of the time addresses are not coded single denary digits, as is the case with IEC timecode, so the denary value 57 has the digital code 0011 1001, the first 4 bits being carried by the most significant nibble of the pair, the last 4 by the least significant. With the exception of the 'hours' byte, all unused leading bits are set to zero. The hours byte always has its MSB (bit 7) set to 0, and bits 5 and 6 carry a code indicating the timecode frame rate. Figure 6.3b illustrates. Table 6.1 gives the time data ident codes; Table 6.2 gives the frame rate codes.

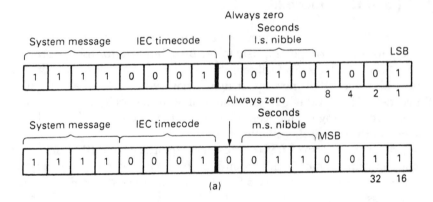

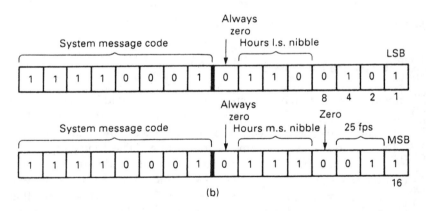

Figure 6.3 Frames, Seconds and Minutes are carried in 6 of the system message bytes, each preceded by a header byte. The most significant nibble of each message byte identifies the detail of the data (a). Hours information is carried in 2 message bytes, each preceded by a header byte. The most significant nibble carries details of the frame rate (b).

Binary code	Time data carried
000	Frames count l.s. nibble
001	Frames count m.s. nibble
010	Seconds count l.s. nibble
011	Seconds count m.s. nibble
100	Minutes count l.s. nibble
101	Minutes count m.s. nibble
110	Hours count l.s. nibble
111	Hours count m.s. nibble

Table 6.1 MTC quarter-frame time identification codes.

Binary code	Frames per second
00	24
01	25
10	30 (drop frame)
11	30

Table 6.2 MTC codes for IEC timecode frame rates.

Quarter-frame codes sent at 25 fps require a data rate of 1600 bits/second within a total MIDI data rate of 31 250 bits/second. This means that MTC will occupy just 5% of the available data space.

Full-frame messages

There are three types of full-frame message. One carries real-time data, another the binary user group data associated with IEC code, and the last carries set-up messages for peripheral devices. They are sent as required, and take precedence over all other messages, even to the extent of breaking into a message stream. 'Header' and 'end' bytes ensure that they can be recognized among the other data. Full-frame MTC messages are carried in consecutive bytes, following a single header byte. The header byte is the system exclusive message code 11110000 (&F0). An end system exclusive message byte terminates the full time message. A minimum of 8 bytes is required to carry the data, making a minimum of 10 data bytes for the complete message. Full time messages can carry machine-specific instructions as well as time data. By their use, machines can be instructed to go to specific time locations and either park or play. If parked, the machine will wait until the corresponding quarter-frame message arrives, then action the instruction.

Real-time message

This carries time information to frame resolution and the frame rate. It does not carry the user bits. Ten bytes are required to carry the whole message. Eight bytes carry time data, preceded and terminated by 'start' and 'end' bytes. The full message has the syntax: &F0 &7F <CH> <ID1> <ID2> <HH> <MM> <SS> <FF> &7F. (Information in triangular brackets is variable). The details are covered in Table 6.3.

Message byte	Binary value	Legend	Information
1	11110000	&F0	System exclusive header (start of message)
2	01111111	&7F	Start of universal real-time message
3		CH	MIDI channel indicator. &7F indicates that the message is intended for the whole system
4	00000001	ID1	Sub-identifier 1. MTC identification byte (&01)
5	00000001	ID2	Sub-identifier 2. Full MTC message identification byte (&01)
6	OXXHHHHH	HH	Hours and frame rate encoding. XX = the frame rate as in Table 6.2. HHHHH = binary encoded hours (0–23). The unused bit is set to zero
7	00MMMMMM	MM	6-bit binary encoded minutes (0–59). Unused bits are set to zero
8	00SSSSSS	SS	6-bit binary encoded seconds (0–59). Unused bits are set to zero
9	000FFFFF	FF	5-bit binary encoded frames (0–29). Unused bits are set to zero
10	11110111	&F7	End system exclusive message

Table 6.3 Details of real-time message bytes.

Binary group message

This carries the 32 bits of the IEC user groups. Fifteen bytes are required, thirteen of which carry the message. The syntax is: &F0 &7F <CH> <ID1> <ID2> <ID2> <UB1> <UB2> <UB3> <UB4> <UB5> <UB6> <UB7> <UB8> <UB9> &F7. Table 6.4 gives the details.

Byte 14, the identification byte, has the form 0000 00YY. The bits designated YY are the binary group flag bits. They perform the same functions as their counterparts in the EBU/SMPTE code. The assembly of the bits into ISO 646 or 2022 characters is:

aaaabbbb ccccdddd eeeeffff gggghhhh

User bit data is not sent on a regular basis. It is sent on request, usually from a peripheral device requiring the data in order to executive a command.

Message byte	Binary value	Legend	Information
1	11110000	&F0	System exclusive header (start of message)
2	01111111	&7F	Start of universal real-time message
3		CH	MIDI channel indicator. &7F indicates that the message is intended for the whole system
4	00000001	ID1	Sub-identifier 1. MTC identification byte (&01)
5	00000010	ID2	Sub-identifier 2. User bit message identification (&02)
6	0000aaaa	UB1	Binary group 1 data
7	0000bbbb	UB2	Binary group 2 data
8	0000cccc	UB3	Binary group 3 data
9	0000dddd	UB4	Binary group 4 data
10	0000eeee	UB5	Binary group 5 data
11	0000ffff	UB6	Binary group 6 data
12	0000gggg	UB7	Binary group 7 data
13	0000hhhh	UB8	Binary group 8 data
14	000000yy	UB9	Binary group 9 data. yy are the binary group flag bits
15	11110111	&F7	End system exclusive message

Table 6.4 Details of the binary group message bytes.

Set-up message

A set-up message makes it possible for a controlling microcomputer to handle individual devices. The message indicates (among other things) the device the message is intended for, what the machine must do, and when it must do it. 128 different messages are possible (remember, the leading bit of a message byte is always zero), but at the time of writing only nineteen messages have been defined. The basic 'set-up' message comprises a minimum of 13 consecutive bytes, but there is a provision to incorporate additional information, which may include MIDI channel messages. The syntax is: &F0 &7E <CH> <ID1> <ID2> <ID2> <HH> <MM> <SS> <FF> <ff EL> <EM> <AI> &F7. Table 6.5 gives the details. Note that Byte 10 carries fractional frame information to a resolution of 1/100 frame. Not all machines are capable of this degree of resolution.

The additional information bytes carry MIDI channel messages, split into nibbles, with the least significant nibble being sent first. The leading bits in each AI byte are set to zero. The following example illustrates the process. Suppose we wish to incorporate a 'pitch bend' message to channel 7, with a (change) value of 157. The channel message header byte will be:

Message byte	Binary value	Legend	Information
1	11110000	&F0	System exclusive header (start of message)
2	01111110	&7E	Start of non-real-time message
3		CH	MIDI channel number. Devices will only respond to this message if their channel number matches
4	00000100	&04	Sub-identifier 1. MTC event message indicator
5		ID2	Sub-identifier 2. Set-up message indicator. See Table 6.6 for details
6		HR	Hours and frame rate code. The form of this byte is 0 rr hhhhh. rr is the frame rate (see Table 6.2 for details) hhhhh is hours code (0–23).
7		MM	Minutes code (0–59)
8		SS	Seconds code (0–59)
9		FF	Frames code (0–29)
10		ff	Fraction (hundredths) of frame (0-99)
11		EL	Event number (least significant bits)
12		EM	Event number (most significant bits)
Bytes as needed		AI	Additional information
13	11110111	&F7	End system exclusive message

Table 6.5 Details of the set-up message bytes.

$$11100111 = \&E7 \qquad \text{(1st byte)}$$

Code for pitch bend   Channel 7

Denary 157 has the binary code: 10011101

Leading zeros are added to make a 14-bit number:

00000010011101

This binary number is split into two 7-bit parts:

0000001 = &1D (most significant part)   (2nd byte)
0011101 = &01 (least significant part)   (3rd byte)

The channel message will have the form &E7 &1D &01. It will be set in six consecutive additional information bytes with the least significant nibble of each byte being sent first, each AI byte having the 1st nibble set to zero:

&07 &0E &0D &01 &01 &00

The 'set up indicator' byte (ID2) can be used to carry 19 possible global messages to peripheral devices. Fourteen of these messages are carried within the byte itself. Table 6.6 gives the functions of the individual ID2 values. The functions are detailed below.

Punch-in (&01) and Punch-out (&02): programmed start and stop of recording. The event number bytes (EL and EM) are used to indicate the track number.

ID2 Value	Indication
&01	Punch-in point
&02	Punch-out point
&03	Delete Punch-in point
&04	Delete Punch-out point
&05	Event Start point
&06	Event Stop point
&07	Event Start point with Additional Information
&08	Event Stop point with Additional Information
&09	Delete Event Start
&0A	Delete Event Stop
&0B	Cue point
&0C	Cue point with Additional Information
&0D	Delete cue point
&0E	Event name in Additional Information

Table 6.6 Full-frame message ID2 byte details.

Delete Punch-in (&03) and Delete Punch-out (&04) erase the punch-in and -out points from the cue list on the peripheral. The time and event number indicated within this message must have the same values as the punch-in and -out.

Event Start (&05) and Event Stop (&06) trigger and stop the execution of an event. The event number indicates the event to be played on the peripheral (e.g. CD track, sequence number of sequencer, lighting cue etc).

Event Start with Additional Information (&07) and Event Stop with Additional Information (&08) perform the same functions as &05 and &06, and also indicate that additional information is being carried. This additional information takes the form of channel messages. The scope of this additional information will depend on the peripheral involved.

Delete Event Start (&09) and Delete Event Stop (&0A): delete the start and stop points from the event list. The time and event number indicated within this message must have the same values as the event start and stop.

Cue Point (&0B) is a registration mark. It can trigger events without the need to specify an 'out' point, and enables the positioning of edit registers.

Cue Point with Additional Information (&0C) is identical to message &0B, except that the presence of additional information (held in the relevant bytes) is indicated.

Delete Cue Point (0D) erases the cue point, with or without additional information. The time and event numbers must have the same values as those held in the cue point.

Event Name AI (&0E) indicates that an event name or remarks have been inserted (manually) in the Additional Information byte/s.

A further five special (directed) messages which do not require the primary function of the event number bytes (EL and EM) may be carried in these bytes by putting the indicator byte to &00. Table 6.7 gives the detail of these directed functions.

There is a fundamental difference between MTC & MIDI clock synchronizers. MIDI clock pulses do not carry time information. Separate Start, Stop and Continue messages, in combination with Pointers are used to control sequences. With MTC, the messages carry the complete time information, and slave devices lock to and follow the timecode.

Synchronization between IEC, MTC and MIDI clocks

When a MIDI system is being used in film or video it must process and act on real-time messages, as opposed to those related to tempo. Two approaches are possible: use a synchronizer to convert time addresses to MIDI clock or MTC messages which can then be used by the controlling sequencer; or use a synchronizer with an integral timecode-to-MTC converter. Which one to use will depend on the complexity of the system and the ability of the individual devices to act on the various message types. Figure 6.4 illustrates various possibilities.

ID2 bits	Event bits	Information carried
&00	&00	Timecode offset. The time value of the peripheral receiving this message is shifted relative to the master MTC value, according to the offset introduced manually.
&00	&01	Event enable list. Allows the peripheral receiving the message to execute messages received from the controlling computer upon arrival of corresponding MTC value.
&00	&02	Disable event list. Prevents the peripheral from executing set-up messages received from the controlling computer. Useful for disabling a peripheral temporarily without having to alter the program.
&00	&03	Clear event list. Erases all set-up messages received by peripheral devices from the controlling computer.
&00	&04	System stop. Immediately stops peripherals from executing orders.

Table 6.7 Full-frame message ID2 byte directed code details

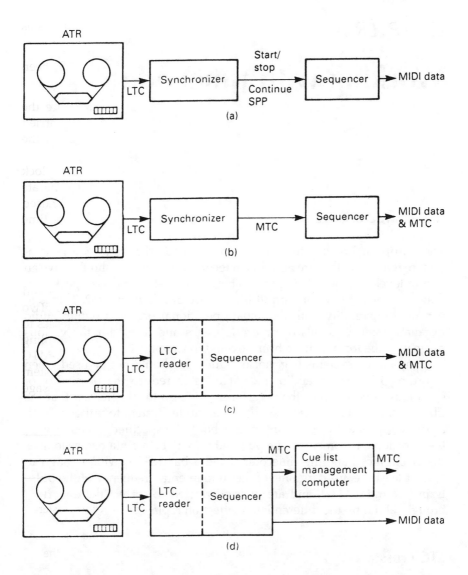

Figure 6.4 Possible TC/MIDI combinations. At (a) timecode off tape is converted to MIDI clock messages and song position pointers. The synchronizer could output MTC (b), letting the sequencer generate MIDI clock and SPPs. The TC reader and sequencer can be combined into a single unit, outputting MIDI and MTC. The integral reader/sequencer could interface with a cue list management programme on computer (d), which will control MTC-capable devices.

CHAPTER 7

Working with timecode

LTC characteristics

The European Broadcasting Union recommends that timecode genera-tors/regenerators that are built into a recorder or a system should have an output level capable of being varied between 0.5–4.5 V peak-to-peak, and that they should have an output impedance of less than 30 Ω. This is to permit compatibility with the usual operational practices within audio installations. The details of timecode tracks and levels for the various magnetic tape formats have been covered in Chapter 4.

Companding systems (e.g. noise reduction) should not be used when recording LTC on an audio track. This is to reduce the possibility of cumulative distortion of the waveform. It is also for this reason that the EBU recommends that the response of an audio system to pulses as well as to steady-state tones or pink noise should be specified, together with the traditional parameters. The pulse edges will be maintained as long as the electronics handling timecodes have a bandwidth wide enough to read at least the 3rd harmonic of the fundamental frequency of the pulse train (around 2 kHz), and are phase-corrected to correct the distortion brought about by the differentiation effect on replay.

LTC crosstalk

The LTC signal is composed of pulses having finite rise and fall times, with a 'sin²' shape to the transition. This shaping ensures that the harmonic content of the wave is kept low. Consequently, crosstalk should be a problem only if poor operational practices are employed. However, the fundamental frequency of the pulse train is one to which the human ear is very sensitive.

A blank track should always be left between timecode and the nearest audio track on multi-track machines. On $1/4$in twin-track tape machines employing centre-track timecode, the audio tracks should be the NAB option, as discussed in Chapter 4. This allows a suitable guard band between timecode and audio to minimize the possibility of crosstalk.

Many operators have reported hearing apparent LTC breakthrough when off-tape monitoring during recording, particularly on location analogue recorders. Later replay has shown no evidence of timecode breakthrough, so what has happened? The apparent breakthrough has been due partly to electromagnetic coupling within the wiring looms connecting the record and play amplifiers to their respective tapeheads, and partly to the lack of a Dolby decoder in the off-tape monitor path of a location VCR.

Despite wave-shaping, the LTC signal does contain a significant proportion of energy in its harmonics. To drive sufficient current through the inductance that forms the record head, a proportionally greater voltage than for a non-inductive load is required. The comparatively low inductance of the wiring loom, and the high amplification factor of the replay amplifier, give a level of timecode that can be heard when off-tape monitoring during recording. Figure 7.1 illustrates the process.

Much has been said about breakthrough of timecode onto audio tracks. The reverse can apply, with low-frequency audio signals affecting the

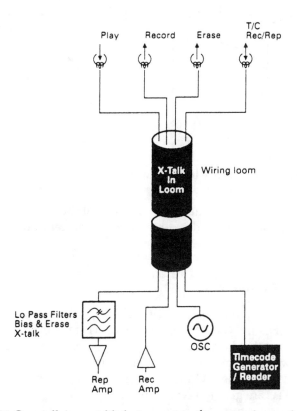

Figure 7.1 Crosstalk is most likely to occur in the wiring loom of a machine. It will be amplified by the replay amplifier, which has a high gain.

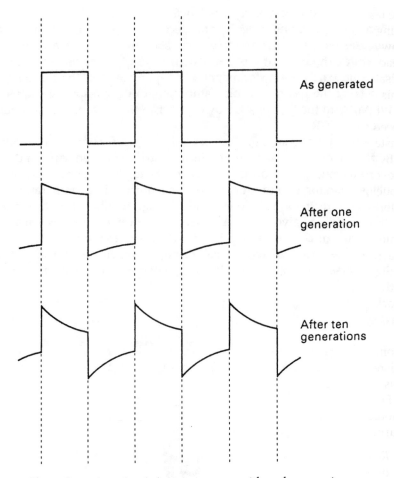

As generated

After one
generation

After ten
generations

Figure 7.2 Phase distortion of code becomes worse with each successive generation unless equalized or regenerated.

timecode track on multi-track machines. To prevent this, if a guard track
cannot be left, do not record audio containing a significant proportion of
low-frequency energy next to the LTC track.

Regeneration of timecode

Whenever a tape is copied together with its longitudinal timecode, it is
imperative that the timecode be regenerated. There are a number of
reasons for this. Firstly, there is the differentiation effect on LTC replay.
This distortion will be aggravated with each successive generation. Fig.
7.2 illustrates the point. The IEC specifications for the waveform shape of
both LTC and VITC are given in Appendix 2.

Tape machines suffer from an effect known as 'scrape flutter' or 'timing
jitter'. This takes the form of small but rapid variations in tape speed
superimposed on the nominal play speed. It is caused by the friction of

the tape-to-head contact combining with the slight elasticity of the tape to bring about a stick-slip effect similar in many respects to that of a violin bow scraping over a string. This effect is more pronounced if the tape-to-head pressure is increased as a result of increased tape tension or misalignments in the tape path, and as the longitudinal tape speed drops. This jitter may be small, but becomes worse with succeeding generations.

When replaying material off VTC or VCR machines, variations in tape speed which may be of little or no consequence for audio result in highly unstable video. These variations are corrected by a 'timebase corrector' (TBC). The TBC will also maintain the special timing relationship between the colour sub-carrier and both line and field synchronizing pulses (touched on in Chapter 1 and to be dealt with in detail later). The timing jitter on LTC recorded on the third audio track of a C-format VTR or one of the longitudinal tracks of a Hi-Band U-Matic will not be corrected unless dedicated electronics are provided. Component analogue machines provide regeneration as a matter of course.

Signal levels coming off analogue tape machines can vary, particularly if the tape concerned has undergone a high number of passes of the head block. (Try recording a steady-state tone and replaying it after a few passes of the head; there will be observable variations in level on a meter.) In addition there is always the possibility of dropout on the tape causing momentary but severe level reductions on code which may cause it to be misread. Tape hiss also becomes worse with successive generations, and this can eventually cause code to be misread.

For the above reasons, raw longitudinal timecode coming off tape should be fed to a regenerator before being passed on to another machine during dubbing. A regenerator may provide the following facilities:

1 *Reshaping*: restoring the LTC signal to its proper form. This is usually done by evaluating the zero crossing points of the replayed waveform, and using these points to generate a steep-sided waveform. This waveform is then passed through a filter to restore the $\sin^2$ shape of the transitions.
2 *Reclocking*: extracting the original clock frequency from the LTC waveform and, using the incoming zero/one pulse train as data, forming a completely new pulse train. Timing jitter is eliminated, but longer-term variations in the incoming data rate (perhaps due to variations in play speed of the tape) can be followed, usually over set limits – say ± 6%. Figure 7.3 illustrates.
3 *Retiming*: When the lock range of the timecode unit is exceeded, retiming takes place. This involves full decoding of the incoming serial LTC data, followed by re-encoding.

Because the regenerator has to examine each complete timecode word for validity prior to re-encoding, a process that will also require a finite time, there will be a one-frame delay (1 LTC word) between timecode into the regenerator and timecode out. This delay must be compensated for within the regenerator for the time information bits in the timecode word

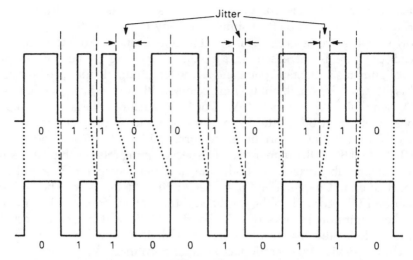

Figure 7.3 Reclocking will even out jitter over a long time period, usually several seconds, and can accommodate small variations in the data rate.

if the correct colour framing relationship is to be maintained, as it will have to be if frame-accurate editing is to be performed from these bits. If time information is also being carried in the user bits within the word, it is important that the 'plus one frame' process is applied to these bits as well. A good regenerator will have this option. If it is switched on, and non-time data are being carried in the user bits, the regenerator may well increase the last digit by 1. The 'add one frame' process on the user bits may be enabled/disabled deep in the menus or on internal DIP switches.

Adjusting for the decoding delay

When a timecode reader/regenerator performs a complete retiming operation, the sequence (illustrated in Fig. 7.4) is as follows.

The incoming LTC signal is first decoded into blocks of serial data representing the 0s and 1s of the timecode word. The synchronizing word is also examined to determine whether the code is running up or down in time. Depending on the result of this examination, the data will be modified to compensate for the decoding delay. Under the control of a clock (perhaps driven from external sync pulses) this data train is then fed either to another register or to a microprocessor, from where it is read out to another biphase mark encoder. The LTC reader/regenerator performing a full retiming operation will continue to clock out timecode at standard rate, within small limits, no matter what the speed of the tape supplying the timecode data, as long as the code can be read (one manufacturer quotes a reader/regenerator as reading over a range of one-fiftieth of standard speed to eighty-times standard speed), though this will depend on the ability of the machine to replay the signal at these

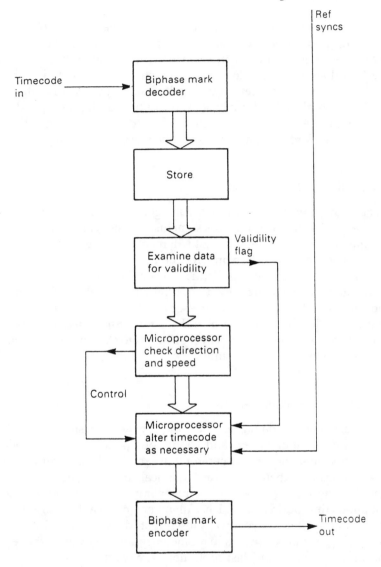

Figure 7.4 Complete regeneration involves checking code validity and direction, together with reprocessing and generation of missing bits. A completely retimed, reclocked and reshaped signal is fed out. The whole process can be under the control of an external reference signal to ensure correct colour framing.

speeds. Obviously, if the data rate deviates too far from standard, then words will either be lost (play speed too high) or repeated (speed too low).

Machine-to-machine operation

If timecode is to be transferred to another video recorder, or a digital audio recorder, both machines must be locked to common syncs, though these could come from the replay machine, via a TBC. If a VCR is providing guide video for sound post-production, the synchronizer(s) driving the audio machine(s) must be fed with the same syncs as the VCR. Any 'stand-alone' timecode regenerator should also be fed with these syncs, because the reprocessed timecode must be generated at the correct rate. For example, a VCR can be locked to a time address supplied from a sound station. As soon as the VCR has locked up, both it and the sound station will lock to reference syncs via the master synchronizer.

Regeneration of damaged code

A regenerator can be used to repair damaged timecode if it is run in a jam-sync mode. As long as it receives some usable code, and is run at exactly the same rate as the off-tape data, it will regenerate the missing addresses. Even if real-time code is being regenerated, as long as good code is present at the start of each take, and sufficient pre-roll time is allowed, the regenerator will recognize good code and regenerate it. Do remember (and this cannot be too highly stressed) that whenever you are regenerating timecode, the regenerator and player *must* be fed with common syncs. Do not assume that the player is locked to station syncs – it may not be, especially within an edit suite.

Momentary and continuous jam-sync

When regenerating damaged code the regenerator should be able to operate in both momentary and continuous (auto) jam-sync modes. In momentary jam-sync the regenerator will examine the incoming timecode for a few frames, then regenerate identical time data, locked to syncs. Should the incoming code fail, the regenerator will continue generating contiguous time addresses which will increment up at frame rate. Should the incoming code have any subsequent discontinuity in the time addresses, this will be ignored in momentary jam-sync mode, the regenerator carrying on from the last contiguous time address.

In continuous (auto) jam-sync mode, a regenerator will again examine the incoming code and regenerate identical time addresses. It will also continue contiguous time addresses if incoming code fails. If, however, there is a discontinuity in the time addresses the regenerator will re-jam to the incoming code. Figure 7.5 illustrates the differences between the two modes.

Using VITC

Most UK companies incorporate VITC on lines 19 and 21. It is as well not to put it too early in the field interval as when 1 in VTR machines are

Momentary Jam sync	Incoming Discontinuous Code	Auto Jam sync
	00:23:14:16	
	00:23:14:17	
	00:23:14:18	
	00:23:14:19	
----------------	00:23:14:20	----------------
00:23:14:21	00:23:14:21	00:23:14:21
00:23:14:22	00:23:14:22	00:23:14:22
00:23:14:23	00:23:14:23	00:23:14:23
00:23:14:24	00:23:14:24	00:23:14:24
00:23:15:00	00:23:15:00	00:23:15:00
00:23:15:01	00:23:15:01	00:23:15:01
00:23:15:02	00:23:15:02	00:23:15:02
00:23:15:03	00:23:15:03	00:23:15:03
00:23:15:04	**********	00:23:15:04
00:23:15:05	**********	00:23:15:05
00:23:15:06	**********	00:23:15:06
00:23:15:07	00:37:42:23	00:23:15:07
00:23:15:08	00:37:42:24	00:37:42:24
00:23:15:09	00:37:43:00	00:37:43:00
00:23:15:10	00:37:43:01	00:37:43:01
00:23:15:11	00:37:43:02	00:37:43:02

Figure 7.5 Momentary jam-sync will ensure that regenerated time addresses increment up from the last valid address received. Any following valid addresses will be ignored until the jam-sync operation is repeated. Auto sync will increment time addresses up from the last valid address received, but will re-jam when new valid code is received.

playing at other than standard speed, perhaps using a Dynamic tracking (DT) or Auto sense tracking (AST) head for track following during post-production, the new relationship between video head and recorded tracks will result in more than the usual 12 lines (10 lines in NTSC) being lost. The timebase corrector will replace these lost lines, but it cannot replace timecode that has not been scanned by the video head. Of course if the C-format sync head option is employed the 18.75 lines (15.75 in NTSC) recorded by this head will supply the missing data.

At the time of writing no particular lines are specified for VITC; it is thus perfectly possible to end up with two different sets of VITC on different line pairs, and also to over-record one line (or both) of a VITC pair with fresh code. Should this happen, the reader will not be able to cope with the ambiguity. It will need to be reprogrammed to read either one or both lines of an unambiguous code. It is perfectly satisfactory to set a VITC regenerator to read one VITC line and one non-VITC line, but in this case it should be set to continuous (auto) jam-sync, and fed with corresponding external syncs to protect the data in the event of dropout. It is particularly important that internally regenerated code should be recorded on the correct lines during any editing operation. The VITC lines setting of the generator should also be checked, particularly if the intention is to put a second set of time addresses on tape. Some VITC generators have the options of generating a single line of VITC or a block of lines.

Timecode corruption

The causes of timecode corruption have been mentioned briefly earlier (pp. 23–27). They are different for LTC and VITC, so will be examined separately, with possible remedies suggested.

LTC data corruption can be due to a variety of defects on replay; dropout has already been mentioned. VCR machines run at extremely low longitudinal tape speeds. If timecode is recorded onto an unmodified audio track, with perhaps a relatively poor frequency response, even a small amount of dirt or oxide on the replay head concerned can cause problems. Regular cleaning of the longitudinal timecode heads will prevent many such problems.

LTC can be corrupted on a location shoot by a hum-loop, especially if an unbalanced line is being used to send the code from camera to recorder. Make sure the generator and any associated equipment are fed from the same mains outlet. To minimize the risk of data corruption from mainsborne spikes, interference suppressors should be fitted. They are expensive, but the expense will quickly be repaid in the reduction of down time, and the minimizing of the risk of a system crash which could result in total loss of data in disc-based post-production equipment. To minimize the risk of induced mains hum appearing on LTC data, and possible RF interferences, the signal should be distributed via screened, balanced lines, ideally with screened transformers or opto-isolators at either end of the circuit. Electronically-balanced inputs may not provide sufficient electrical isolation. Radio links are sometimes used for sending timecode between camcorder and audio recorder, and these are suscept-ible to fading. If the recorder has momentary (one-time), or, better, auto jam-sync facility, use it. If using momentary jam-sync, make sure that timecode is running (and incoming) before jamming to it. This might seem obvious, but it is traditional in film to start the sound recorder before running up the film camera (film stock is more expensive than audiotape). If code is not running, either it will not be recorded at all, or the wrong time addresses will be recorded. With film, there is the risk of the camera running at the wrong speed if incoming timecode fails.

To minimize the possibility of loss of code on recording, the following procedures should be adopted:

1 Use a balanced link for cable feeds of timecode.
2 If mains-powered equipment is being used, try to connect camera and recorder to the same mains point, or use an isolating transformer to feed 'floating' mains, with no earth reference, to the equipment.
3 Check all cables regularly. This will minimize the risk of connector failure.

4 If using a radio link, consider using a 'diversity' system to minimize the risk of fading.

5 If feeding timecode from a master to a number of slave units, do not loop through. If one connector fails, all downstream devices will lose code. Use a distribution amplifier (Figure 7.6).

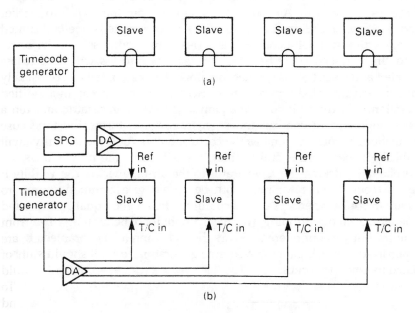

Figure 7.6 Recording timecode with no reference syncs, or using loops through (a) is asking for trouble. Feed everything with reference syncs and distribute all signals via DAs (b).

6 If the recorder has no visual display of incoming code, try to check the incoming level or use a separate display unit.

7 When using a field audio recorder, if possible use continuous or auto jam-sync mode. The use of jam-sync on location will be discussed in Chapter 8.

Dealing with LTC corruption

Timecode readers/regenerators can cope with corrupted LTC in a number of ways, and there are a number of associated techniques for replacing corrupted code with fresh code. Selection of a particular technique will depend on the exact circumstances but all techniques are based on one of the following:

Momentary jam-sync restriping

If the recorded code on a videotape is badly corrupted it may be possible to use a good section of code to start up a generator in momentary jam-sync mode. The video format used must allow timecode to be laid down independently of video and control track (perhaps a longitudinal audio track can be used). The videotape recorder should be set to record just LTC and put into play at the start of bars at the head of the tape. The timecode generator, which must be locked to the off-tape, timebase corrected video, will jam to the off-tape timecode as long as just a couple of frames can be read. As soon as this happens put the VTR into record mode *only on the LTC track* (Figure 7.7). The regenerated code laid down on tape will consist of a contiguous series of time addresses. If there are discontinuous sections of timecode on tape the process will have to be repeated at the start of each timecode block. This can only be successfully done if each recorded section has sufficient run-in to accommodate the operation, which will involve the jamming of the regenerator, and time for the operator to confirm the regeneration and throw the timecode channel into record. As long as the corruption was not due to faulty tape (unlikely if the video is still usable) this will solve the problem. As an alternative to locking the regenerator to the off-tape video, the VTR and the timecode regenerator may both be locked to a common source of video sync pulses, perhaps from a common SPG. A good quality timecode generator, even free-running, will have a stability of better than 1 frame in 11 hours, but without reference syncs the code cannot be guaranteed to be colour-locked. If using an internal time generator the VCR should still be locked to reference syncs.

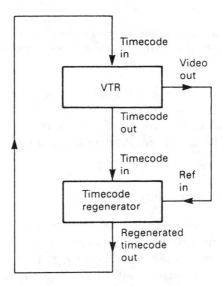

Figure 7.7 Damaged code from a VTR can be regenerated and fed back for re-recording. The process will be successful if the machine is switched into timecode record only a few seconds before the associated programme material starts.

Auto jam-sync restriping

If 'time-of-day' code was used at the time of recording, the regenerator should be placed in the auto or continuous lock mode. As soon as it has received valid code, it will generate a contiguous sequence of time addresses. It will continue to generate contiguous time addresses in the event of the incoming code being corrupted, and will update when a discontinuous time address arrives.

Neither of the above remedies will work effectively for long stretches of corrupted code from an analogue audiotape, as without good code to control the speed of the tape via a synchronizer there is bound to be a degree of slippage due to the friction nature of the drive, even if tacho pulses are being used to control the speed of the transport.

Recording code onto an audio track of a VCR

If it is not possible to lay timecode track down independently of video and control tracks, it may be possible to record regenerated code onto a spare longitudinal audio track. The timecode output should be fed to the spare audio record input. The VCR should be set to record just on this spare audio track, and put into play at the start of bars at the head of the tape. As soon as the regenerator has jammed, the recorder can be put into record and regenerated code will be recorded onto the spare track. If it is not possible to regenerate the code, a separate timecode generator, locked to the off-tape, timebase-corrected video, can either be momentarily jammed to a good section of code, or if all else fails, be set to approximately the same time as indicated in the tape's log sheet. In either case, code should be locked to video syncs. If a slate was put at the head of each take, the difference between the re-recorded code and the original code (the offset) can be calculated for the purpose of post-production.

If it is proposed to do colour-framed edits during post-production, the timecode generator must be locked to video from the VTR in order that the 8-field (4-field in NTSC) sequence is followed by the fresh code. This also means that the generator must be reset at the start of each new recorded sequence.

Dubbing with fresh code

If regeneration or restriping is not possible (perhaps because the LTC is totally corrupted or missing, there is no VITC present, the format does not permit independent recording of LTC, or both audio tracks have programme material on them which cannot be lifted off), there are a couple of options possible. The first of these is to dub the programme material across to another tape, relaying timecode at the same time. The video material should be copied via a timebase corrector fed from station syncs or a sync pulse generator. Fresh timecode can be added from a generator locked to the same source of syncs. If a proper log was kept at the original recording stage it should be possible, if somewhat tedious, to stripe the copy tape with close approximations of the original code. Of course, this method will result in an additional generation of tape, though perhaps the opportunity could be taken to 'lay-off' the audio together with this fresh code, if it is intended to post-produce the audio anyway.

Control track editing

If the worst comes to the worst, and if nothing subtle is required in the way of editing (no 'invisibles' etc) then it may be possible to edit using the control track pulses. There are distinct problems with this form of editing. There will be slippage caused by the misreading of the pulses as the machines stop and start, which will usually prevent frame-accurate editing. This will be particularly so if the edit is previewed a number of times before the edit is done. There will be no colour framing so there is the possibility of picture disturbance over the edit point.

All the above assumes there is no usable VITC code on the tape. Matters become much easier if VITC is present since any regenerator can be fed with this form of the code, in which case the regenerated LTC will have time addresses that correspond exactly to the VITC recorded on the video tracks. This will permit the dubbing or restriping of identical longitudinal timecode. It will also allow the audio tracks from a machine where the separate recording of timecode is not possible to be dubbed onto a separate audiotape recorder, together with LTC regenerated from the original VITC, for post-production.

VITC corruption

VITC is far less likely to be corrupted than LTC, being recorded as a part of the video signal, where the FM method of recording reduces the effects of partial dropout. It is also recorded twice per field, four times per frame, so if one VITC word is corrupted the chances are the other three words will be valid. If tape dropout is so bad that all VITC words in a frame are affected then the programme video is likely to be unusable too.

Note that since the VITC word is recorded as a part of the video it cannot be restriped without dubbing the video at the same time.

Record-run and time-of-day codes

There are two modes in which timecode can be recorded. In the 'record-run mode the timecode generated represents the cumulative recorded duration of the tape. The use of record-run mode has the advantage that the time addresses recorded on tape are contiguous, that is to say they increment up in sequence, with no gaps in the time addresses. In the record-run mode many VCRs will backwind slightly when put in the pause mode from record, with the tape being held against the head drum. When they go back into 'record', the code (and the video) will pick up from where they left off, maintaining continuous (i.e. no gaps in the signals) and contiguous (i.e. no gaps in the addresses) timecode. This option may well be of benefit in situations such as newsgathering, where events may preclude pre-roll time, since the editor can pre-roll from the preceding scene. This contiguous sequence of numbers might also be of use during post-production, as the editor knows that the difference in time between two timecode addresses on tape also represents the difference in tape time. The disadvantage from the operator's point of view is that holding a recorder (including a camcorder) in this mode is costly in terms of battery life, as the head drum continues to rotate.

Power supply back-up

'Time-of-day' (sometimes erroneously called 'real-time') code will run from the moment it is set, and will continue to run no matter what mode the recorder is in, as long as power is available. Most recorders contain an internal back-up power supply, either in the form of a large internal capacitor (2 farad or so), or a NiCd battery on permanent trickle charge from the d.c. supply; which will continue to run the timecode generator for a short time while batteries are changed. Most recorders will continue to run timecode even when they are switched off, as long as the batteries are in circuit, until they are exhausted. One audio field recorder will run timecode for up to three months when left switched off with a fresh set of batteries. However, a word of warning would not be amiss regarding the ability of the internal backup battery to keep the timecode generators running while main batteries are changed. The internal batteries will of course go through the charge/discharge cycle each time the recorder is turned off or has its main batteries removed, or if the batteries go flat, and then is turned on again with fresh batteries. There is a limit to the number of cycles a NiCd battery can undergo before its efficiency drops, and with an elderly internal battery there is the possibility that the recorder may not keep time of day code running with the power off for main battery changing. In field recorders employing large capacitors to maintain the timecode generator (the Nagra IV-S TC is one such), time is required to charge up on first use, or after a prolonged power failure. This recharging time may take a few tens of seconds. During this period the timecode generator will not be available for setting. It is a good operational practice to have fresh batteries ready before removing the old ones, as this will minimize the drain on the backup system. If timecode is lost while changing batteries in a recorder with an internal battery back-up, even if the time taken for the change is short, it is likely that the back-up batteries are life-expired. They are designed to have a long life – 5 years or so – but they will eventually fail. Get them replaced in good time.

Setting the timecode

On some VCRs, including those in camcorders, it is possible to record two sets of timecode. Record-run code can be set into the time-address bits of the timecode word (both LTC and VITC), and time-of-day code can be set into either the time-address bits of both LTC and VITC, or into the user bits of the VITC code. It is thus possible to have both codes present. Figure 7.8 illustrates the facility as provided on the Sony DVW-700P. The REAL TIME switch provides ON/OFF facility to record time of day code in the user bits; the SET position allows the setting of the code in this mode. The F-RUN/SET/R-RUN switch provides free (real-time) run or record-run facility in the time-address bits of both LTC and VITC; the SET position allows setting of both time address and user bits.

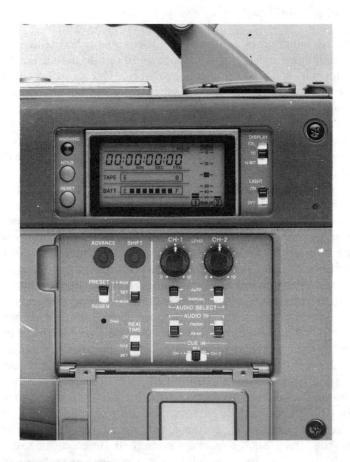

Figure 7.8 Sony DVW-700P

Multiple machine continuous jam-sync

If a number of recorders are to run with time-of-day code there are two options open: 'slave lock' (continuous jam-sync) or 'one-time lock' (momentary jam-sync). If slave lock is being employed then one machine or timecode generator should be designated 'master', and LTC feeds taken off this, via distribution amplifiers (DAs), to all other recorders. If composite video is being recorded, all items of equipment, including any master timecode generator, must be genlocked to the same pulse generator. This will either be a camera feeding the master recorder, or a stand-alone SPG. This requirement is necessary for two reasons. Firstly, if the timecode generator and the recorders are not locked to a common pulse train the timing of each may well drift with respect to the others, or their individual timecode/video frame relationship will drift, causing major problems if timecode is to be used in post-production. Secondly, the 8-field (4-field in NTSC) relationship between timecode and colour sub-carrier can be established only if the code generator is fed with reference video. In this respect, note that a feed of sync pulses alone (e.g. mixed syncs) is not sufficient, as these contain no colour information. A feed of 'Colour Black' or 'Black and Burst' will be required at least, though a feed of video from the master camera will also suffice. On no account should a system be slaved to timecode supplied from an analogue audiotape machine, as this will have no established relationship with the colour framing sequence. Shooting to audio playback is possible, and is covered in Chapter 8.

Multiple machine momentary jam-sync

It is, of course, perfectly possible to have the video and audio recorders run time-of-day code independently of each other. The timecode generators on the video recorders should be set from a master generator, remembering first to connect the video genlock feed from the master to ensure correct colour framing. An audio recorder can be fed momentarily with timecode from one of the video recorders to lock its generator. If it is an R-DAT machine it should also be genlocked to the video signal. Once this is done, all recorders will then run timecode-locked to the video. An analogue audio machine, though not synced, will generate timecode with a high degree of accuracy, but should be re-jammed from time to time to minimize any drift.

Control tracks and tacho pulses

When neither LTC or VITC can be read, perhaps because the shuttle speed is too high, audiotape machines will read 'tacho' pulses generated from a transducer coupled to a rotating idler wheel within the tape path. These pulses will be converted into an estimate of elapsed time. There is the possibility of slippage due to the friction nature of the drive, particularly during start/stop operations; and during the shuttle process the microprocessor controlling the operation will probably slow the machine down from time to time so that the timecode track can be examined. If the timecode recorded was time-of-day code there will probably be gaps in the number of sequence time addresses. The tacho pulses cannot take account of these gaps, so when the machine slows down to examine the code the microprocessor may see that it has overshot the time called for, so will put the machine into reverse shuttle. Again it will slow down to examine the code, and again will see that it has overshot. The process repeats itself all over again until the operator calls a halt to it. The answer to the problem is good logging of the recorded material so that the operator can instruct the machine to shuttle to just before the gap in the incremental sequence of addresses, and take it over the time-address discontinuity by hand.

R-DAT recorders, as we saw in Chapter 3, can read timecode at the highest shuttle speed. However, they shuttle so fast that some edit controllers, unless programmed with the ballistics of the R-DAT machine, cannot easily cue them up on a particular time address. This makes locating a pre-roll time tedious. This can be avoided by the use of an 'emulator'. This device will make the machine appear to have the characteristics of a VCR. Video recorders, as we have seen, can be set to read control track. They can be set to read this if neither LTC or VITC can be read. The same arguments apply regarding gaps in the timecode address sequence as with audio machines. The control track will contain colour framing information.

Telecine machines will generate 'biphase' pulses as a matter of course. These are not timecode, but are the equivalent of control track pulses. As this pulse train is directly linked to the rotation of the sprocket reels, there is no slippage.

Digital audio synchronization

Digital audio signals are composed of discrete samples. The sampling process is controlled by a highly accurate clock. Operations that require digital audio signals to be mixed or connected between different machines must be in synchronism. This is done by ensuring that the machines' internal clocks are locked together to bit accuracy. Locking is often achieved in a large installation by means of a master clock generator. The AES recognizes two standards for these clocks: Grade 1 clocks are accurate to within 1 part per million (ppm), Grade 2 clocks are accurate to within 10 ppm. Grade 1 clocks are for use in studio centres or when a high degree of accuracy is required. Grade 2 clocks are suitable for single

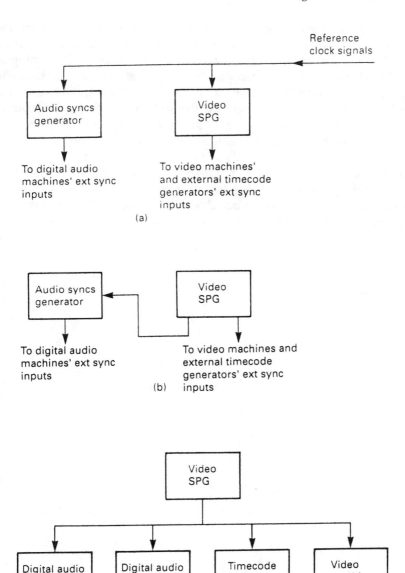

Figure 7.9 Possible ways of locking digital audio machines, VCRs and timecode generators include (a) locking to a common reference, (b) locking audio clock to video syncs, or (c) locking everything to common video syncs.

studios. A digital audio recorder will usually have a number of sync input options, as well as a highly stable internal clock. If it has to interface with a video machine, it should be locked to video black and burst, either directly if it will accept such an input, or via an external sync clock genlocked to reference video. The video frame rate and audio sampling rate must be correct, and in particular the sampling rate on replay must match that on recording (avoid having the internal clock running at 44.056 kHz on replay if the recording was made at 44 kHz). Digital audio machines rely on their internal clocks to control their transports. If the clock is running at an incorrect rate, the audio machine will drift out of sync with video in replay. Figure 7.9 illustrates some possible methods of achieving lock between digital audio clocks and video syncs.

If a recording has been made with an unlocked digital recorder, the situation may be recovered by replaying unlocked, and resyncing sound with pictures as necessary. This, however, could be time-consuming (and expensive), and might not be possible with a long continuous recording (e.g. an opera) which cannot be resynced.

CHAPTER 8

Timecode on location

Synchronization of video and audio machines

When shooting drama or similar material, sound is often recorded on a separate audio recorder with or without sound back-up on the video recorder. It will help the post-production process if both audio- and videotapes have identical timecodes. It will also help the process if the videotape contains at least a guide audio track. The audio recorder can be fed timecode from the VCR, as this will have the correct colour framing reference.

The audio machine's internal timecode generator must be either slaved to code coming from the VCR, in which case it will need to be set to 'external', or some form of 'momentary jam-sync' must be used. If the audio recorder's timecode generator is to slave-lock to that from the video recorder via a cable, precautions must be taken in the event of a momentary loss of code. Most field audio recorders will have the option of disregarding a few frames containing errors, substituting a regenerated code that will increment up from the last time a valid time address was received. They will revert to the incoming code as long as it becomes valid again within the limits set. If it does not, the timecode generator in the field audio recorder will run independently of any incoming code until reset. If this happens it is important to rejam as soon as possible as the time addresses will gradually drift apart. The audio recorder's timecode generator must not stop generating code at the first non-valid address received. If the camcorder and separate audio recorder need total independence of movement a radio link can be employed. In this case precautions need to be taken against loss of the radio link. If continuous slave lock is employed, some form of diversity radio link may be used. Such a link employs two aerials spaced apart, feeding the receiver unit, which selects the strongest signal received, usually with some form of indication as to relative signal strengths, and thus minimizes the risk of signal loss as the camera moves. This system is of little use if the audio recorder has to move around as well, and is prodigal of available radio channels. A better solution would be to employ some form of automatic jam-sync. In this mode the timecode generator in the audio recorder will lock to incoming code, when available, free-running to its internal oscillator in the absence of signal. It will automatically revert to incoming code when this becomes valid again. When running code in the 'auto' mode it is important that the sound recordist ensures that the audio recorder's timecode generator is re-jammed to timecode from the VCR at the start of each fresh take. This is not just because the two free-running codes (generated by the video recorder, and by the audio recorder respectively) will have drifted; they are driven by highly accurate and stable oscillators. It is because there is always the possibility that one of the generators may have stopped generating code during power-down mode (for example while changing batteries). There is also the possibility that the video recorder may not send code to its output during the stop mode. In Chapter 5, mention was made of the need to ensure that valid code is being received before jamming to it. There are timecode monitors available to provide readout of incoming code. Their use is recommended if the field audio recorder has no integral timecode display.

Radio links

Since LTC is an audio signal it is possible to employ a radio-microphone link to transmit it from one recorder to another. The level of code coming from a generator is likely to be too high for use in its raw state. It will need reducing in level by some 20-40 dB. Having done this the transmitter can be adjusted in the usual way.

There is no need for a dedicated timecode radio link. If the sound recorder is equipped with the auto jam-sync facility then a simple switch arrangement at either end of the radio link, coupled with a clear method of operational practice, will permit the link to be switched between audio and timecode (Figure 8.1). In essence, send code over the link prior to the take, and use this code to jam the audio recorder's timecode generator to it. Confirm the audio generator has jammed, then switch the link back at each end to audio and confirm audio is being received. Recording of the take may now proceed. It is probably sensible not to put the audio recorder into record mode until the radio link has been switched to send audio, in order to avoid the post-production personnel receiving an unwanted burst of timecode at the start of each take! One manufacturer makes a dual-channel radio link which can be used to send timecode, and guide audio to the VCR from the audio recorder. The timecode will not be colour-framed, but could be placed in the user bits of the video timecode, or recorded on a spare audio track.

Portable links capable of transmitting video information are also available. With one of these units taped to the camera, and a receiver at the audio recorder, a locking source is available for the audio timecode generator, though precautions should be taken in the event of loss of

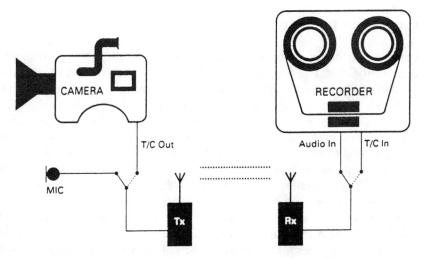

Figure 8.1 Timecode need not occupy a separate radio channel. The link can be switched and the field recorder put in the auto jam mode. Synchronization will be maintained over several minutes.

signal. More importantly, timecode can be 'burned in' to the video for display on a small monitor. This can be most helpful for the PA, who is not usually in a position to read code from the camera, for logging purposes. Figure 8.2 illustrates one possible arrangement, using a small inserter. The operator contemplating the use of such a link should check its legality in the country concerned.

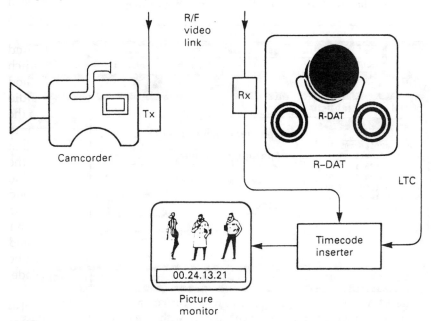

Figure 8.2 A suitable radio link can provide a video feed for a timecode inserter. This burnt-in code can be displayed on a small picture monitor.

Logging for non-linear editing

Perhaps the one drawback to non-linear editing is the time taken to digitize the material shot, and, of course, the finite amount of memory available to hold that material. Both these drawbacks can be minimized if a pre-selection is made of material to be digitized. This in itself can be time consuming, but the process can be speeded up considerably if material shot is accurately logged at the time of recording, not only with start and end timecodes but also such details as scene and take numbers, shot description, person/s shot, lighting/weather conditions, sound track/s and production comments (e.g. N/G, Use this! etc). Devices are available, and they are hand-held, which permit such details to be pre-programmed in. They will automatically log start and end timecodes, via a radio link from the camcorder or film camera, together with relevant shot detail. They permit the sorting and editing of logged material, and can produce either an EDL or Logging Database for export to either a linear or non-linear editor. These devices will run on either Macintosh or PC and will produce EDLs or Logging Databases for all commonly encountered linear and non-linear editors. They usually have the sync options of record-run, free-run or jam-sync and have clocks stable enough to remain in sync for several tens of minutes in the event of the radio link failing. Figure 8.3 illustrates one such device, which the author has used to great effect while shooting on location for later non-linear editing. As with any radio link the operator is advised to ensure that the frequency used complies with the regulations in the area of use.

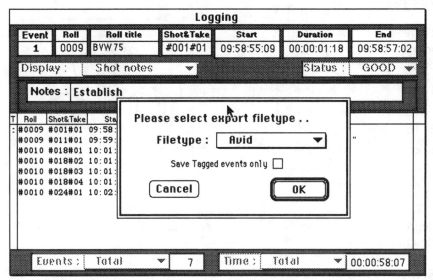

Figure 8.3 An automatic logging device which runs off a radio link from camcorder or film camera. Used in conjunction with a computer it can produce on-shoot timecode logs and Logging Databases for export to non-linear editors. Courtesy of Electronic Visuals Ltd.

Running unlocked with film

At one time, running a field audio recorder and a film camera unlocked was anathema. However, the advent of film cameras with crystal-controlled transports, loaded with pre-timecoded film stock, and fitted with in-camera timecode generators (see Chapter 5), made it possible to run both camera and audio recorder unlocked. With pre-timecoded film there is no need for a clapperboard, as the offset between the codes on audio tape and film (or the subsequent video off-line copy of the film) can be calculated by a microcomputer on transfer.

Running unlocked with video

Although video and analogue audio can run unlocked as long as the timecode generators are accurate and stable, this mode of working should be treated with care if using a field R-DAT recorder. The sampling clock on R-DAT will need to have a known relationship with video syncs if relative slippage is to be avoided in post-production. Over short periods the clocks in both professional camera and R-DAT will probably be accurate enough to permit unlocked recording as long as the R-DAT's timecode generator is re-jammed at regular intervals. However, some domestic and semi-professional R-DAT machines do not have clocks stable enough to allow this. In any event, long continuous takes should be undertaken only with R-DAT locked to the camera's video reference.

The playback shoot

There is an increasing requirement for shooting pictures to a pre-recorded sound track (e.g. for a pop video). The pictures will then be post-produced. In this event it will be necessary to provide the following facilities:

1 Audio replay machine to run at *exactly* the same speed as the video recorder

2 Timecode on the video recorder that is colour-framed

3 Some method of identifying synchronization between pictures and sound in the absence of a clapper slate, or if there is no slating signal recorded on tape

There are a number of ways of achieving the above with varying degrees of complexity, depending on equipment available. These are described below.

Self-resolving of timecode

Some audio field recorders can run locked to their internal timecode generators, rather than running at a nominal speed dependent on the

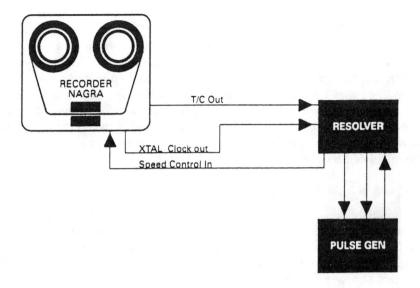

Figure 8.4 For short vision recording runs a Nagra can be made to self-resolve. It uses pre-recorded timecode as a control track, comparing this with its internal clock to control tape speed.

degree of slippage in the friction drive system (Figure 8.4). The tape to be replayed must first have been striped with timecode when being copied from the final mixed audio master, and it would be helpful if a 'click track' is put at the head to aid the performers in vision. If the guide audio can be recorded onto an audio track of the video recorder it will aid synchronization during post-production.

Resolving to video

Although more complex to achieve than self-resolving, resolving to an external video source is much more elegant. This involves comparing the off-tape audio timecode with that being generated by the video recorder (Figure 8.5). The replay speed is now under the control of the timecode from the video recorder. Guide audio can be recorded on one track of the videotape, and timecode from the audio recorder onto the other. The recorded videotape will now have both sets of code available, that generated by the video recorder or camcorder will be colour-framed. The other, recorded from the audio field recorder will correspond to the code laid on the audio master tape. From these two codes the offset can be easily calculated for post-production purposes.

The use of R-DAT for field recording

One of the many advantages digital recorders have over analogue is that synchronization and timing are made much easier as digital data can be stored and clocked out precisely to order under the control of an

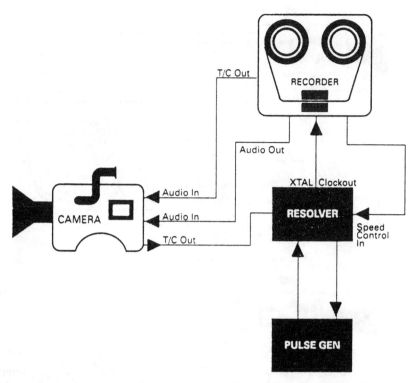

T/C Out

RECORDER

Audio Out

XTAL Clockout

RESOLVER

Speed
Control
In

Audio In

Audio In

T/C Out

CAMERA

PULSE GEN

Figure 8.5 A Nagra can resolve to timecode coming from a camcorder. This will lock audio and video firmly together. Guide audio and LTC can be recorded on the audio track of the videotape to act as a guide in post-production.

extremely accurate clock. If the R-DAT machine is capable of being synchronized to an external source of composite video, it will run at exactly the same rate as the camera. If it will accept timecode from the video recorder (earlier R-DAT field recorders will not do this), the code striped onto the audio tape and that striped onto the video tape will be identical (Figure 8.6a). It will, of course, record its own internally-generated timecode, so it will be necessary to put a clapper or some other slating signal at the head of both video and audio recordings at the start of each tape to ease the process of synching the sound to the pictures in post-production.

If an R-DAT recorder has no facility for recording continuous timecode then record, at the head of the take, incoming longitudinal timecode from the video recorder onto an audio channel for a few seconds – 20 seconds is a good duration, since R-DAT machines can take up to 10 seconds to lock up under the control of an edit controller or synchronizer in post-production (they lock up much faster if fed with an external reference signal) – and then switch the channel back to incoming audio before the actual take. This code can then be used in post-production for calculating the offset between pictures and sound. Figure 8.6b illustrates the

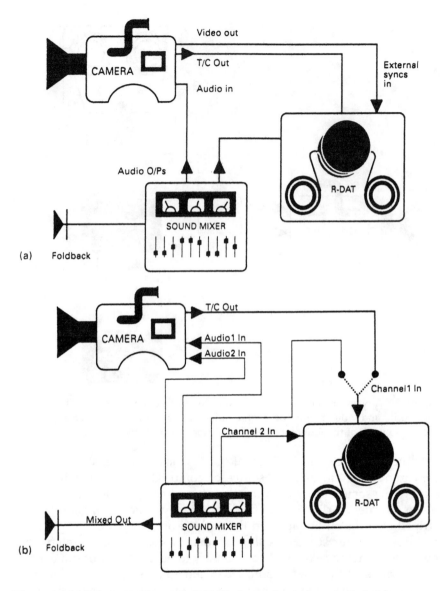

Figure 8.6 (a) When working with R-DAT, timecode can be recorded either on a dedicated track, or a spare digital audio track if working in mono. (b) If working in stereo with older machines without timecode facility, a few seconds of LTC can be recorded at the head of each take on one audio channel, which should then be switched back to audio.

procedure. Of course it is important not to stop the R-DAT machine recording between laying down each LTC leader and the take to which it relates. Unlike ordinary analogue machines the same rotating heads, locked to an internal control signal, attend to both record and replay so there is no offset to compensate for when the tape is replayed.

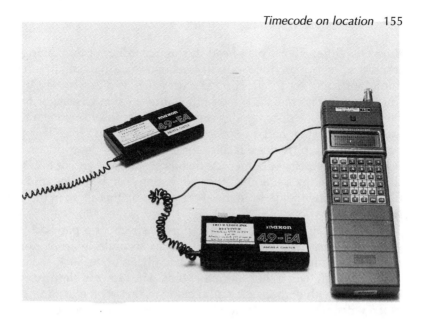

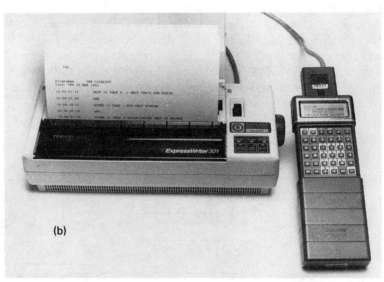

Figure 8.7 (a) A Psion Organizer used as a timecode reader. A radio link is optional. (b) Shot lists being typed up at the end of the day from a Timecode Organizer. (Courtesy of Chris Thorpe Projects.)

Not all R-DAT field recorders provide indication of the timecode recorded. This is not only a nuisance when it comes to logging the takes, but, perhaps more important, it means that there is no way of checking that a timecode has been received. As the timecode is placed in a subcode within the actual programme sound data stream, the ability to read the timecode either from a play head during recording or by playing back a test recording prior to the take will give assurance that both timecode and audio are being recorded. An accessory such as a Timecode Organizer, illustrated in Figure 8.7a, which plugs into a Psion Organizer to give a display of received timecode, can prove very useful. Incoming code failure is indicated, and an optional radio link is available. This piece of equipment also provides a facility for entering shot descriptions into the organizer, together with timecode details at start and end of takes, and at the end of the day's shooting, the shot listings can be edited and printed out, thus freeing the PA from the chore of typing this all up in the evening (Figure 8.7b).

R-DAT certainly makes the operational aspects of a playback shoot a great deal easier. Locked to its extremely accurate internal clock, and playing back material recorded via an equally accurate clock, there will be negligible drift over a short period of time. The tape can simply be played back, again with perhaps the audio being recorded on one audio channel of the video recorder as a guide for post-production, and the timecode on another channel for the offset. Figure 8.8 illustrates. The same rules apply regarding locking the video recorder to the R-DAT timecode: don't do it. There will be no established relationship between the R-DAT timecode and the video recorder's sync pulse generator, and no colour-framing relationship. The R-DAT machine on which the guide audio was recorded must have been locked to video syncs. This will have ensured an established video frame/timecode address relationship.

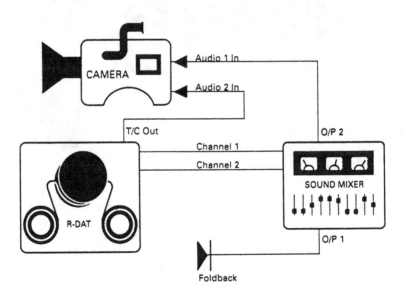

Figure 8.8 An R-DAT machine will be stable enough to run with independent timecode during playback shooting. Guide audio and timecode may be recorded on the audio tracks of the VCR.

Remote timecode generation

If you are using an analogue audio field recorder without an internal timecode generator, then independence from the camera can be achieved if a separate portable timecode generator is used. Its use frees the recordist from both radio links and the need to keep re-jamming to the camera as long as time-of-day code is employed. At the time of writing, portable battery-operated timecode generators have an accuracy of 1 frame per hour, but crystals are coming on the market with a much higher degree of thermal stability, and portable generators with an accuracy of 1 frame in 5 hours can be expected.

Record-run and time-of-day codes

Timecode generators in field recorders allow for two modes of operation. In the record-run mode, when the recorder is put into Pause (not Stop) it will backwind a few frames with the tape loosely laced round the head drum. On pressing Record again, the end section of the timecode and control signals on the backwound tape will be used to regenerate fresh code and control track pulses, which will be laid down seamlessly on tape as soon as the machine goes into 'record'. The contiguous time addresses and the continuous control track will make post-production much easier, as there will be no timecode or control track problems during pre-roll.

Time-of-day code is exactly that. The generator can be set either manually, or jam-synched at the start of the day, and within limits the code addresses recorded will represent the passing of time. This means that time addresses across separate takes will not be contiguous, and there may be problems during post-production if insufficient pre-roll time has been left at the start of a take. This form of code can be useful when a number of independent units have to record an event where it is important to have a record of the time of day, to aid continuity. Most field video recorders have the facility to place record-run addresses in the time data bits of the timecode word, and time-of-day addresses in the user bits.

The problem with midnight

At midnight the timecode generator does not blithely carry on through 24h.00m.00s.00f, but instead resets to 00.00.00.00. If a recording is made over this time there could be problems with some edit controllers and synchronizers, which will not recognize the progression through midnight and so may spool the wrong way when searching for a time address. There are three ways of preventing these problems from arising. The recording of a take could be started sufficiently early for it to end well before midnight. Reels and cassettes should be changed before the post-midnight take so that there are no split days on the same tape – either sound or video. Fresh tape(s) could be put into the recorder(s) and production paused until after midnight has passed. Alternatively, if the nature of the events is such that recording over midnight is necessary, as for example it would be when recording New Year celebrations, then the answer is to reset the timecode generator(s) so that they skip past midnight, re-jamming slave generators if necessary: a sensible way might be to advance the 'hours' address to 12 (noon). This will keep the minutes, seconds and frames unaffected for synching timecode with the actual time of events, which will be a great help during post-production if the events are being shot with multiple independent cameras and recorders.

Cassette changes

It is a good idea to have some indication within the timecode word of the reel number. If time-of-day code is being used this information may be stored in the user bit, and one manufacturer of audio field recorders has provided a facility for easily incrementing the last two digits of the user bits when they are being used in calendar mode. Most people prefer to have the reel number incorporated within the time data, and convention is to put the reel number in the hours digits of the timecode.

If this is done, both video- and audiotapes should be changed together. There will be no danger of the reel number incrementing up accidentally as long as the code is reset to zero and the tape duration is less than 1 hour long. No audiotape recorded on location should ever be split across videocassettes.

Setting the VITC lines

Most field recorders use little thumbwheels to set the two lines on which VITC will be recorded independently of each other. These thumbwheels are often marked with the hexadecimal sequence of symbols 0–F. While there are sixteen symbols in the Hex system, the IEC allows VITC to be placed on any line between 6–22 (319–335) inclusive when used with 625/50 systems, a total of 17 possible lines. It might be supposed that these would permit VITC to be placed either in lines 6–21 to 7–22. This is not the case. Component analogue recorders use line 8 or 10 to record vertical interval sub-carrier: line 7 may be used in PAL systems to carry a pulse identifying the eight-field sequence (it is recorded in field 1); lines 7–15 (320–328) carry field identification signals in SECAM. Most factory settings put VITC in lines 19 and 21. If you are considering altering the VITC lines also bear in mind that 1 in C-format machines have a format dropout that will increase when running at other than standard speed.

The tape logs should state which video lines carry VITC, together with any non-standard codes such as a secondary code in the user bits or on an audio track.

Shooting without a slate

It is possible to shoot without the need for a slate if in-camera real-time code is also recorded on the audio tapes by the sound recordist, and the 'ready-to-roll' time (day, hour, minute) is written on the tape box as soon as the tape is loaded onto the recorder. This ready-to-roll information is necessary as the audio recorder timecode may not carry data information, so saving the colourist having to hunt to find the sound reel corresponding to the film negative. If the recorder has no timecode generator, or has one that cannot be jam-synched, a master clock can be used to provide the correct code. If no dedicated timecode track is available, code can be laid down on a spare audio track.

If Aaton code is being used, the later R-DAT recorders will accept the Nagra/Aaton user-bit organization which carries the date, and modifications are available to allow some R-DAT machines to accept TTL timecode levels, so easing the interface problems with some cameras. Check with your supplier whether or not you have the correct soft- and hardware in the recorder.

Although in-camera codes are quite tolerant of over- or under-exposure, do check the settings of the LEDs' intensity – timecodes burned in on a 50 ISO film with the intensity set to 500 ISO could be difficult to read on transfer. A test transfer prior to shooting could save much angst later. If shooting monochrome film, relying purely on real-time code for sound sync on transfer, be aware that most black and white emulsions are relatively insensitive to the red light from the in-camera code generator – a 250 ISO monochrome negative stock could have a sensitivity of 80 ISO in the red end of the spectrum – so have a transfer test done before shooting starts. Check also, each time film is to be loaded, that the LEDs generating Aaton code are twinking equally brightly; no particles of dust should cover any of the LEDs. Regularly, say every couple of years, check the stability of the timecode generators. They should have a stability better than 1 part in a million (approx 1 frame in 10 hours). A good check of picture/sound time clock accuracy is to shoot a marble bouncing on a marble or ceramic tiled surface. One last point – a battery which is too low in charge to run the film camera can still keep the real-time clock going for a couple of hours so do not disconnect it until a fresh one is to hand.

CHAPTER 9

Timecode and linear post-production

The transfer suite

After rushes have been viewed to sort the wheat from the chaff, the 'wanted' takes should be identified and transferred to a format suitable for the off-line edit. Traditionally, Hi-band U-matic machines have been used for this, as the format supports timecode. Some post-production houses, at least one broadcaster, and some manufacturers, have developed VITC generators that will lay code onto Lo-band and VHS. Laying down a proper time-address signal is preferable to burning-in the code, as the off-line editor has the options of switching it in or out, whether to put it in a 'letter-box' or superimpose it, and – important – where to place it on the screen. If code has to be burnt in, consideration should be given as to where to place it within the image. Some editors will wish to see the bottom of the picture, as footsteps can be used to help sync pictures with sound. Superimposed code can be more difficult to read, but is less obtrusive than code in a letter-box. Whatever method is used, the time addresses must correspond with those on the rushes. If the off-line tapes are from film transfer, both KeyKode® and the in-camera recorded code should be transferred, and the time addresses also stored in a computer database for later conforming and negative cutting once the off-line edit has been done.

Whatever method is used to marry code with the off-line copy, it should always be transferred via a regenerator, which should be set to 'external' and 'auto'. If possible, both VITC and LTC should be transferred to the off-line copy. It is important that they should be identical. If they are not, the addresses could unexpectedly change during the off-line edit as the play VCR switches automatically between the two.

Off-line editing

It can be cost-effective to make the major edit decisions off-line, away from the expensive (both in time and personnel terms) edit suite that will be used to complete the final master edited tape. The tape format, edit controller and other hardware used for off-line editing will be less expensive, and the off-line editing may be personally undertaken by the director. At its very simplest the off-line edit may be a 'paper' edit, where the director sits down with a VHS copy of the road tapes, with timecode 'burned in' within a letter-box-shaped window in the picture (a 'window' dub), and writes down the 'in' and 'out' times by hand (Figure 9.1). The decisions may be stored in a timecode organizer or, in more sophisticated systems, on floppy or hard disc by means of a controlling microcomputer, for later transfer to the on-line edit controller.

EDIT LIST

Page. *1*...of. *8*...   Date ..../..../...

Production. *Industrial Estate Promo*   Producer. *J. Grundleton*..........
Client.. *Clitheroe C. of C.*....   Director. *R. Sawley*............

Reel	Slate	Hrs	Min	Sec	Frm	Hrs	Min	Sec	Frm	Comments
1	14–5	1	34	15	20	1	34	36	24	Fade in
7	3–1	7	12	04		7	14	20		Intro A/V
					MIX TO					
13	17-5	13	17	12		13	17	25		Crane shot. Cut before car enters
6	18-1	18	02	47		18	02	47		Entry through doors
13	15-1	13	01	15		13	01	27		Pan of empty space
				MIX TO						
13	16-1	13	12	18		13	12	30		Completed installation. End after
										zoom to company logo.
7	5-1	7	15	27		7	17	15		Interview with M.D. (Paul
										Slaidburn.
7	6-1	7	18	40		7	20	40		Reverse angles for M.D. Int.
8	7-2	8	04	50	12	8	06	13	20	Interview with Secretary
										CCC (Variable audio)
8	10-7	8	15	42	15	8	15	58	21	Lorry entering site
8	11-1	8	17	01		8	17	18		Lorry unloading (cut before
										offloading office desks).
10	12-1	10	02	04		10	02	12		Phone installation
10	14-3	10	12	20		10	14	14		Interview Bank Representative.
										(Name Super "Richard Weddington")
10	15-1	10	16	10		10	17	04		Reverse angles for R.W. Int.
13	20-3	13	17	24	21	13	17	41		Bank Rep arrives for Site Meeting
14	2	14	04	57	07	14	05	18	11	Bank Rep greets Paul Slaidburn.

Figure 9.1 In its simplest form an EDL can be handwritten.

The two most common off-line edit methods will obtain a 'rough cut' of the final version by means of assembly or insert editing. It may be that little thought will be given to the problems of the 8-field sequence when editing composite pictures, the edit controller being switched to 2- or 4-field. Some off-line editors may even work from the control track. In both cases, the matter of the correct sequence will be attended to during conforming, prior to the on-line edit. For this reason any audio post-production should be done only after conforming.

Assembly editing

Assembly editing consists of adding successive video, audio, control track (in the case of video and some digital audio formats) and timecode onto a tape which is effectively virgin. The new information is butt-joined to that already on tape, using the control track, and maybe timecode, to ensure a seamless join (Figure 9.2a). (In this respect it should be noted that assembly editing on Prodigi and some implementations of the R-DAT format require pre-striping.) The video, audio, control and timecode tracks are extended as the process continues. Before each edit the tape is backwound to a point before the end of the previous sequence, and on the approach to the edit point the previously-laid control track is used to guide the servo systems to ensure correct continuation of synchronization. If the edit controller can generate a list of both original and corresponding off-line edit master time addresses during this process, the

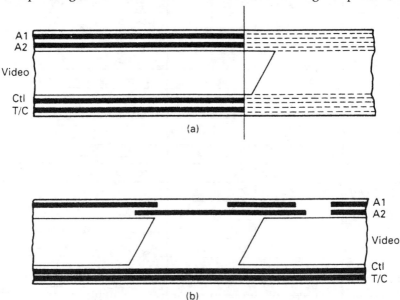

Figure 9.2 In assembly editing (a) programme, control and timecode tracks are laid down together consecutively as the edit proceeds. Insert edits (b) involve striping the tape with control track prior to the edit. Video and audio can be recorded individually. When striping the tape, the opportunity is often taken to lay LTC as a stripe of contiguous time addresses.

record machine can be set up for record-run code. This will result in a continuous and contiguous code on tape, with the corresponding original addresses on disc. This will permit later insert-editing of the tape, should this prove necessary. If this degree of sophistication is not available, the recording machine should be set to 'external' and 'regenerate'. The time addresses recorded will be those of the working copies of the original tapes. If VITC is being recorded, the lines should be the same as those on the working copies of the road tapes. If this is not done there is the possibility of a VITC reader receiving different information from different lines, if it is set to auto. If an edit list is stored on disc, it should be printed out in hard copy each time it is modified, to protect against loss in the event of a system crash.

During assembly editing, both video and sound must be laid down together; in particular, audio alone cannot be laid down because of the need for a control track. Note that later insert-editing on the tape can be performed only if continuous control track is present without any disturbance at the edit point, together with a timecode address track that is both continuous and contiguous.

Insert editing

Insert editing permits video, audio and sometimes timecode to be laid down individually. The process requires the tape to be pre-striped with both control track and longitudinal timecode (LTC). This is usually done by pre-recording 'picture black' or 'black and burst' (Figure 9.2b), though some editors prefer a coloured video field. Reference to the colour sub-carrier will be necessary for sophisticated editing in a composite environment, to prevent picture disturbance at the edit point. Component videotape recorders do not, in themselves, require reference to colour sub-carrier. However, a line of colour sub-carrier is recorded during the vertical interval when recording from a composite source.

VITC cannot be pre-striped as it will be overwritten when video information is recorded. It is important that longitudinal timecode is not overwritten while insert-editing, otherwise any subsequent editing or audio post-production will be made very difficult. It is sensible to generate VITC from the pre-striped LTC during the video insert edit as both timecodes will be present and identical. The recorder's internal regenerator should be set to 'internal' and 'regenerate'. The videotape machines employed later in the post-production process will then have the choice of both timecode forms, for maximum flexibility.

Pre-roll requirements

Since all machines require a few seconds of pre-roll in order to synchronize before performing an edit, it is important that the timecode addresses over this period are contiguous. If they are not, the edit controllers/synchronizers may pick up the discrepancy and abort the edit. The pre-striped timecode and picture black must be synchronous (and colour-framed when working in composite). If not, lack of synchronism between timecode and video frames will cause edits to abort, and lack of correct colour framing in composite will cause problems with sophisticated edits. If the recorder has an inbuilt timecode generator this will need to be set to 'internal'. If a separate regenerator is used, it must be fed with the same syncs as the video machine by way of reference. It is not a good idea to momentarily jam-sync a timecode regenerator, then remove its reference. It may well not be stable enough to maintain accurate synchronization for more than a few minutes.

If timecode on the edit master has lost synchronism with the video, it may be possible to retrieve the situation by replaying the tape from the head with the internal timecode generator set to regenerate, then switching the LTC track into record. This will ensure that the regenerated code will remain in sync with the video. If an external timecode generator is used the same procedures apply, but it must be fed with reference video from the videotape recorder, not station syncs.

When insert-editing, conventional practice is to have the edited programme start at 10 h 00 m 00 s 00 f. It is not a good idea to start the programme at '00' hours because of the 'midnight crossing' problem. One way of doing this is by laying down timecode from the head of the tape starting at 09 h 57 m 00 s 00 f. This will allow the recording a leader at the head of the tape.

The edit decision list

In its basic form the edit decision list will be a written list containing reel numbers, in and out times of the edits with corresponding start and finish times of the source tapes and details of the individual edits, such as video only, cut, wipe etc (Figure 9.3). At its most sophisticated, the EDL will also contain details such as colour grading of the source tapes, details of split edits etc, with this information included in the EDL before autoconforming to permit most efficient use of time. Whatever its sophistication, compilation of the EDL will rely on timecode. Both on- and off-line editing sessions are greatly helped by having accurate production logging (shot lists) with timecode.

Editing and the colour frame sequence

As discussed in Chapter 1, the relationship between colour sub-carrier and video syncs varies over an 8-field sequence in PAL, 4-field in NTSC and SECAM. For this reason, when editing together material from a variety of composite sources, the sub-carriers on either side of the edit

```
                              Title: Sample Edit List
                               Customer name here
        V A1 A2                                                    00:06:58:17
                           In          Out        Duration        Time-code
                 Mstr    01:06:23:11                              PLA N-01:17:06:05
    Dissolve
    C to A 060   A-077   12:10:37:20  12:10:44:04  00:00:06:14   Cue N-12:10:34:00
                 B-0 05  12:35:18:28  12:35:18:28                STP N-12:35:19:08
    Autotrim     C 084   12:39:18:24  12:39:18:24                LOS D-12:42:06:20
    Sort rec-in  AUX                                             REC OFF DISK ON
    Event =020   Black                                           CO N-13:31:25:14
    A mode assembly, events:


    014 084 A1/V  C          12:39:13:20  12:39:18:24  01:06:18:07  01:06:23:11
    015 081 AA    C          12:35:01:06  12:35:18:28  01:06:23:11  01:06:41:03
  > 016 084 V     C          12:39:18:24  12:39:18:24  01:06:23:11  01:06:23:11 <
  > 016 077 V     D    060   13:10:37:20  13:10:44:04  01:06:23:11  01:06:29:25 <
    017 077 V     C          13:26:17:02  13:26:22:02  01:06:29:25  01:06:34:25
    017 084 V     W019 045   12:35:04:03  12:35:10:11  01:06:34:25  01:06:41:03
    018 081 AA,V  C          12:37:08:02  12:37:11:02  01:06:41:03  01:06:44:03
    018 081 AA V  K B        12:37:11:02  12:37:18:23  01:05:44:03  01:06:51:24
    018 AX  AA V  K    030   00:00:00:00  00:00:06:21  01:06:44:03  01:06:50:24
    019 077 A2/V  K B  (F)   12:19:37:19  12:19:44:12  01:06:51:24  01:00:58:17
    019 084 A2/V  K 0  090   12:53:00:19  12:53:04:12  01:06:51:24  01:06:55:17
```

A CMX edit decision list 1, menu area; 2, system message area; 3, edit decision list (*Courtesy of F W O Bauch Limited*)

Figure 9.3 A computer-generated EDL showing menu (1), system messages (2), and the actual EDL (3) with information concerning the individual edits.

must be brought into phase. If this is not done there may be picture disturbance following the phase discontinuity, when the edited material is replayed. This is caused by the sub-carrier regenerator in the receiver or picture monitor changing frequency and/or phase in order to resync. To prevent this happening, the timebase corrector(s) (TBCs) associated with the source tape machine(s), in combination with the edit controller, will time-shift the picture information to ensure the correct phase relationship exists both sides of the edit.

When undertaking simple editing, i.e. cutting or mixing between dissimilar programme material, the TBC corrects for phase discontinuities by time-shifting the video signal (in theory in either direction, but in practice inserting a delay), usually horizontally, by multiples of one quarter-cycle with respect to the horizontal sync pulses, and/or down by a line to obtain a half-cycle phase shift, to bring the sub-carriers in phase across the edit. On cuts or mixes between dissimilar material this horizontal or vertical shift is not going to be noticeable unless the monitor is underscanned. Certainly, without any common spatial reference point within the picture, the small shift in the position of the programme material is irrelevant.

The situation is different when cutting or mixing between identical picture material, for example during an animation sequence with a common background, or when shortening or lengthening a scene, a process known as 'invisible' editing. Here, any timing shift will be noticeable as horizontal and/or vertical picture displacement. The way of dealing with this is to instruct the edit controller to perform a colour-framed edit. This is done by amending the IN point(s) of the source machine(s) so that the sub-carrier(s) when extrapolated across the edit will be in phase with the sub-carrier on the edit master.

The correct phase relationship cannot be obtained by decoding the composite signal into its components, then re-encoding with correctly phased sub-carrier, because decoded composite video carries a residual colour sub-carrier, which cannot be filtered out without degrading the signal (colour sub-carrier lies within the luminance bandwidth). This residual sub-carrier, carried across a non colour-framed edit, will interfere with the luminance signal, causing various degrees of cancellation. Final phasing may have to be performed manually if the S-C/H phase relationship is not close enough (± 20° is the recommended tolerance). Material acquired and edited totally within a component environment will not have these constraints.

Whatever technique is used to match sub-carrier phases, the edit controller and TBC need to know the phase of all sub-carriers so that the correct time shift can be inserted. This is done most conveniently if there exists a fixed and standard relationship between timecode addresses and sub-carrier to horizontal phase because the timecode(s) on source and record machines can be examined to establish the various phase relationship(s). The fixed and standard relationship between timecode and colour sub-carrier is indicated by the presence of the colour frame flag. If this flag is present in all source tapes and the pre-striped record master tape, the phase relationship can be established. It is for this reason more than any other that no composite video source should ever be fed with timecode that it is not referenced to a colour sync pulse generator. All sync pulse generators intended for use in composite editing suites, or component suites where composite sources may be handled, must generate a correctly colour-framed sequence of pulses and colour burst. Not all SPGs maintain the correct sub-carrier-to-sync relationship. If relaying damaged timecode on a road tape, the timecode regenerator must be fed with the off-tape video as reference.

The relationship between timecode and the 8- or 4-field sequence will be correct only if the sub-carrier phase is correct with respect to the horizontal sync pulse edges (S-C/H phase). Timebase correctors associated with videotape machines have the ability to vary S-C/H phase incrementally. The phase should be correct within 10° for trouble-free editing, and should always be checked for all source machines to avoid ambiguities. It should be suspect if problems arise when a colour-framed edit fails. A timecode sync monitor can display information about colour framing on a picture monitor (see Figure 3.19, p. 57).

Audio post-production

As audio signals are continuous, it is perfectly possible to slip the audio signal within each timecode frame, something not possible with video, to aid synchronization. With 80 bits per timecode word (frame), offsets are possible down to 1/80 or less of an equivalent video frame, an incremental time of 1/2000 s at 25 fps. One sound station on the market can slip individual channels relative to each other and the master VCR or synchronizer timecode by as little as 1/10 000 s. Analogue and audiotape recorders do not have timebase correctors, so it is important that any control device is able to smooth out any timing jitter on incoming timecode if wow and flutter are to be avoided.

Synchronizers

Synchronizers control all transport functions of the machines, including 'stop', 'play', 'fast forward', 'rewind' and 'speed'; they enable a number of machines to play together in synchronization; they allow timecode offsets between machines both in integer frames and fractions of a frame. They may emulate the characteristics of a VCR in order to allow an audio machine to be controlled from an edit controller. To do this efficiently each device will require details of its machine's ballistics (acceleration, deceleration, spooling speed, variable speed play range, nature of tachometer pulses). Commonly a synchronizer can be programmed either by software or by hardware changes such as resistor links, to 'recognize' the tape machine associated with it. Some synchronizers have the ability to 'learn' a machine's ballistics, and some, although pre-programmed, can still confirm the ballistics on switch-on.

Masters and slaves

As a rule, one synchronizer is designated 'master'. This is normally the one controlling the videotape recorder in video/audio post-production. This is because it is more difficult to make a videotape recorder slave to an external source than it is an audiotape recorder. Designating more than one synchronizer as master causes total confusion, as each of the synchronizers concerned tries to control the others. With some audio formats this can cause physical damage. If one synchronizer is designated 'master', the other synchronizers control the slave machines, which are thereby forced to run in synchronism with the master. It is important that the synchronizers controlling these machines do not lock them too firmly to the master, as any speed variation in the master would then be reflected in the slave machines. It is also important that the slave synchronizers 'roll-over' any short breaks in timecode which may be caused, for example, by dropout on the master, if the edit is not to crash. All synchronizers should have a selection of locking ranges available, and a selection of timecode dropout limits. Some may have the ability to reference to incoming timecode on machine start-up, switching to incoming reference syncs once the slave machine is locked. One point to remember is that when a tape machine stops, its parked position will depend on its braking ballistics; so it may well not be parked in synchronism with the master. If this is the case, it will have to search for synchronism on start-up. This will take some time, depending on its ability to play over a range of speeds: the smaller the range, the longer the lock-up time.

Chase synchronizers

Chase synchronization is the simplest form of control. Under this system the slave machine follows the master. The slave cannot park until the master has parked. Its speed follows that of the master, within limits. The slave will lock to timecode supplied to it from the master. Should the master shuttle at a faster rate than the slave is able to follow, the slave's capstan drive will disengage, the tape will lift off the heads, and the slave machine will go into spool. This may result in the slave running out of control (a 'speed hit'). The consequence is a possible run-off at the end of tape. More likely, the result will be excessively long synchronization times. To prevent this happening, audiotape machines intended for post-production will have methods of controlling and monitoring spooling speeds when under the control of a synchronizer.

Since a chase synchronizer can only follow the master, both master and slave will have to roll back to a point several seconds before an edit point, as the master has first to reach a stable play speed before the slave machine can lock up to it. It is important that timecode is contiguous during this time, otherwise the slave machine will not be able to lock, and the edit will abort. If necessary, the timecode may have to be restriped if a section of a videotape used as master in post-production has a rogue section of timecode.

The synchronization procedure for the slave machine via a chase synchronizer has three stages: first, the slave cues up to approximately the same position as the master, using timecode as the reference; next, as the master goes into play, the slave machine also goes into play, but with large speed variations possible (up to ±50% or so) until the timecode error between the two is less than 1 timecode frame; finally, small speed variations (usually less than ±1%) are used to bring the slave into synchronism with the master, often referenced to individual timecode bits. The slave now locks to the master. Figure 9.4a illustrates.

Control synchronizers

Chase synchronizers are ideal when only one slave machine is required to follow a master. However, when a multi-machine edit facility is required it can be advantageous to employ central control, with a keyboard for addressing individual machines via individual synchronizers, each one programmed with the machine's ballistics. Such a system is referred to as 'modular'. In this way a cue-time address, together with any offsets, can be entered into master and slaves, and all machines, master and slaves, go to their respective addresses individually, in their own time. This will

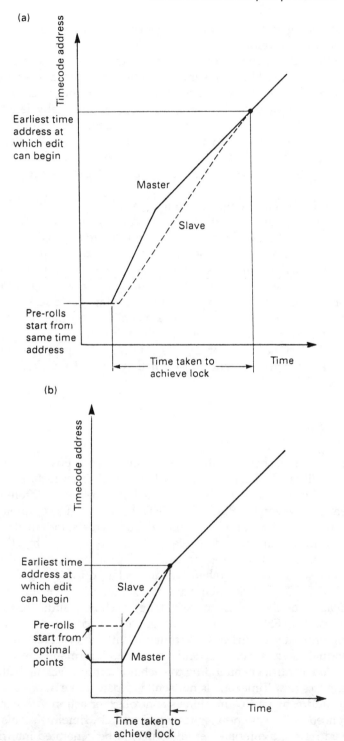

Figure 9.4 A chase synchronizer (a) will accelerate the slave machine, following the master. A control synchronizer (b) will park the slave at an appropriate point, according to its ballistics, and accelerate both together, handing lock over to an external reference.

reduce cueing time, and allow a system to grow as the requirements expected of it develop.

'Intelligent' synchronizers will park machines at a pre-roll point determined for each machine individually, and reduced to a time suitable for the machine with the longest lock-up time. Some synchronizers may park machines with a short pre-roll time, automatically lengthening it incrementally if one machine cannot achieve lock until success is achieved. This facility can be useful where a variety of machines are expected to lock up, and the synchronizer does not recognize a particular machine. This situation can arise when a machine is brought in from outside.

Synchronizers may employ a compromise between locking slaves to the master, and locking everything to external syncs. Known as auto-lock, this system first locks the slaves to the master, to bit accuracy. Control of both master and slaves is then passed to an external reference (Figure 9.4b). This obviates the possibilities of wow and flutter being introduced to the slave transport system from the master. When using auto-lock it is important that the master (usually the videotape recorder) and slave are locked to the same sync source. If a machine is on internal sync it may drift out of sync with the others and the edit will fail.

R-DAT machines used for lay-offs within a video post-production suite will achieve synchronization faster if they are fed with reference syncs (genlocked).

The ESbus

Communications between the various elements of a post-production suite have traditionally been specific to individual manufacturers, with the user unable to transfer such data as EDLs between different editing systems. However, the EBU and SMPTE have agreed a common standard for communication, known as the 'ESbus'. This standard specifies the manner in which individual elements are connected together, signal levels, connectors to be used, data rate and protocol. The complete specification is extremely comprehensive, and is laid down in EBU TECH-3245 and SMPTE 207M, and their various supplements which deal with the application of the ESbus to videotape machines, audio recorders and telecines. The ESbus system is based on the concepts of 'distributed intelligence' and 'virtual machines'. With distributed intelligence, individual devices interpret and act on the information received, their individual controllers attending to such matters as machine ballistics and locking to syncs. Timecode is not sent as a part of the data stream, but as a time address sent to a machine's controller for action. All machines are referenced to a common sync signal called 'Timeline'. This may be derived from a common external source, or be generated internally by a machine synched to a common reference. In this way, messages sent through a system can be kept to a minimum. A virtual machine is an individual machine addressed via its associated controller. This may be a remote-control panel or a synchronizer.

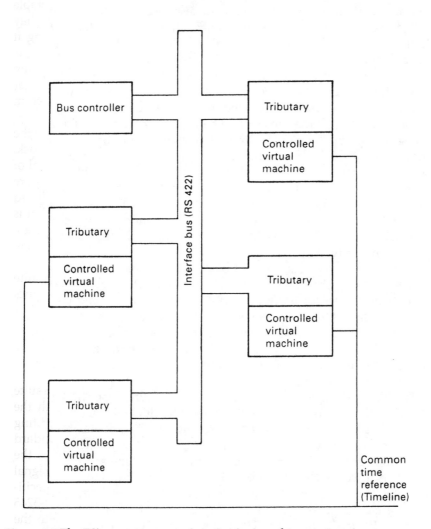

Figure 9.5 The ESbus system controls individual machine via interfaces (tributaries). According to system needs, common timecode, sync, MTC etc will be required as ESbus communication data do not carry these on a continuous basis, but as individual 'go-to' or 'event' addresses.

The interface between a virtual machine and the system is called a 'tributary'. The tributary transfers messages to and from virtual machines according to a fixed protocol. Each virtual machine will act on appropriate messages, received from other tributaries, the whole being regulated by a 'bus controller'. Figure 9.5 illustrates.

ESbus messages

There are two types of ESbus message, 'virtual machine' and 'system service'. Virtual machine messages pass data between individual virtual machines, and result in either action or response (reply) from the device called. System service messages control the whole system. Data are transmitted asynchronously in serial form at 38.4 kbaud, using RS422 interconnection standards. Each message consists of a series of 8-bit bytes, each preceded by a start bit and followed by a stop bit. The LSB is transmitted first. The connectors used are 9-pin D-type. If twisted-pair telephone cable is used, terminated in 100 Ω, a 1200 m cable run should be possible, though the runs should be kept as short as possible. Typical messages will be Time data, Orders (commands) and Status. Time data messages will be used as a reference by the virtual machine controller section, and will consist of standard timecode addresses. Offsets may be sent, and for audio machines these may contain trimming information down to 1/100 frame. User bit data may also be sent. The messages are not sent continuously, but in response to a command, which will be actioned when the timeline address corresponds to the time data message previously received.

Commands will be used to control a machine, which will respond with a status message by way of acknowledgement. The machine controller will attend to the detail of implementing the command and issuing the status message. Orders include such commands as go to, play timecode source, track select etc. Whenever an order is sent a response is required. Status information is sent by a virtual machine's controller to the system in response to an order. It indicates the activity of the device (stopped, record enabled, playing etc).

The big advantage of the ESbus over manufacturer-specific systems is that only the controllers associated with individual machines need to be ESbus-capable. This means that, for instance, an ESbus synchronizer can be used with a variety of machines as long as it will interface. Synchronizer manufacturers usually provide machine-specific interface software to cover a wide range of machines at the time of purchase. Updates are available at reasonable cost, so a system may grow with relative ease. Figures 9.6 and 9.7 illustrate a typical small ESbus audio post-production installation. The top synchronizer is the bus controller, the tributaries are interfacing with R-DAT and multi-track machines.

Synchronizer features

It is essential that a synchronizer for audio post-production should allow a tape to be slipped out of sync by a controlled amount, not just by an integral number of timecode frames, but by timecode bit increments. Synchronizers should also have the option of hard or soft lock. Hard lock will follow the master timecode precisely; soft lock will 'flywheel' over

Figure 9.6 Audio Kinetics ESbus synchronizers. The top module is the master.

Figure 9.7 ESbus synchronizers controlling multi-track and R-DAT machines from a VCR master during audio post-production.

any momentary loss of code and timecode jitter. It can be useful to alter the slew rate in soft lock to permit the best compromise between picture/ sound synchronization and minimum audio disturbance. For example, lip-sync requires sync accuracy of better than a frame; but speech is quite tolerant of small degrees of wow. Music, on the other hand may be more tolerant of small picture/sound sync displacements, but is not tolerant of wow.

It can be useful to trim the offset value of timecode down to bit accuracy, particularly 'on the fly' (i.e. dynamically), and for this fresh value to be loaded automatically into the synchronizer for recalculation of the 'in' and 'out' points. The term 'offset' commonly refers to whole (integer) timecode frame shifts, whereas the term 'trim' commonly refers to shift of a fraction of a frame. All synchronizers should be able to read tachometer pulses if any serious audio post-production is to be undertaken. They should also be capable of preventing tape run-off at the end of a reel during spooling. This latter facility should not be needed, but even in the best-regulated world there will still be occasions when timecode has not been recorded contiguously on the master tape, and the slave machines may try to spool through, counting tacho pulses. In this respect, if there is a hole in the timecode addresses the slave machine will have to be taken past the point manually. Unless you are particularly unlucky there will be sufficient contiguous pre-roll timecode the other side of the hole. If not, re-stripe and enter in the new offsets.

An automatic cycling facility will allow an edit to be rehearsed using a play-rewind-play sequence between edit points, or rather between pre- and post-roll points. Coupled with dynamic offsetting and trimming of the slave machine(s), this can be a great help in speeding up the editing process.

Synchronizers can also be set with pre-determined timecode limits. This will prevent a tape spooling off unexpectedly.

Synchronizer problems

If a tape spools unexpectedly, if it spools in the wrong direction, if the play speed varies unexpectedly, you should suspect one of the following causes:

1   No timecode present

2   Gaps in the recorded timecode

3   Timecode is not contiguous

4   The synchonizer is not set for the machine concerned

5   The machine is not under the control of the synchronizer

6 Timecode addresses on the master are not ascending

7 Synchronizers and video machine set at different frame rates

8 The play speed and timecode speed of the slave machine are different (e.g. slave playing at 38 cm/s; timecode striped at 19 cm/s)

9 Synchronizer not programmed with correct tacho pulses data

10 Machine not playing at correct speed for tacho pulses loaded into synchronizer

11 Unwanted offsets in the slave synchronizer(s)

12 Time address limits (if available) not set

13 Different VITC and LTC time addresses on the working copy of the video edit master

14 The R-DAT player is set to a different clock rate from that used to record the tape

If timecode is present but not being read correctly check the following:

1 Dirty timecode heads

2 Unregenerated code coming off tape

3 Timecode at incorrect frame rate

4 Timecode low in level

5 Timecode corrupted

On this last point, timecode is usually recorded on track 24 of an audio multi-track machine. Do not route it through the desk. Opening the wrong fader may be disastrous; there is the possibility of the output crosstalking onto audio, and of audio crosstalking to it, and audio may be inadvertently routed to the same bus as timecode, corrupting it. If an edit keeps aborting, check the following:

1 Pre-roll times are long enough for the slowest slave to lock-up

2 Synchronizers and master videotape machine are all fed with the same reference

3 Master videotape machine set to external syncs

4 Contiguous timecode present during pre-roll

5 Contiguous timecode present during the edit (if the synchronizers require this)

Timecode and stereo pairs

With a 24-track audiotape machine it is possible to record 10 stereo pairs (track 24 is timecode, track 23 is guardband, track 1 is unused edgetrack, track 2 is spare). When more stereo pairs are required another 24-track machine can be run in synchronism, both machines being locked together by separate synchronizers. Chase mode synchronizers are not suitable for this, as they will try to follow any speed variations in the master. Sets of stereo pairs having a significant proportion of common phase-coherent information should not be placed on separate machines. The machines are best locked by some form of control sync process, so that, once synchronized, they lock to a common and stable reference. Any offset introduced into the synchronizer of one machine should also be entered into those controlling the others.

CHAPTER 10

Timecode and non-linear post-production

This chapter has been the most difficult to write for this second edition, not because the subject is intrinsically difficult, indeed manufacturers of data management and non-linear editing systems have been spectacularly successful in making their products intuitively easy to use. No, it has been difficult to write because of the enthusiasm these products have engendered in the author! I have tried to avoid turning this chapter into a pocket textbook on how to edit, and I hope I have been successful, but any discussion of timecode application in video-assisted film post-production is bound to touch on the business, if not the art, of editing.

What timecode to record

In the *Preface* to this edition timecode was likened to a 'business manager', and like any business manager it can do its job most efficiently if it is involved, and thought given to what type/s of code are to be involved, at the very start of a project, no matter how simple the making of the finished product is likely to be. It is also advantageous to appreciate just how non-linear editing systems handle timecode when material is digitized.

Non-linear systems vary in their timecode requirements. Some will accept only LTC, some are happy with either LTC or VITC, and yet others will call for – and accept – timecode in the ESbus data sent down the RS422 (9-pin) interface used to control the VCR or Telecine remotely. Some non-linear editors will not accept LTC directly, but will record it onto one of the audio channels, from where it can be loaded into their databases. At the time of writing no non-linear editors will accept raw KeyKode® data straight off the telecine, though will accept databases containing such codes generally externally. Most non-linear editors allow material to be loaded in (digitized) without timecode, in which case timecode data will have to be entered for both pictures and sound if accurate EDLs are to be generated. If timecode data is not sent at the time pictures and sound are digitized it will be a great help if 'burnt-in' code (BITC) is displayed within the picture area, and (if appropriate) a matching picture and sound slate (Digislate) is placed at one end or the other of each take. Most non-linear editors can display audio waveforms so a tone slate will greatly ease the synching of sound with picture.

Non-linear editors do not, by and large, store timecode data on a frame-by-frame basis – it takes up valuable memory. Instead they load the time address of the first selected frame of a take, and from there onwards calculate the time address, when needed, using the frame count from the last event as an offset. To this extent, it is usually regarded as good operational practice to set any timecode break detection to ON. If set to OFF when digitizing the result could be an inaccurate EDL, as the discontinuity in the code will be ignored.

Options are also available for the loading of the start KeyKode® number of the take, and again there are differences between non-linear editors as to how this is handled, and for the form in which the final EDL will be presented on disc. Thought should be given as to how any on-line video edit or negative cutting is going to be undertaken. The organization/s undertaking these tasks should be consulted before the non-linear process is begun, and manufacturers of non-linear editors are invariably encouraging when it comes to asking advice. After all they have a vested interest in making their systems as trouble free as possible. One manufacturer, with a refreshing honesty that does them credit, acknowledges that at the time of writing (late 1994/early 1995) everyone involved with non-linear editing is on a fairly steep learning curve, and that there are several data and material handling and management strategies available to progress the route from loading raw stock and blank tape into cameras and recorders to the presentation of the final product on videotape and/or film.

Basic organization of film production using non-linear editing

The organizational principles are the same for both traditional film conforming and non-linear editing to produce a cutting list. Briefly, the following steps are involved:

1 Negative is shot in camera.
2 Negative has edge number to uniquely label every frame.
3 A print is made from the negative. This also carries the edge numbers.
4 The print is edited to produce a cutting copy (pull list).
5 The negative is cut to match the cutting copy (including any lab process work such as dissolves etc) using the edge numbers as a guide.
6 A final release print is made from the cut negative.

Figure 10.1 illustrates the process. The key to the whole process is that each frame of film has a unique *Label* to identify it. As long as the labels on the original negative and the cutting copy are identical, the conformed cutting list will be what the film editor wanted.

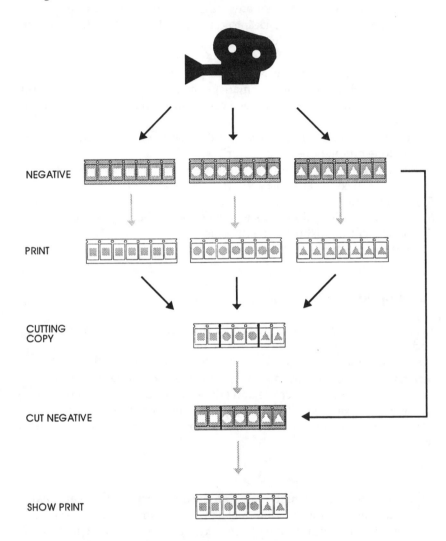

Figure 10.1 The basic process by which film is post-produced. Courtesy of Lightworks Editing Systems Limited.

In non-linear editing the processes are similar, but powerful data management systems allow the editor to perform the cuts (and a limited but growing number of special effects) non-destructively, permitting a degree of experimentation along 'what if' lines with an ease that is not possible on film. The data management systems track the various timecodes (original Aaton/Arri, KeyKode®, recorder), check for errors, match pictures and sound shot at different timecode frame rates, and produce EDLs and cutting lists in a variety of formats to suit most online film and video conformers.

As stated earlier, there are many ways of arriving at the final product from the insertion of raw stock into camera and blank tape into recorder. One option could be as follows:

1 Telecine transfer film neg or print to videotape.
2 Create databases to hold and manage the relationship between the film codes (e.g. KeyKode®) and video codes (this can be done on most non-linear editors).
3 Convert databases into a form that the non-linear editor can handle (if not done on the non-linear editor).
4 Record video into non-linear editor (this may be automated using the database to control the play VCR).
5 Do the edit.
6 Merge the various databases (can be done on the non-linear editor).
7 Produce cutting list from the database/s.
8 Print the cutting list.

Label options

Labels are the means by which individual frames of film or videotape, and the corresponding audio tracks (either analogue or digital), are identified. Traditionally, electronic editing has treated these labels as separate entities, but it is more helpful if they are thought of generically, with in-camera code, timecode and edge-codes (such as KeyKode®) being thought of as examples. It is also helpful for non-linear editing if timecode is regarded as a label to identify a film or video frame, and not time as such.

Edge numbers

These are recorded as latent images on the film stock. As they carry a code that uniquely identifies the film reel as well as frame number, these codes uniquely identify each frame of film. They are both machine and human readable once the stock has been developed. Edge numbers cannot be used to label sound since they are unreadable on unprocessed film.

Timecodes

Used as labels on both videotape, film and audiotape, they do *not* uniquely identify every frame as they repeat every 24 hours, and may not carry information about the camera number. The reel or camera number can be placed in the 'hours' digits, the data can be placed in the user bits (see Appendix 7), and at the time of writing there are developments in the ways in which non-linear editors are able to handle user bits information.

It helps if the sound is shot at the same timecode frame rate as the video, as it simplifies the digitizing process, but it is not essential – remember that non-linear editors only regard timecode as a label to identify the first frame of a take – think of audio tape as something that runs at 7.5 inches/second (or whatever) and not as so many frames/second.

Camera code

Both Aaton and Arriflex use in-camera labelling of film. The labels are recorded as latent images at the time of shooting, and identify each frame, though only Aaton code identifies the date and camera number in the time data. If date and camera number are not recorded with the time data, they should be placed within the user bits, or logged separately, and burnt-in for the digitizing process.

Rubber numbers (Acmade or Ink numbers)

Where picture and sound are synched up on film print and sepmag, the sync rolls are stamped with rubber numbers (Figure 10.2) to help maintain sync during film cutting.

Synching options for sound and pictures

As picture and sound are recorded on different media, thought needs to be given as to how they will be combined for editing. For non-linear editing a number of options are open:
1 Film negative/print and segmag sound can be synched up prior to telecine transfer.
2 Film and segmag sound can be synched up in telecine. The process can be automated using camera-generated codes if they correspond.
3 Synchronization can be done on videotape, using an edit controller.
4 Sync can be achieved at digitization (chase sync).
5 Sound can be synched to picture within the non-linear editor (most of which have easy to use utilities or 'tools' to achieve this, and will also give a visual indication when sync has been lost).

However synching up is achieved, it is important that all the labels will allow accurate tracking back to the original pictures and sound. Each of the above methods has its own pros and cons (invariably trading off simplicity against cost) and it is helpful if either the non-linear manufacturer is approached for advice, or specialist advice is sought at an early stage from a specialist organization, such as a sync suite. A variety of such organizations exist, often using relatively cheap audio workstations (with professional quality sound) and simple edit controllers, and usually equipped with a range of DAT, Beta, Nagra or even disc-based recorders such as SADIE.

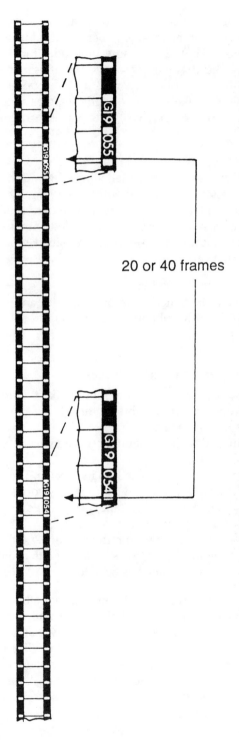

20 or 40 frames

Figure 10.2 Super 16 print showing rubber numbers.

Maintaining labels

There are two basic strategies for maintaining the labels during non-linear post-production:

1 Store the various labels in a separate database (such as Excalibur or OSC/R) and digitize together with a single timecode such as LTC or VITC (or if available use the facility to have it sent down the RS422 interface). The database must generate matching lists so that the various label types can be correlated to produce the cutting list.

2 Place all the labels somewhere on the videotape prior to digitizing (only possible if the non-linear editor is able to handle data placed in the timecode user bits).

Whichever method is chosen it is essential that, for the pictures, KeyKode® and/or rubber numbers and/or camera code plus camera roll or date, and, for sound, rubber numbers and/or timecode plus sound roll or date are maintained. It is also helpful if the videotape reel ident is available on the database for cross-checking.

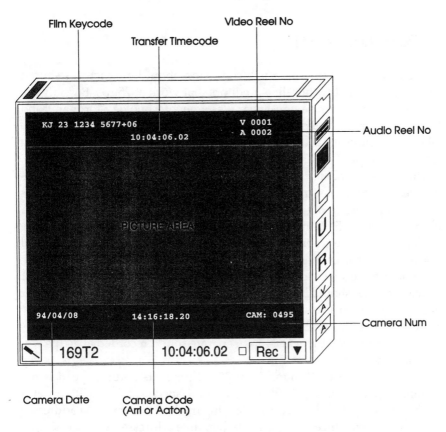

Figure 10.3 'Burnt-in' display on a non-linear editor, displaying the various time- and film-codes. Courtesy of Lightworks Editing Systems Limited.

If a separate database is created prior to loading into the non-linear editor, it will be converted by the editor into a form that can be used, but it must be in a format and disc operating system that the editor can read. Most non-linear editors accept a range of database files, and the manufacturer can usually give advice as to whether or not a particular database format is acceptable. Aaton's Keylink, Evertz's Keylog, FLEx, Keyscope and FilmLab's Excalibur are commonly acceptable. If commercially manufactured databases are not an option, one can usually be created on the non-linear editor, often 'customized' from one of a range of standard templates provided.

Whether you write information into your database manually, or create it automatically, do remember that the accuracy of the final product will depend on the accuracy of the information held in that database, and (if used) the accuracy of any burn-ins. Figure 10.3 shows an example of a non-linear display of a 'burn-in' plus timecode label, and Figure 10.4 illustrates a typical film database display.

24 fps pictures in PAL

In the past, there has been much confusion about how pictures shot at 24 fps are handled by non-linear editors that work at 25 fps. Possibly the confusion arose because non-linear was a new technology for many, and few editors appreciated that timecode addresses were used mainly as labels to identify starts of shots. Handling film material shot at 24 fps is in fact quite simple.

The telecine transfer is done at 25 fps, straight frame-for-frame. This ensures that each film frame has a corresponding video frame. If sound is synched up prior to digitizing (options 1, 2, 3 and 4 on page 181) it should be played in at 25/24 times its original speed. This is possible on some analogue machines, some recent DAT machines and on earlier digital machines if a correspondingly higher speed word-clock can be provided. If sound is to be synched up in the non-linear editor (option 5 on page 181 or wild track) it should be played in at its original speed. As the non-linear editor will record pre-synched pictures and sound at 25 fps and replay them at 24 fps they will remain in sync. As the editor will record pictures at 25 fps and replay them at 24 fps, separate sound recorded at 24 fps will maintain sync.

If the option to play sound in at 25/24 times its natural speed is not available, it can be digitized at its natural speed, and it will run at a slightly lower pitch in the editor. Keeping track of the timecode addresses is not a problem since, as we saw earlier, time addresses are used simply to label the selected starts of takes.

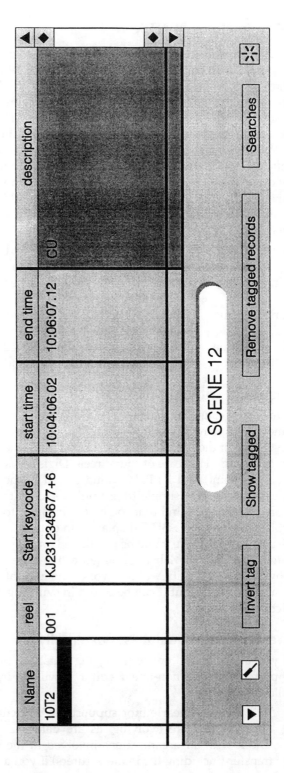

Figure 10.4 A typical film database display on a non-linear editor. Courtesy of Lightworks Editing Systems Limited.

24 fps pictures in NTSC

In Chapter 5 the business of transferring film shot at 24 fps to 30 fps video using 3/2 pull down was examined. Some non-linear editors ignore the extra pull down fields when digitizing, on the basis that these cause movement to appear somewhat jerky. To ignore these extra fields the system must know where they are located. This it usually does by examining the timecode at the sync point and calculating the pull down fields for the rest of the clip from this point. This can be done automatically on some external database generation and management systems, or by examining a few frames over the sync point on the VCR and checking whether the timecode changes in value from field 1 to field 2. If the film frame at the sync point has been keypunched prior to digitization life will be easier:

For an A frame: There will be two keypunched fields, timecode value will not change from field 1 to field 2.

For a B frame: There will be three keypunched fields, timecode value will change between field 2 and field 3.

For a C frame: There will be two keypunched fields, timecode value will change between field 1 and field 2.

For a D frame: There will be three keypunched fields, timecode value will change between field 1 and field 2.

Digitizing without timecode

If material (sound or vision) is recorded into a non-linear editor without timecode, this need not pose a problem as long as BITC is present. The first frame of the sequence can be located (non-linear editors have a utility for this), and in the case of sound reels, Digislate is a great help in locating the sync point) and its BITC value placed in the database (again, non-linear editors have simple to use utilities to do this). In this respect it is worth bearing in mind that some non-linear editors have a BITC facility, which will provide a BITC display, with options as to how much detail is displayed and where it will be positioned on the screen, the value/s being calculated from the labels provided at the time material was digitized. Obviously this facility will not work if no accurate timecode was logged in at digitization, but it can be of use in synching and labelling sound to pictures.

Creating logging databases externally

If you are going to create a logging database prior to digitizing, and import it into the non-linear editor it will be important to check the following points:

- Will the non-linear editor support the particular database? All non-linear editors are evolving, as are database management systems. Check with all organizations involved in the database creation and transfer (including the manufacturers) if you are unsure.

```
000 Manufacturer Aaton      No. 021 Equip Keylink    Version  5.1    Flex 100
010 Title SOUP AXIS TRANSFER FILE

012 Shoot Date 02-06-95  Transfer Date 02-02-95

100 Edit 0001            Field A1  PAL
110 Scene        Take         Cam Roll 9        Sound         10:21:27:22.
120 Scrpt
200       16 25.00 000001           000008+17 Key EASTM KL265232 004129+01 p
300       Assemble  00000001 At 01:00:25:09.0 For 00:00:07:02.0

100 Edit 0002            Field A1  PAL
110 Scene        Take         Cam Roll 9        Sound         10:26:10:16.
120 Scrpt
200       16 25.00 000001           000009+05 Key EASTM KL265232 004139+11 p
300       Assemble  00000001 At 01:00:33:19.0 For 00:00:07:10.0

100 Edit 0003            Field A1  PAL
110 Scene        Take         Cam Roll 9        Sound         10:54:54:08.
120 Scrpt
200       16 25.00 000001           000029+08 Key EASTM KL265232 004150+04 p
300       Assemble  00000001 At 01:00:42:07.0 For 00:00:23:13.0

100 Edit 0004            Field A1  PAL
110 Scene        Take         Cam Roll 9        Sound         11:05:35:11.
120 Scrpt
200       16 25.00 000001           000030+02 Key EASTM KL265232 004181+05 p
300       Assemble  00000001 At 01:01:07:03.0 For 00:00:24:02.0

100 Edit 0005            Field A1  PAL
110 Scene        Take         Cam Roll 9        Sound         11:07:04:21.
120 Scrpt
200       16 25.00 000001           000029+05 Key EASTM KL265232 004212+17 p
300       Assemble  00000001 At 01:01:32:10.0 For 00:00:23:10.0

100 Edit 0006            Field A1  PAL
110 Scene        Take         Cam Roll 9        Sound         11:22:50:16.
120 Scrpt
200       16 25.00 000001           000036+00 Key EASTM KL265232 004244+05 p
300       Assemble  00000001 At 01:01:57:13.0 For 00:00:28:20.0

100 Edit 0007            Field A1  PAL
110 Scene        Take         Cam Roll 9        Sound         11:24:09:04.
120 Scrpt
200       16 25.00 000001           000053+17 Key EASTM KL265232 004281+11 p
300       Assemble  00000001 At 01:02:27:09.0 For 00:00:43:02.0

100 Edit 0008            Field A1  PAL
110 Scene        Take         Cam Roll 9        Sound         11:26:27:05.
120 Scrpt
200       16 25.00 000001           000073+05 Key EASTM KL265232 004337+11 p
300       Assemble  00000001 At 01:03:12:04.0 For 00:00:58:15.0

100 Edit 0009            Field A1  PAL
110 Scene        Take         Cam Roll 9        Sound         11:34:57:00.
120 Scrpt
200       16 25.00 000001           000036+04 Key EASTM KL265232 004412+05 p
300       Assemble  00000001 At 01:04:11:23.0 For 00:00:28:24.0

100 Edit 0010            Field A1  PAL
110 Scene        Take         Cam Roll 9        Sound         11:56:03:04.
120 Scrpt
200       16 25.00 000001           000026+02 Key EASTM KL265232 004450+06 p
300       Assemble  00000001 At 01:04:42:09.0 For 00:00:20:22.0
```

Figure 10.5 Printout of a typical film logging database containing information on time, footage, roll number, scene, take and date. Courtesy of Wren Communications.

- Will the negative cutters be able to read the pull-list that will eventually be created?
- What time/film data is to be handled at each stage of the post-production process, not just for pictures but also for sound? Ensure that all relevant codes are loaded into the database.

Different non-linear editors require their externally generated databases to be provided in different formats. All, however, will require the information regarding video and sound parameters (e.g. 25 fps, 48 kHz digital), a header that describes the database layout, and the entries themselves. Figure 10.5 illustrates a part of a typical logging database and Figure 10.6 illustrates three options for logging edge-number and timecode during film-to-videotape transfer.

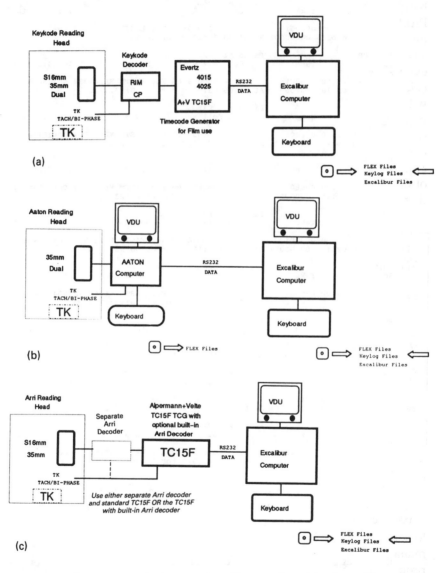

Figure 10.6 Three options for logging time/footage data: (a) using a film-use timecode generator, (b) using an Aaton computer such as Keylink, (c) using a timecode generator with built-in Arri Decoder. Courtesy of Filmlab Systems International Limited.

Working with external databases

It has been the creation of powerful data management systems that have 'empowered' timecode. Systems such as Excalibur, Keylink, Keylog etc are more than just databases. They can play a key part at any and every stage of film-with-video-assist post-production. They can not only store time- and footage-related data for film, video and audio tapes, but will handle roll numbers, date, camera number and position (set-up), carry PAL field and NTSC pulldown field information, and even provide a means of logging information needed by the colourist. They may generate VITC for the video that will be digitized into the non-linear editor, and even log external GPI events such as might come from the telecine's colour controller, such as Pogle®. Not all of this data can be transferred with the video, certainly not in the user-bits of a single frame of traditional timecode. One manufacturer arranges for all this data be carried as 'tags', stored in three VITC lines (lines 19, 20, 21), within the user bits of one VITC line, with another line (the KeyKode® line) carrying edge numbers in full, and the third line (the real-time line) carrying time-of-day. Figure 10.7 illustrates a typical display provided to a colourist at the end of a transfer session.

```
Film title  :  Shadows in the shade      Production id :  AA0003
Lab. spool  :  910004 Post-Lab / London  Transfer date :  93 04 01 09:59:40
Video tape #:  048 (25fps PAL)           Data base file :  AG910004.T01

                              day      film time     video tc        keycode
Ev   001   scene 32A    92 04 24   11:26:46+17   01:42:21:18   KM090106 3591+08
Snd  026   take   05    cam 0853   11:28:12+13   01:43:44:03   KM090106 3694+08
                                                       one stop under-exposed

Ev   002   scene 33     92 04 24   11:28:25+08   01:44:57:24   KM090106 3695+14
Snd  026   take   01    cam 0853   11:30:15+22   01:46:44:03   KM090106 3828+08
          Reverse shot, low angle, better than last take, sound may be N.G., light red

Ev   003   scene 33     92 04 24   11:30:46+10   01:47:42:02   KM090106 3828+09
Snd  026   take   02    cam 0853   11:32:30+00   01:49:21:13   KM090106 3952+15
                                                                       sound OK

Ev   004   scene 34A    92 04 24   11:32:41+17   01:50:01:13   KM090106 3954+03
Snd  026   take   01    cam 0853   11:33:32+13   01:50:50:08   KM090106 4015+03
                                                          check foreground focus
```

Figure 10.7 At the end of a session the colourist can view and print the details of the transfer. Courtesy of Aaton des Autres.

With much television material being shot on film (for quality, the film look and the wide-screen format) for later mastering onto videotape, data management systems can be used at all time-critical stages of post-production; for negative logging, providing an edge-number edit list for a rough-cut assemble of the negative and, after assembly of the rough-cut, an accurate EDL for auto-conforming the on-line. Figure 10.8 illustrates a typical sequence of operations.

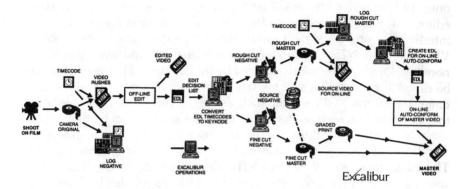

Figure 10.8 Options for film-to-video post-production using a data management system. Courtesy of Filmlab Systems International Limited.

When the final product is to be released on film, data management systems can be involved at the initial logging of the negative; for later conversion of the off-line video EDL to a matching KeyKode® list; for organizing a frame-accurate cut list for providing the check print; and lastly for providing any modified cut list for the fine-cut of the source negative. Figure 10.9 illustrates two typical film-to-film post-production processes.

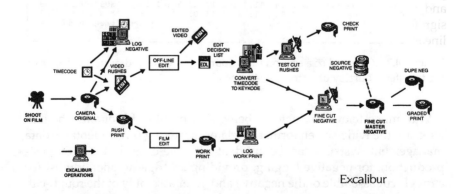

Figure 10.9 Options for film-to-film post-production using a data management system. Courtesy of Filmlab Systems International Limited.

Doing away with the external database

Top-of-the-range non-linear editors no longer require external databases for the management of time and footage codes. Camera and Telecine manufacturers provide options that permit 3-line VITC to be encoded onto the videotape at the time of transfer from Telecine, and non-linear editor manufacturers have developed a range of 'template' options for internal database management systems. The data thus encoded into 3-line VITC (see Chapter 5 and Appendix 8 for details) can be loaded into the non-linear editor at digitization, being carried either in the video signal to be digitized, or via a separate physical link. Once in the editor, internal database management systems, coupled with EDL and cutting list generators can provide just about any option required.

The future?

Manufacturers of non-linear systems are working on increasing the time-data options that they can accept during digitizing (as opposed to relying on databases generated externally), more and more routes are being mapped out for the journey through film-to-film and film-to-video post-production. Video with 3-line VITC will, within a few months of this edition being published, be available to the non-linear editor straight from the camera's video assist facility (though obviously without key numbers). This will allow an off-line editor, on location, in conjunction with the Director, to decide whether or not a scene needs to be reshot for editability and/or continuity. At least one manufacturer of non-linear editing systems is actively exploring the possibility of transferring digital audio data to audio workstations without having to do it in real time. The same manufacturer is currently developing a database management system that will permit sync sound to be digitized separately from the pictures, using 3-line VITC to marry up sound to picture within the editor, and an option to discard unwanted audio. Finally, and perhaps most significantly, with the cost and size of memory both coming down, non-linear editing will soon be available in broadcast quality.

CHAPTER 11

Timecode and the AES/EBU digital audio interface

Introduction

Timecode has moved into new areas of use. It can be carried in the AES/ EBU digital interface and transmitted within the NICAM stereo sound signal. This chapter explains how it is incorporated into the digital bit stream.

AES/EBU digital interface

This interface is primarily intended to permit the sending of two channels of stereo sound in digital form around a studio centre, using existing traditional (balanced, twin-screened) audio circuits. Digital recorders have the ability to accept digital audio data in this form. Within the code is provision for carrying time data. This is compatible with IEC code, though as yet there are no practical applications in wide use. One can envisage time data in the digital audio bit stream being processed by a database to aid post-production. Since audio is sent to the transmitters in AES/EBU form, it would be possible to place the time data into the 11-bit additional data word incorporated in each NICAM data block. Perhaps the data could carry some form of 'advertised' programme time to automatically reprogram home videos in the event of late changes to the transmission schedules. The data carried in the AES/EBU digital interface are organized into blocks, each block containing 192 frames. Each frame is further divided into two subframes, with each subframe carrying alternate left and right channel audio data (though the interface does allow for data other than audio to be transmitted). Each subframe, and the start of each block, carries at its head a unique identifier, called a 'preamble'. The data, with the exception of the preambles, are coded into biphase mark form; the preambles are straight NRZ code. Figure 11.1 illustrates the process.

Each subframe consists of 32 bits. Bits 0–3 carry the preamble. This can take one of 3 forms:

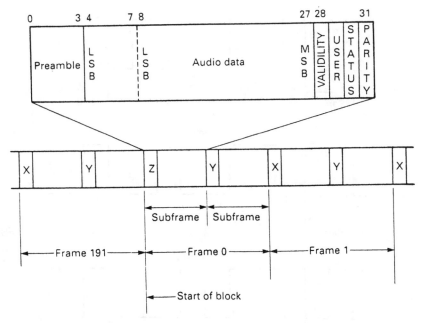

Figure 11.1 The AES/EBU interface assembles data in blocks of 192 frames. Each frame carries 2 subframes. Each pair of subframes comprises 32 bits. One of these bits, STATUS, can carry timecode, referred to as ProDIO code.

1   Preamble X (11100010 or 00011101) indicates the start of subframe 1 (left audio channel in stereo).

2   Preamble Y (11100100 or 00011011) indicates the start of subframe 2 (right audio channel in stereo).

3   Preamble Z (11101000 or 00010111) indicates the start of subframe 1 and the start of the block. This is necessary for synchronization, and for correct assembling of the time address bits embedded in the data stream. Figure 11.2 illustrates the three different pre-ambles.

Bits 4-27 carry either audio data alone (in the case of 24-bit-long audio data words), or audio data preceded by 4 bits of auxiliary information (in the case of 20-bit long audio data words).

But 28 is the validity bit. If set to logical 0 it indicates that data contained in bits 4–27 are suitable for conversion into analogue form.

Bit 29 is the user bit. The bits in the 192 successive subframes within each block can be used for any purpose by the interface user. They can be formed into 24 bytes.

Bit 30 is the channel status bit. These bits within each block combine to form the channel status frame, which can carry time information.

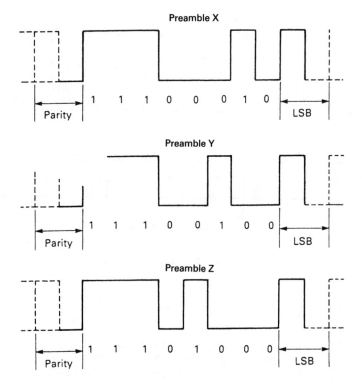

Figure 11.2 The preambles enable synchronization and identification. The preamble code is NRZ.

Bit 31 is the parity bit for bits 4–31 of the subframe (even parity is explicit in the preamble). Even parity is employed.

The channel status frame

This frame is formed from the individual channel status bits carried in each subframe. There are 192 of these bits within each block, assembled into a frame of 24 bytes, each byte having a specific purpose. Figure 11.3 illustrates these bytes and their functions. Since most of the bytes formed by the assembled channel status bits are unconnected with either time or synchronization they will not be described here, but a brief discussion is given in Appendix 6. Bytes 0, 4, 14–17 and 18–21 can carry time information.

Byte 0, bit 6 and bit 7 indicate the sampling frequency. This information is necessary to permit transcoding between time addresses held within the channel status frame and traditional timecode or time-of-day. The information is held in the following form:

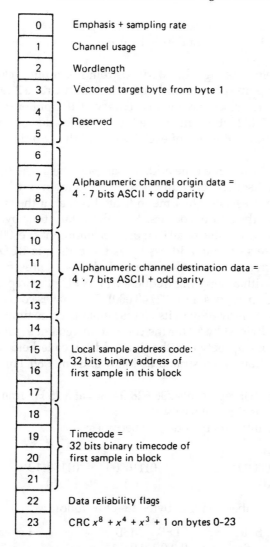

Figure 11.3 The 24-byte sequence of the channel status data formed from the 192 status bits associated with an AES/EBU audio block.

Bit 6	Bit 7	
0	0	Sampling frequency not indicated. Manual override permitted.
0	1	48 kHz. Manual override disabled.
1	0	44.1 kHz. Manual override disabled.
1	1	32 kHz. Manual override disabled.

Byte 4, bits 0–1 form the digital audio reference signal according to the following table:

Bit 0	Bit 1	
0	0	Not a reference signal
0	1	Grade 1 reference signal

| 1 | 0 | Grade 2 reference signal |
| 1 | 1 | Not defined – use is reserved |

A Grade 1 reference signal is derived from a sampling clock having an accuracy of 1 ppm (part per million) or better. A Grade 2 reference signal is derived from a clock having an accuracy of 10 ppm or better.

Bytes 14–17 (32 bits) contain the local sample address code. This is, in effect a tape timer. Bits 0–7 of each byte send the LSB first. Details of the code are given below.

Bytes 18–21 carry the time address sample. This is the time of day laid down during source encoding and will remain unchanged during subsequent processing. The time indicated is that at the start of the data block in which the address occurs. As with the tape time bytes, LSB is sent first in each byte. A value of all 0s indicates 'midnight', i.e. 00h 00m 00s 00f.

For both sets of time address bytes the coding is BCD. In each, the addresses increment up each successive channel status frame (in effect, each block). With a sampling frequency of 48 kHz this represents a count incrementing up every 4 ms (192/48 000). This makes conversion into IEC timecode particularly easy in its 25 fps version, as the time address needs simply to be divided by 10 for the count to increment at video frame rate.

The relationship between the time address code held in Bytes 18–21 and real time can be illustrated as follows, using 08h 11m 05s 03f as an example:

08h 11m 05s 03f represents 736 628 frames at a 25 Hz frame rate. This is 7 366 280 x 4 ms time intervals.

Converted into binary code this becomes:

MSB			LSB
00000000	01110000	01100110	10001000
(d)	(c)	(b)	(a)

These will be embedded into bytes 18–21 as follows:

Byte	LSB MSB	Legend
18	0 0 0 1 0 0 0 1	a
19	0 1 1 0 0 1 1 0	b
20	0 0 0 0 1 1 1 0	c
21	0 0 0 0 0 0 0 0	d

Byte 22, bit 6 indicates the reliability of the data held in bytes 14–17, with logical 0 indicating reliable data. Byte 22, bit 7 indicates the reliability of the data held in bytes 18–21, with logical 0 indicating reliable data.

Alternatives for timecode in AES3 channel status

Timecode is generated at one of a number of frame rates, and really needs to be independent of audio sampling rate. Equipment design would also be simpler (cheaper?) if timecode in channel status were in hours, minutes, seconds and frames rather than requiring to be transcoded into a 'number of audio samples' form, though any organization which is not totally equipped to carry audio in AES/EBU digital interface form at all stages of post-production might find that the complexities and cost of transcoding are prohibitive. At least one UK organization however, already carries time data 'in-house' as BCD hh.mm.ss.ff within the channel status, though only allowing for synchronous timecode. In 1992 a proposal (Rumsey) was submitted to the AES SC2-5-1 working party on synchronization which would free timecode in channel status for the need of synchronicity.

A data byte indicates the offset between the timecode frame start and the start of the first AES/EBU block of a new timecode frame, the first frame in a new block being flagged with a single bit. The video frame rate can be carried in 2 data bits. A 'timecode unlocked' flag could also be incorporated to indicate asynchronous operation.

Sample address code data

Either bytes 14–17 and/or bytes 18–21, which currently carry sample address codes, could carry BCD timecode data, using byte 22, bit 3 (currently reserved) as a flag.

28 of the 32 bits available can carry time data in BCD form, the remaining 4 bits indicating picture frame rate and the first block of the frame:

Bits 0–27

Frames units	4 bits
Frames tens	2 bits
Seconds units	4 bits
Seconds tens	4 bits
Minutes units	4 bits
Minutes tens	4 bits
Hours units	4 bits
Hours tens	2 bits

Bits 28–29

24 fps	00
25 fps	01
29.97 fps	10
30 fps	11

Bit 30
Set to '1' in the first block of a new timecode frame

Bit 31
Set to '1' to indicate timecode asynchronous with audio sampling rate

Indication of offset

A byte is needed to indicate the offset between the start of the timecode word and the start of the channel status block, either to accommodate asynchronous timecode, or to accommodate 625/60 and 525/60 operations, where there is not an integer number of audio samples in a video frame. There can be an offset of up to 191 samples. Byte 5 of the channel status has the only space available, currently being reserved with all bits set to zero. This byte could indicate the number of audio samples offset between the start of the timecode frame and the start of the first AES/EBU channel status block containing the new timecode frame value.

Currently work is being carried out by various working groups to define the addressing structure of AES/EBU ancillary data.

The colour frame sequence and timecode

The PAL 8-field sequence

In the PAL system the colour sub-carrier frequency is calculated as fsc = (284 − 0.25) fh + 0.5 fv, where fsc is the colour sub-carrier frequency, fh is the line (horizontal) frequency, fv is the field (vertical) frequency.

This gives fsc = (284 − 0.25) x 15 625 + 0.5 x 50

= 4 433 618.75 Hz.

This means that there are 4 433 618.75/15 622 = 283.751 6 cycles of colour sub-carrier per line.

With 625 lines to each frame, there are 283.751 6 x 625 = 177 344.75 cycles of sub-carrier per frame.

Not until 4 frames have passed (177 344.75 x 4 = 709 379 cycles of sub-carrier) do we get matching (extrapolated back) sub-carrier phases at the start of the first line of each frame.

Another way of looking at the matter is to say that 709 379/283.751 6 = 2 500 lines = 4 frames (8 fields).

The NTSC 4-field sequence

The NTSC system does not employ the line-by-line phase alternation of the PAL system, so the mathematics is simpler.

In NTSC,

fscs = 3 579 545 Hz

fv = 29.97 002 617 Hz

and there are 525 lines per frame. Therefore there are 3 579 545/(29.970 026 17 x 525) = 227.5 cycles of sub-carrier per line.

With 525 lines per frame there are 227.5 x 525 = 119 437.5 cycles of subcarrier per frame. Therefore, not until 2 frames (238 875 cycles of sub-carrier) have to pass before we get matching (extrapolated back) sub-carrier phases at the start of the first line of each frame.

Another way of looking at the matter is to say that 238 875/227.5 lines = 1 050 lines = 2 frames (4 fields).

The relationship between the colour sub-carrier and the video sync pulses is complicated. However, it must be respected during video editing if picture disturbance is to be avoided. For NTSC, SECAM and simple editing in PAL the sequence cycles over four fields. In more complex (invisible) editing in PAL an eight-field sequence must be respected.

These sequences can be accurately followed by using the timecode signal as a guide. This can be done only if there is a known relationship between each timecode word and the position of its associated frame in the sequence. The IEC has established a standard for this relationship for PAL, SECAM and NTSC systems.

The 625/50 field sequence

When a timecode generator is locked to the 8-field sequence then the remainder (R) obtained from the equation $R = (S + F)/4$, where S is the number of seconds and F the number of frames, will be

0 for fields 7 and 8
1 for fields 1 and 2
2 for fields 3 and 4
3 for fields 5 and 6

Let the bits of the longitudinal timecode word be labelled

bit 0 = A
bit 16 = B
bit 1 = C
bit 8 = D
bit 17 = E
bit 24 = F

For correct colour framing of timecode in the 4-field sequence (SECAM and simple PAL editing):

fields 1 and 2 shall occur when $A \oplus B = 1$
fields 3 and 4 shall occur when $A \oplus B = 0$

where + represents the exclusive-OR function.

Thus the first field of the day at 00h 00m 00s 01f has A = 1 B = C = D = E = F = 0, and A + B = 1

At 09h 11m 03s 07f, A = 1 B = 1 and $A \oplus B = 0$
At 12h 22m 10s 12f, A = 0 B = 0 and $A \oplus B = 0$
At 21h 59m 47s 10f, A = 0 B = 1 and $A \oplus B = 1$

For correct colour framing in the 8-field sequence, the same conditions as above apply, together with the following relationship:

fields 1 – 4 shall occur when $(A \oplus B) \oplus C \oplus D \oplus E \oplus F = 1$
fields 5 – 8 shall occur when $(A + B) \oplus C \oplus D \oplus E \oplus F = 0$

where $\oplus$ represents the exclusive-OR function.

If the timecode is displayed in decimal numbers, let S and P designate the values of seconds and pictures respectively.

The 4-field condition is met when

$(S + P)/4$ is odd for fields 1 & 2 and fields 5 & 6

$(S + P)/4$ is even for fields 3 & 4 and fields 7 & 8

The 8-field sequence is met when in addition to the above the remainder on dividing $(S + P)$ by 4 is:

0 for fields 7 & 8

1 for fields 1 & 2

2 for fields 3 & 4

3 for fields 5 & 6.

Editing in SECAM

In the SECAM system the two colour sub-carriers (having different frequencies) are modulated on alternate lines by two signals, designated D'b and D'r. For correct colour framing of timecode, frames in which the second field begins with a line having sub-carrier modulated by D'b, require the sum of the numbers of frames and seconds in the associated timecode address to be odd.

Where the second field of the frame starts with a sub-carrier modulated by D'r then the sum of the numbers of frames and seconds is even.

The relationship can also be defined as follows:

Let bit $0 = A$; bit $16 = B$

Then the timecode generator must be locked to the video so that

$A \oplus B = 1$ for fields where line 24 (or 336) is modulated by D'b

$A \oplus B = 0$ for fields where line 24 (or 336) is modulated by D'r

Editing in NTSC

For correct colour framing in the 4-field sequence, even-numbered frames will contain fields 1 and 2, odd-numbered frames will contain fields 3 and 4. Fields 1 and 2 are commonly referred to as together constituting Colour Frame A; fields 3 and 4, Colour Frame B.

To permit correct selection of 2- or 4-field editing the following relationship between timecode and the associated video signal is that LTC bit no. 0 contains:

0 for fields 1 & 2

1 for fields 3 & 4

Colour framing and VITC

For the VITC word the logic is identical. The bit representation differs because the distribution of data through the 90-bit VITC word differs from the 80-bit LTC word:

bit $2 = A$, bit $22 = B$, bit $3 = C$, bit $12 = D$, bit $23 = E$, bit $32 = F$.

LTC and VITC specifications

Specification of the 625/50 longitudinal timecode waveform

Rise and fall times:	50 (+15, −10) μs, measured between the 10% and 90% amplitude points of the waveform
Shape of pulse edges	$\sin^2$
Maximum overshoot, undershoot and tilt	5% of peak-to-peak amplitude
Nominal clock period	500 μs
Maximum timing error of any clock period	±2.5 μs
Maximum timing error of 1 transition	±2.5 μs

Specification of the 625/50 vertical interval timecode waveform

Pulse amplitude, logic 0	0–25 mV
Pulse amplitude, logic 1	550 ± 50 mV wrt blanking level
Clock period	0.556 μs approximately. The bit rate is specified as fh x 115 ±2%. Note: the bit rate is fh x 116 ± 200 bits/s (where fh is the line frequency)
Rise and fall times of transitions	200 ± 50 ns
Maximum overshoot or undershoot	5% of peak-to-peak amplitude

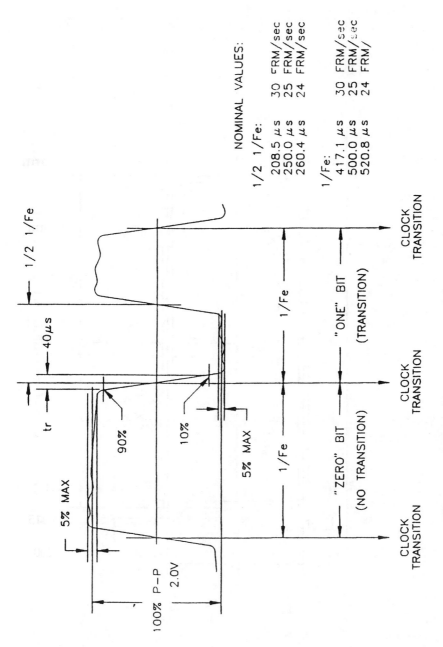

Figure A2.1 LTC waveform specification. Courtesy of *SMPTE Journal*.

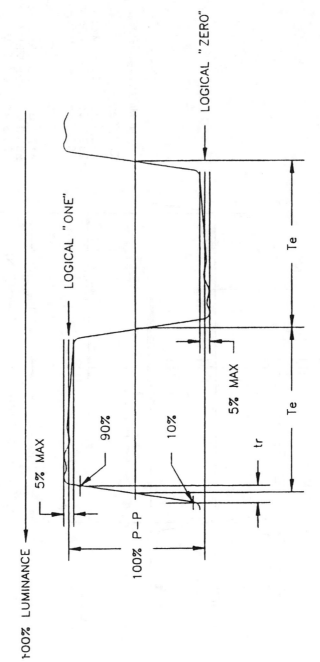

Figure A2.2 VITC waveform specification. Courtesy of *SMPTE Journal*.

Specification of the 525/60 longitudinal timecode waveform

Rise and fall times	25 ± 5 μs, measured between the 10% and 90% amplitude points of the waveform
Maximum overshoot, undershoot and tilt	2%
Clock period	416.7 μs
Maximum timing error of any clock period	± 4.2 μs
Maximum timing error of 1 transition	± 2.1 μs

Specification of the 525/60 vertical interval timecode waveform

Pulse amplitude, logic 0	0–10 IRE
Pulse amplitude, logic 1	70–90 IRE
Clock period	0.552 μs approximately The bit rate is specified as fh x 115 ± 2% (where fh is the line frequency)
Rise and fall times of transitions	200 ± 50 ns
Maximum overshoot or undershoot	5% of peak-to-peak amplitude

APPENDIX 3

Timecodes conversion

A   To convert from IEC timecode to Pro-R time (Figure A3.1):

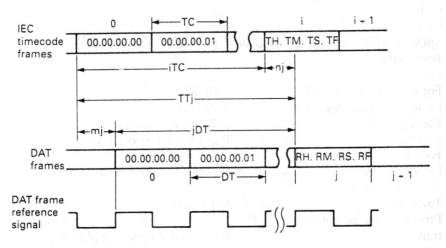

Figure A3.1 IEC timecode and DAT frame timecode conversion factors illustrated.

TH = Hours stored in the ith IEC timecode frame
TM = Minutes stored in the ith IEC timecode frame
TS = Seconds stored in the ith IEC timecode frame
TF = Frames stores in the ith IEC timecode frame
TC = period of timecode frame
DT = period of DAT frame
nj = time difference between the start of the jth DAT frame and the start of the IEC timecode frame current at the start of the jth DAT frame
TTj = time of the IEC timecode frame current at the start of the jth DAT frame
mj = time difference between TTj and jDT
Tfs = periodic time of sampling clock used for the IEC timecode conversion from the IEC timecode to the Pro-R time
TCM = timecode marker, which expresses time difference in terms of Tfs

TC, DT, nj, TTj, mj & Tfs are expressed in the same units

The relationship between EBU, SMPTE or Film (24 fps) timecode and ProR time is as follows:

The R time and the TC marker identify the time of the IEC timecode at the start of a DAT frame reference signal, the period of which corresponds to a group of audio data recorded on a positive azimuth track, and the following negative azimuth track. A DAT frame is identified by the DAT Frame Reference Signal, as defined below.

$TTj = nj + iTC$

$j = INT (TTj/DT)$

$= 120000RH + 2000RM + 33RS + INT(RS/3) + RF$

$mj = TTj \ MOD \ (mj/Tfs)$

where

j = total number of DAT frames from zero up to the start of a DAT frame

i = total number of IEC timecode frames from zero up to the start of the
  IEC timecode frame current at the start of the jth DAT frame

For EBU timecode,

$i = 90000TH + 1500TM + 25TS + TF$

For SMPTE drop-frame timecode,

$i = 107892TH + 1798TM + 21NT(TM/10) + 30TS + TF$

For SMPTE non drop-frame,

$i = 108000TH + 1800TM + 30TS + TF$

For 24 fps film,

$i = 86400TH + 1440TM + 24TS + TF$

To convert from Pro-DIO code to Pro-R time (Figure A3.2):

Pro-DIO code is recorded in the Pro-R time pack as a 32-bit binary code, transmitted over the Channel 1 sub-pack. The conversion obeys the following rules:

$TLO = TB + n$ where

TLO = the 32-bit binary code corresponding to the 1st sample (LO) of a DAT frame

TB = the 32-bit binary code in the channel status data of the DIO block current at the start of the DAT frame

n = time difference (unit:sample) from the start of the DIO block to the start of the DIO frame

To convert from TLO (32-bit binary) to Pro-R time:

Sample number = TLO MOD(DTs)

where DTs = number of audio samples in one DAT frame

If Fs = 48 kHz then DTs = 1440 (0–1439)

If Fs = 44.1 kHz then DTs 1323 (0–1322)

If Fs = 32 kHz then DTs = 960 (0–959)

Hours (RH), Minutes (RM), seconds (RS), and frames (RF), recorded in packs PC4 to PC7 are recorded in 2 digit BCD form. The following ranges apply:

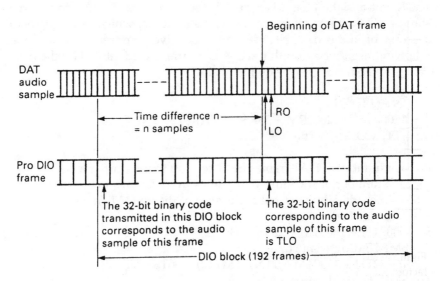

Figure A3.2 Sampling clock, DAT audio samples and ProDIO frame sequences compared.

RH, 00–99
RM, 00–59
RS, 00–59
RF, 00–33 (if RS MOD 3 = 2); 00–32 (if RS MOD 3 = 1 or 0).
k = INT(TLO/DTs) MOD 100
RF = k MOD(33) + 33 INT(k/99)
RS = 3[INT(TLO/100DTs) MOD 20] + INT(k/33) – INT(k/99)
RM = INT(TLO/2000DTs) MOD 60
RH = INT(TLO/120000DTs)

D   Conversion from Pro-R time to TLO (32 bit binary)
TLO = [12000RH + 2000RM + 33RS + INT(RS/3) + RF] x DTs + Sample number

Conversion between IEC timecode and ProDIO code (Figure A3.3).
The conversion from IEC timecode to ProDIO code, the 32-bit code, (TLO) corresponding to the 1st audio sample (LO) of a DAT frame, is calculated as followed:
TLO = [120000RH + 2000RM + 33RS + INT(RS/3) + RF] x DTs + TC marker
To convert from ProDIO code to IEC timecode, let the start of the zero frame IEC code (00h 00m 00s 00f) correspond to all zeros of the 32-bit binary code (TLO). Then the relationship between TLO and TTj is:

$$TLO \times TFs = TTj = nj + iTC$$
$$i = INT[(TLO \times Tfs)/TC]$$
$$nj = (TLO \times Tfs) \; MOD \; TC$$

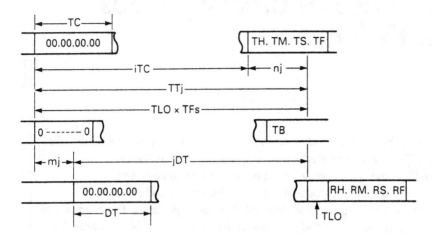

Figure A3.3 IEC timecode frame, ProDIO block and R-DAT frame conversion factors compared.

The use of binary groups with film

Use of the binary groups to carry additional data as specified in SMPTE RP135-1990 is indicated by setting the flag bits as follows:
bit 43 of the type C code or bit 67 of the type B code to 0
bit 59 of the type C code or bit 83 of the type B code to 1.

As several types of additional data are specified, they cannot all be carried in one timecode frame. If the data were to be carried over a number of frames, the corruption of a single frame could result in the data being lost. The different types of data are each incorporated within a single frame, the specific type being paged by a code held within the frame.

In essence, the principle is that of a directory system, with Binary Group 1 of each timecode frame (bits 4–7 in type C, bits 28–31 in type B) identifying the type of data held in User Groups 2–7 by means of an index. Binary Group 8 carries an error detection code (checksum). The data in each of the 8 binary groups are arranged such that the lowest numbered bit in each group carries the LSB, the highest numbered bit the MSB, of a 4-bit (16 character) code. Figure A4.1 illustrates the directory index.

Index	Data	Digits reqd	Format
0	Flags	24	Binary
1	Date (DD:MM:YY)	6	BCD
2	Production no	6	BCD
3	Equipment ID no	4	6-bit character code
4	Scene number	4	6-bit character code
5	Take number	4	6-bit character code
6	Roll number	4	6-bit character code
7–14	Unassigned	–	–
15	Extended directory	–	–

Table A4.1 Details of RP135-1990 Binary Groups Index.

Binary Group number

	1	2	3	4	5	6	7	8
Flags	Index		24-bit binary code					Checksum
BCD	Index	Units of day of month	Tens of day of month	Units of month	Tens of month	Units of year	Tens of year	Checksum
		Least significant no.	Number	Number	Number	Number	Most significant no.	
6-bit char.	Index	Least significant character		Character		Character	Most significant character	Checksum

Figure A4.1 The SMPTE RP135-1990 binary group formats.

The index

Binary group 1 carries the index to the directory of data held in binary groups 2–7, according to Table A4.1. Each frame of film then can carry only one type of data, as specified in the index, so a sequence of several frames will be needed to carry the various possibilities of data types carried in the various directories (as we shall see when considering the Aaton timecode system) though, as stated earlier, the choice and scope of the additional data provided is a matter of discretion.

The directory

Each directory may either carry up to six discrete 4-bit items of information in the six-binary groups available, with each 4-bit item having the ability to carry either pure numeric information in BCD or hexa-decimal form; alternatively the groups may be combined to provide a greater range of values, such as a subset of the ISO 2022-1982 (ASCII) codes. The type of data being carried is indicated by an entry in the index.

Bit no.		Data flagged	
B-format	C-format	'0'	'1'
36	12	Pictures	Sound
37	13	Sync sound/picture	No sound/picture
38	14	Print	Do not print
39	15	Sync speed	Not sync speed
44	20	Daylight photography	Night photography
45	21	Daylight	Tungsten light

Table A4.2 Detail of binary group bits flagged by Index entry '0'.

Bit numbers B-format	C-format	Weighting
36, 37, 38, 39, 44, 45	12, 13, 14, 15, 20, 21	Least significant character
46, 47, 52, 53, 54, 55	22, 23, 28, 29, 30, 31	Character
60, 61, 62, 63, 68, 69	36, 37, 38, 39, 44, 45	Character
70, 71, 76, 77, 78, 79	46, 47, 52, 53, 54, 55	Most significant character

Table A4.3 Details of binary groups bits when carrying 6-bit characters.

Entry 0
When the index is set to zero, the bits of binary groups 2–7 are set as flags to indicate the nature of the shot material according to Table A4.2. Unused bits are set to zero.

Entry 1
When the index is set to one, binary groups 2–7 carry date information in BCD format. The groups are assigned as follows:

Group Number	Contents
2	Units of day of month
3	Tens of day of month
4	Units of month (January = 1)
5	Tens of month
6	Units of year
7	Tens of year

The lowest-numbered bit in each group is the LSB, the highest-numbered bit the MSB. The data is displayed in increasing quantities of time, i.e. DD MM YY.

Entry 2
When the entry is set to two, binary groups 2–7 carry a 6-character numeric code identifying the production. The format is BCD.

Entry 3
When the entry is set to three, binary groups 2–7 are combined to form a 4-character alphanumeric equipment identification code (for example, to determine the camera on a multi-camera shoot). The bits in the user groups are combined together in the manner illustrated in Table A4.3. As can be seen, each character comprises six bits, so 64 separate characters are possible. These are specified in Table A4.4. The code values are identical to USS-128 (values 0–63), the barcode used in the KeyKode® system. The code is a subset of ISO 2022-1982.

Entry 4
When the entry is set to four, binary groups 2–7 are combined to form a 4-character alphanumeric scene number. Tables A4.3 and A4.4 give the details of the code format and values.

Entry 5
When the entry is set to five, binary groups 2–7 are combined to form a 4-character alphanumeric take number. Again, Tables A4.3 and A4.4 give the details of the code format and values.

Entry 6
When the entry is set to six, binary groups 2–7 are combined to form a 4-character alphanumeric roll number. Again, Tables A4.3 and A4.4 give the details of the code format and values.

Entries 7–14
At present these are unassigned. The SMPTE reserves their use.

Entry 15
When the index is set to 15, an extended directory is possible, User Group 2 becoming an extended directory index identifier for User Groups 3–7.

Appendix 4 gives details of the SMPTE standards for the extended use of binary groups. Possible uses are the carrying of a second timecode, equipment control (e.g. cueing), colour correction information, remote machine control and so on.

Character	Binary equivalent	Decimal equivalent	Character	Binary equivalent	Decimal equivalent
SPC	000000	0	@	100000	32
!	000001	1	A	100001	33
"	000010	2	B	100010	34
#	000011	3	C	100011	35
$	000100	4	D	100100	36
%	000101	5	E	100101	37
&	000110	6	F	100110	38
'	000111	7	G	100111	39
(	001000	8	H	101000	40
)	001001	9	I	101001	41
*	001010	10	J	101010	42
+	001011	11	K	101011	43
,	001100	12	L	101100	44
–	001101	13	M	101101	45
.	001110	14	N	101110	46
/	001111	15	O	101111	47
0	010000	16	P	110000	48
1	010001	17	Q	110001	49
2	010010	18	R	110010	50
3	010011	19	S	110011	51
4	010100	20	T	110100	52
5	010101	21	U	110101	53
6	010110	22	V	110110	54
7	010111	23	W	110111	55
8	011000	24	X	111000	56
9	011001	25	Y	111001	57
:	011010	26	Z	111010	58
;	011011	27	[	111011	59
>	011100	28	\	111100	60
=	011101	29	]	111101	61
<	011110	30	^	111110	62
?	011111	31	–	111111	63

Table A4.4 The 6-bit character code used in RP135-1990.

User Group 8

This carries error detection in the form of a checksum. It is the negative of the modulo-16 sum of groups 1–7.

The extended use of binary groups

In 1993 the SMPTE published a standard (SMPTE 262M:1993) and recommended practices (SMPTE RP 173:1993 and RP 179:1994) for the extended use of binary groups to carry an additional timecode, media address data and applications data. The general principle is of grouping several timecode frames of binary groups together to form a 'directory', organized into 'pages' and 'lines'. This use of binary groups is flagged in BGF 0–2, with BGF0 at '1', BGF1 at '0' and BGF2 at '1'. Table A5.1 illustrates the binary group flag values for LTC and VITC in 24, 25 and 30 fps systems. Data can be organized into bytes to carry 8-bit character sets, with binary groups 1 and 2 forming byte 1, groups 3 and 4 forming byte 2, groups 5 and 6 forming byte 3, and groups 7 and 8 forming byte 4.

Binary groups 7 and 8 form a directory index, with group 7 specifying a directory line of 16 lines per page and group 8 specifying a directory page of 16 pages. Figure A5.1 illustrates the page-line directory.

All address data in pages 0, 1 and 2 relate to programme timing. Auxiliary time address data are stored in lines 0–9 of pages 0 and 1, and lines 0–3 of page 2 in the following manner:

LTC bits	VITC bits	Binary group	Assignation
4–7	6–9	1	Units of frames
12–13	16–17	2	Tens of frames
14	18	2	Drop frame flag
15	19	2	Colour frame flag
20–23	26–29	3	Units of seconds
28–30	36–38	4	Tens of seconds
31	39	4	Unassigned
36–39	46–49	5	Units of minutes
44–46	56–58	6	Tens of minutes
47	59	6	Unassigned
52–55	66–69	7	Units of hours (line index)
60–61	76–77	8	Tens of hours (page index)
62–63	78–79	8	Zero (page index)

Page (Binary Group 1)	Line (Binary Group 2)															
	0	1	2	3	4	5	6	7	8	9	10 (A)	11 (B)	12 (C)	13 (D)	14 (E)	15 (F)
0				Auxiliary time addresses (Tens and units of hours)							Media address data					
1																
2																
3							Applications data									
4																
13 (D)							Applications data									
14 (E)																
15 (F)							Control/command data									

Figure A5.1 Possible page-line applications of the Hours binary group. Page-line combinations 00 to 23 are reserved for the carrying of timecode in user bits. F0 to FF could carry control data. Courtesy of *SMPTE Journal*.

Media address data (other than time) are stored in lines 10–15 of pages 0 and 1, and lines 4–15 of page 2.

Control data are stored in page 15.

As well as time data, either single or multiple frame messages may be sent, carrying such information as film transfer data (film manufacturer, emulsion type, film batch, edge number, roll number, film footage, footage frame offset and transfer data), static production data (scene, take, video reel number, film roll number, sound roll number, production number, date and message strings), and sync point data (film latent number sync point, film edge number sync point, film manufacturer's edge number sync point, ink number sync point and film and audio timecodes).

As can be seen, the applications possible with extended use of binary groups are very comprehensive, and it is apparent that extended use of binary groups can form the vehicle for carrying the vast amount of data for processing by a non-linear editor's database management system and the reader is referred to the various SMPTE standards mentioned earlier for the details.

Binary group flag	Bit value	24- and 30-fps systems		25-fps systems	
		LTC bit	VITC bit	LTC bit	VITC bit
BGF2	1	59	75	43	55
BGF1	0	58	74	58	74
BGF0	1	43	55	27	35

Table A5.1 Binary group flag values for 24, 25 and 30 fps page-line encoding. Courtesy of *SMPTE Journal*.

AES/EBU interface channel status data

The 24 bytes (0–23) are arranged as in the following table:

Byte	Bit	0	1	2	3	4	5	6	7
0		a	b	c	c	c	d	e	e
1		f	f	f	f	g	g	g	g
2		h	h	h	i	i	i	r	r
3		j	j	j	j	j	j	j	j
4		k	k	r	r	r	r	r	r
5		r	r	r	r	r	r	r	r

Byte	
6 7 8 9	Alphanumeric channel origin data

Byte	
10 11 12 13	Alphanumeric channel destination data

Byte	
14 15 16 17	Local sample address code 32-bit binary

Byte	
18 19 20 21	Time-of-day sample address code 32-bit binary

22	Reliability flags

23	CCRC

The specific organization of the data is as follows:

Byte 0

a Bit 0		0	Consumer use of channel status block
		1	Professional use of channel status block
b Bit 1		0	Normal audio mode
		1	Non-audio mode
c Bits	2–4		Encoded audio signal emphasis
bit	2 3 4		
	0 0 0		Emphasis not indicated. Manual selection enabled
	1 0 0		No emphasis. Manual selection disabled
	1 1 0		50/15 μs. Manual selection disabled
	1 1 1		CCITT J.17 emphasis. Manual selection disabled

All other bit states are reserved

d Bit 5		1	Source sampling frequency unlocked
		1	Sources sampling frequency locked
e Bits 6–7			Encoded sampling frequency
	bit 6 7		
	0 0		Sampling frequency not specified. Default is 48 kHz. Manual selection enabled
	0 1		48 kHz. Manual selection disabled
	1 0		44.1 kHz. Manual selection disabled
	1 1		32 kHz. Manual selection disabled.

Byte 1

f Bits 0–3		Encoded channel mode
bit	0 1 2 3	
	0 0 0 0	Mode not indicated. Manual selection enabled
	0 0 0 1	Two channel mode. Manual selection disabled
	0 0 1 0	Single channel (Mono) mode. Manual selection disabled
	0 0 1 1	Primary/secondary mode (sub-frame 1 is primary). Manual selection disabled
	0 1 0 0	Stereo mode (channel 1 is left). Manual selection disabled
	0 1 0 1	Reserved for user-defined applications
	0 1 1 0	Reserved for user-defined applications
	1 1 1 1	Vector to Byte 3. Reserved for future use

All other states are reserved

g Bits 4–7   Encoded user bits management
bit   4 5 6 7
       0 0 0 0   Default mode. No information indicated
         0 0 0 1 192-bit block structure. Preamble Z indicates the
                  start of the block
       0 0 1 0   Reserved for future use
       0 0 1 1   User defined use
    All other states are reserved

Byte 2

h Bits 0–2   Encoded use of auxiliary sample bits
bit   0 1 2
       0 0 0   Maximum audio sample is 20 bits (default). Use of aux
                  sample not defined
       0 0 1   Maximum audio sample is 24 bits. Aux sample bits
                  used for audio data
       0 1 0   Maximum audio sample is 20 bits. Aux sample bits
                  used to carry voice quality (talkback) signal
       0 1 1   Reserved for future use
i Bits 3–5 Encoded audio sample word length

bit	3 4 5	Audio sample wordlength if maximum wordlength is 24 bits as indicated in bits 0-2 above	Audio sample wordlength if maximum wordlength is 20 bits as indicated in bits 0-2 above
	0 0 0	Not defined (Default)	Not defined (Default)
	0 0 1	23 bits	19 bits
	0 1 0	22 bits	18 bits
	0 1 1	21 bits	17 bits
	1 0 0	20 bits	16 bits
	1 0 1	24 bits	20 bits

    All other states are reserved
r Bits 6–7   These are reserved for future use

Byte 3

    j Bits 0–7   Vectored target byte from byte 1. Reserved for future use
                  and currently set at logical 0

Byte 4

k Bits 0–1   Digital audio reference signal (per AES11)
bit   0 1
       0 0   Not a reference signal (Default)
       0 1   Grade 1 reference signal
       1 0   Grade 2 reference signal
       1 1   Reserved for future use
r Bits 2–7   Reserved for future use and currently set at logical 0

Byte 5

r Bits 0–7   Reserved for future use and currently set at logical 0

Bytes 6–9

Alphanumeric channel origin data. First character in message is byte 8
Bits 0–7   7-bit ISO 646 characters with no parity bit. LSBs are
(each byte)   transmitted first, with logical 0 in bit 7. Non-printed control
                 characters (&01 to &1F and &7F) are not permitted

Bytes 10–13

Alphanumeric channel destination data. 1st character in message is byte 10
Bits 0–7   7-bit ISO 646 characters with no parity bit. LSBs are
(each byte)   transmitted first, with logic 0 in bit 7. Non-printed control
                 characters (&01 to &1F &7F) are not permitted

Bytes 14–17

Local sample address code (32-bit binary). Value is of 1st sample of current block
Bits 0–7   LSBs are transmitted first
(each byte)

Bytes 18–21

Time-of-day sample address code (32-bit binary). Value is of 1st sample of current block.
Bits 0–7   LSBs are transmitted first
(each byte)

Byte 22

Channel Status Information reliability flags. If information is reliable, the appropriate bit is set to logical 0; if unreliable, it is set to logical 1
Bits 0–3   Reserved and currently set to logical 0
Bit 4   Refers to bytes 0 to 5
Bit 5   Refers to bytes 6 to 13
Bit 6   Refers to bytes 14 to 17
Bit 7   Refers to bytes 18 to 21

Byte 23

Cyclic redundancy check character
Generating polynomial is:
$G(x) = x^8 + x^4 + x^3 + x^2 + 1$
   LSB is transmitted first.

EBU recommendations for the recording of information in the user bits

Although the EBU recognizes that its member organizations can freely use the binary groups in any way, nevertheless a number of specific uses have been devised by individual organizations, for internal use. The EBU has documented these uses for the benefit of all member organizations. Chapter 5 covered one of these uses (panscan data in user bits).

In the UK the BBC has devised a means of carrying date information in the user bits in dd, mm, yy form. The date is normally changed at midnight local time, taking any summer time into account. Each digit of the date is coded in BCD in the following manner:

Binary group 1	Reserved	All bits set to zero
Binary group 2	Units of days	4 bits, LSB in bit 12
Binary group 3	Units of months	4 bits, LSB in bit 20
Binary group 4	Tens of days	2 bits, LSB in bit 28
	Tens of months	1 bit, bit 30. Bit 31 set to zero
Binary group 5	Reserved	All bits set to zero
Binary group 6	Units of years	4 bits, LSB in bit 44
Binary group 7	Reserved	All bits set to zero
Binary group 8	Tens of years	4 bits, LSB in bit 60

3-line VITC for film-to-tape transfer

First line

This line of the code contains Video Tape Time (recorded on the VCR at the time of transfer) in standard IEC form and can also carry Aaton tags or video reel ident (or any arbitrary hexadecimal value) in the binary groups. The CRCC is the IEC standard.

Second line

This line contains KeyKode® information, 3/2 pull-down flags, film manufacturer and film gauge information, and video field ident. The data are carried in the bits that would normally carry both time- and user-data in traditional VITC. The CRCC in this line is the inverse form of the IEC VITC CRCC. The traditional time bits are used to carry the pull-down

VITC bit no.	3-line VITC content	Traditional VITC content
00–05	Prefix 4	Frames units
06–09	Frames 4 LSB	Binary group 1
12–15	Prefix 3	Frames tens
16–17	Frame 2 MSB	Binary group 2 LS nibble
18–19	Max frame count	Binary group 2 MS nibble
22–25	Prefix 2	Seconds units
26–29	Footage 4 (LS digit)	Binary group 3
32–35	Prefix 1 (MS digit)	Seconds tens
36–39	Footage 3	Binary group 4
42–45	Emulsion type (LS digit)	Minutes units
46–49	Footage 2	Binary group 5
52–55	Emulsion type (MS digit)	Minutes tens
56–59	Footage 1 (MS digit)	Binary group 6
62–65	Film manufacturer + gauge	Hours units
66–69	Prefix 6 (LS digit)	Binary group 7
72–74	Pull-down flags (Table A8.4)	Hours tens (LS bits)
75	Field flag (Table A8.2)	Hours tens (MS bit)
76–79	Prefix 5	Binary group 8

Table A8.1 Bit allocation for 3-line VITC 2nd line arranged in bit order.

flags, film manufacturer and film gauge information, emulsion type and part of the prefix digits of the KeyKode® number. The traditional user bits of the codeword are used to carry the rest of the prefix digits of the KeyKode® number plus the footage count, the maximum frame count and the frame offset from the last KeyKode® number. Tables A8.1 and A8.2 give the details of the contents of the traditional VITC time- and user-bits.

VITC bit no.	3-line VITC content	Traditional VITC content
75	Field flag (Table A8.2)	Hours tens (MS bit)
72–74	Pull-down flags (Table A8.4)	Hours tens (LS bits)
62–65	Film manufacturer + gauge	Hours units
52–55	Emulsion type (MS Digit)	Minutes tens
42–45	Emulsion type (LS Digit)	Minutes units
32–35	Prefix 1 (MS Digit)	Seconds tens
22–25	Prefix 2	Seconds units
12–15	Prefix 3	Frames tens
00–05	Prefix 4	Frames units
76–79	Prefix 5	Binary group 8
66–69	Prefix 6 (LS digit)	Binary group 7
56–59	Footage 1 (MS digit)	Binary group 6
46–49	Footage 2	Binary group 5
36–39	Footage 3	Binary group 4
26–29	Footage 4 (LS Digit)	Binary group 3
18–19	Max frame count	Binary group 2 MS nibble
16–17	Frame 2 MSB	Binary group 2 LS nibble
06–09	Frames 4 LSB	Binary group 1

Table A8.2 Bit allocation for 3-line VITC arranged in function order.

Along with the frame count recorded in the LS byte of the user bits data are two flags which identify the maximum frame count for that key number. The flags are carried in bits 18 and 19 and are interpreted according to information regarding film manufacturer and gauge ident carried in bits 62–65. Table A8.3 gives the details of the max frame count, together with film manufacturer and gauge ident.

The three pull-down flags carried in bits 72–74 identify the video frames that result from the 3/2 pull-down sequence. They do not change in the middle of a frame. To these bits is added a fourth bit (bit 75) to identify the video field. In 25 to 30 transfer with 625/25 systems, pull-down sequences A1 and A2 only are identified. Table A8.4 gives the details.

16 mm	35 mm	70 mm	Imax	Ink
Bits 18–19				
0 0 reserved	0 1 16 (4 perf key no/ft & fr)	0 0 reserved	0 0 reserved	0 0 16 (35 mm 4 perf)
0 1 2 (key no & fr)	0 1 21 (3 perf head dot, perf 1)	0 1 16 (5 perf)	0 1 5 (15 perf head dot)	0 1 20 (16 mm)
1 0 4 (ft and fr)	1 0 21 (3 perf centre dot, perf 2)	1 1 10 (8 perf)	1 1 5 (15 perf centre dot)	1 0 40 (16 mm)
1 1 reserved	1 1 22 (3 perf tail dot, perf 3)	0 1 8 (10 perf)	0 1 5 (15 perf tail dot)	1 1 reserved

Bits 62–65 (binary values 0–15)

0	= Ink								
1	= Agra 35 mm	2	= Kodak 35 mm	3	= Fuji 35 mm	4	= not used	5	= not used
6	= Agfa 70 mm	7	= Kodak 70 mm	8	= Fuji 70 mm	9	= not used	10	= not used
11	= Agfa 16 mm	12	= Kodak 16 mm	13	= Fuji 16 mm	14	= not used	15	= Imax

The frame number is encoded in binary in the LS byte of the user bits data, along with two flags which identify the maximum frame count for that key number. This MFC is encoded as two bits (18 and 19) and its interpretation is based on the film manufacturer + gauge ID nibble (bits 26–65).

Table A8.3 Max frame count with film manufacturer and film gauge idents.

Film frame	Video frame	Field no.	Pull-down ident	Bit 72	Bit 73	Bit 74	Bit 75
0	0	1	A1	0	0	1	0
0	0	2	A2	0	0	1	1
1	1	1	B1	1	0	1	0
1	1	2	B2	1	0	1	1
1	2	1	B3	1	1	0	0
2	2	2	C1	1	1	0	1
2	3	1	C2	0	1	0	0
3	3	2	D1	0	1	0	1
3	4	1	D2	0	0	0	0
3	4	2	D3	0	0	0	1

Bit 72	identifies the pull-down sequence.
Bit 73	is `0' for a video frame containing the same film image in both fields.
	is `1' for a video frame containing different film images in each field.
Bit 74	is `0' for a video frame where picture content changes at start of field 2.
	is `1' for a video frame where picture content changes at start of field 1.
Bit 75	identifies the video field, is `0' for field 1 and `1' for field 2.

Table A8.4 Pull-down and field ident bit allocation.

As an example of the above, a 35 mm (4 perf) film frame with key number KJ12 3456 7890+12 would be encoded:

Manufacturer's code	02	letter code K for Kodak, encoded as 02 in 35 mm
Film type	96	letter code J for 5296 emulsion
Prefix	123456	
Footage	7890	

| Frames | &C | hexadecimal representation of 12 frames |
| Field and pull-down | 4_2 | A frame, field 1, represented in binary form (bits 72-75) |

In 3-line VITC, line 2, this will be encoded as:

Time data bits				User groups bits			
hh	mm	ss	ff	12	34	56	78
42	16	12	34	56	78	90	0C

BIBLIOGRAPHY

Videotape time and control codes

ANSI/SMPTE 12M-1986 (amended 1993): American National Standard for television – time and control cycle – video and audio tape for 525 line/60 field systems.

ANSI/SMPTE 230M-1991: $^1/_2$ in Type L – Electrical Parameters Control Code and Tracking Control.

EBU N12-1994: Time and Control Codes for Television Recording.

IEC 461:1986 (amended 1993) and BS 6865:1987 (amended 1993) British Standards Specification for Time and Control Codes for Videotape Recorders.

SMPTE 228M (Proposed): 19 mm type D-1 Cue and Time and Control Code Records.

SMPTE 248M (Proposed): 19 mm type D-2 Cue Record and Time and Control Code Records.

SMPTE 262M: Storage and Transmission of Data in Binary Groups of Time and Control Codes.

SMPTE 266M: 4:2:2 Digital Component Systems – Digital VITC.

SMPTE RP169: Audio and Film Time and Control Codes – Auxilliary Time Address Data in Binary Groups – Dialect Specification of Directory Index Locations.

SMPTE RP179: Dialect Specification of Page-Line Directory Index for Television, Audio and Film Time and Control Code for Video Assisted Film Editing.

SMPTE/ANSI 20M-1991: 1 in Type C Recorders and Reproducers – Longitudinal Audio Characteristics.

Robinson, J. *Videotape Recording* (Focal Press).

Watkinson, J. *The Art of Digital Video* (Focal Press).

Watkinson, J. *The D2 Digital Video Recorder* (Focal Press).

R-DAT, DASH and Prodigi

IEC Draft International Standard: Reference 60A (Central Office) 138.

SMPTE Journal, July 1990: A Professional DAT System.

Watkinson, J. *The Art of Digital Audio* (Focal Press).

Watkinson, J. *RDAT* (Focal Press).

AES/EBU Interface

AES3-199X: Draft AES Recommended Practice for Digital Audio Engineering – Serial Transmission Format for 2-Channel Linearly Represented Digital Audio Data.

AES18-1992 (ANSI 54.52-1992): Format for the user channel data of the AES digital audio interface.

EBU Tech 3250: Specification of the Digital Audio Interface.

Nunn, J. P. (1992) Ancilliary data in the AES/EBU digital audio interface. In *Proceedings of the 1st NAB Radio Montreux Symposium*, 10–13 June, pp 29–41.

Rumsey, F. J. (1992) Timecode in Channel Status. Proposal submitted to AES SC2-5-1 working party on synchronisation, San Francisco, August.

Rumsey, F. and Watkinson, J. (1995) *The Digital Interface Handbook* (Focal Press).

Film Timecodes

Arri press release, 8 September 1992: The Time Machine.

Arri press release, 9 September 1992: Keykode links film and tape editing in big productions.

Eastman Kodak®, Guide to Film and Video Postproduction, November 1993.

SMPTE RP 114-1983: Dimensions of Photographic Control and Data Record on 16 mm Motion Picture Film.

SMPTE RP 115-1983: Dimensions of Photographic Control and Data Record on 35 mm Motion Picture Release Prints.

SMPTE RP 116-1990: Dimensions of Photographic Control and Data Record on 35 mm Motion-Picture Camera Negatives.

SMPTE RP 117-1989: Dimensions of Magnetic Control and Data Record on 8 mm Type S Motion-Picture Film.

SMPTE RP 118-1983: Dimension of Photographic Control and Data Record on 8 mm Type S Motion Picture Prints.

SMPTE RP 135-1990: Use of Binary Groups in Motion Picture Film Time and Control Codes.

SMPTE RP 136-1986: Time and Control Codes for 24, 25, or 30 Frame-Per-Second Motion Picture Systems.

SMPTE 270: Manufacturer-Printed Latent Image Identification (65 mm motion picture film).

SMPTE 271: Manufacturer-Printed Latent Image Identification (16 mm motion picture film).

USS-128: Uniform Symbology Specification, Pub. Automatic Identification Manufacturers, Pittsburgh.

ESbus

EBU TECH 3245 and Supplements 1–4: Remote-control systems for broadcasting production equipment; System service and common messages; VTR, ATR and Telecine type-specific messages.

SMPTE RP113 (Proposed revision of RP 113-1983): Supervisory Protocol for Digital Control Interface.

SMPTE RP139 (Proposed revision of RP139-1986): Tributary Interconnection.

SMPTE 207M (Proposed revision of 207M-1984): Digital Control Interface – Electrical and Mechanical Characteristics.

MIDI timecode

Penfold, R. *MIDI Advanced Users Guide* (PC Publishing).

Rumsey, Francis, *MIDI Systems and control* (Focal Press).

Penfold, R. *The Practical MIDI Handbook* (PC Publishing).

Index